South Asian Colloquium on Human Rights and Development

South Asian Colloquium on Human Rights and Development

Vijay Kumar Gupta

MD PUBLICATIONS PVT LTD
NEW DELHI
www.mdppl.com

Published by :

MD Publications Pvt Ltd
"MD House", 11, Darya Ganj,
New Delhi-110 002
Phone : +91-11-41563325 (Customer Service)
+91-11-41562846 (Editorial)
E-mail (orders) : **order@mdppl.com**
Website : **www.mdppl.com**

ISBN : 978-81-7533-267-6

Published and Printed by Mr. Pranav Gupta on behalf of **MD Publications Pvt Ltd** at Printext, New Delhi.

Dedication

This book is dedicated to

my wife Mrs. Rajni Gupta,

whom I continuously cherished her

memory a lot.

Although your time was short

on this earth, you always

lived it to the fullest taking the time to

give of yourself to anyone

who needed anything.

You will be there always in

every step of my life still much

closer than

yesterday.

In Memory of my late beloved wife

Mrs. Rajni Gupta

(1959 to 2010)

Mrs. Rajni Gupta was born on 25th January, 1959 at Mumbai. She worked actively as a Managing Director in MD Publications Pvt Ltd which is a reputed publishing house that has earned both name and fame across the globe. She was down-to-earth and was an affable character with high moral principles. She was a very supportive and generous person that I have met along the way, have shared joys and sorrows in my journey and given me the encouragement, that I needed to take the next step forward, you are all special wonderful human being and I am blessed to have met you. You have been a very loving wife, mother and a great entrepreneur, who worked very hard to give her children the best in Education and moral values. I'm glad for the time we had together and the life time of memories we made. I patiently wait to be re-united with you in Heaven. Until then may God shower out all his love and blessing's on you.

I will forever miss you.

If ever there is tomorrow
there is something I must always remember.
You are braver than you believe,
stronger than you seem,
and smarter than you think.
But the most important thing is,
even if we're apart..
I'll always be with you.

– Vijay Kumar Gupta

Mrs. Rajni Gupta
(1959 - 2010)

PREFACE

The Colloquium is the starting point, offering intensive training and open space for sharing experiences and best practices among participants. The Colloquium also brings together academics and practitioners who get to know each other and often develop common initiatives. The Colloquium is different from other human rights courses because it combines capacity-building through lectures and readings, with peer learning through the exchange of experiences among participants, speakers and organizers. In its seven years of existence, the Colloquium became a crucial forum in which organizations from the South can think about their common challenges and create new strategies for collaboration.

South Asia is one of the most dauntingly complex regions of the world. All of the South Asian states – Afghanistan, Pakistan, India, Bangladesh, Nepal, Sri Lanka, Bhutan, and the Maldives - are contending with momentous changes, internally, regionally and globally. The region is home to three of the world's ten most populated countries, two of the world's nine nuclear weapons states, and the world's most corrupt country for five of the last eight years. Political instability, economic instability, poverty, natural disasters, and religious, ethnic and cultural clashes are abundant. It is at once one of the worlds most dangerous and most promising of areas.

In South Asia, the judiciary plays a particularly important role in protecting the rights of citizens, in particular of the most vulnerable sectors of society. The trend throughout national courts in the region to developing human rights jurisprudence indicates the judiciary's significance in finding common solutions to common problems. For this reason, strengthening the judiciary, by increasing linkages between pro-active judges in the region, and enhancing the capacity of the courts to protect rights. While reaffirming the general principles stated at past colloquia, the participants reiterated the universality of fundamental rights and freedoms which was declared to derive from the moral principle of each individual's personal and equal autonomy and human dignity.

It is also pointed out that the provision of equal justice requires a competent and independent judiciary and legal profession trained in the discipline of the law and sensitive to the needs and aspirations of all the people. It is fundamental for a country's judiciary and legal profession to enjoy the broad confidence of the people they serve. Public confidence in the judiciary depends not only on the institutional arrangements for protecting its independence from political pressures but also on the transparency and legitimacy of the manner in which judges are selected. Any mechanism, including judicial service commissions, should ensure that persons are selected because of their proven integrity, ability and independence and that the views of the existing judiciary are given appropriate weight.

I am very grateful to Mr. Pranav Gupta, Director of MD Publications Pvt Ltd, New Delhi, for his kind cooperation and support for this book.

Vijay Kumar Gupta

CONTENTS

1

South Asia and the Impact of Globalization on Human Rights

The Asian Human Rights Charter is a reflection of this global trend and it embodies the universality of human rights, even though the people who participated in the drafting process of the Charter were primarily from Confucian cultures and traditions and to investigate whether the so-called Asian concept of human rights, based on cultural relativism, is a valid argument.

The cross-cultural and inter-civilizational human rights norms have been increasingly accepted in a pluralistic contemporary world. Convergence on human rights has been taking place across cultures, which we call the universality of human rights. The concept of human rights can and should apply for all human beings in every human society equally and in equal measure by virtue of their humanity.

THE UNIVERSALITY OF HUMAN RIGHTS

People display enormous diversity in customs, languages, religions, moral norms, values, and political practices. In the article "Clash of Civilizations?", Huntington identifies eight major civilizations-Western, Confucian, Japanese, Islamic, Hindu, Slavic-Orthodox, Latin American and African. The world is also divided by levels of economic development and ideologies into either first, second, and third worlds or a North-South framework. This enormous civilizational diversity has led to a situation where ideas on human rights seem to lack a commonly shared philosophical foundation upon which to promote a uniform interpretation of rights in the international community.

The debate between universality versus cultural relativism is one of the major issues in study of human rights. The cause of this debate is that the modern concept of human rights stems from largely the liberal tradition of Western thought, especially the Lockean theory of natural rights that constitutes an indispensable source of contemporary ideas of human rights. According to the European concept, human rights are composed of principles and rules made available to the individual with the essential ai.n of enabling him to defend himself against the state.

For instance, the idea of natural rights reflects a view of man as natural, autonomous, and private. This derives from Protestantism. The U.S. Constitution states that:

"We hold these truths to be self-evident, that all men are created equal, that they are endowed by their Creator with certain unalienable rights, that among these are life, liberty and the pursuit of happiness...to secure these rights governments are instituted among men, deriving just power from the consent of the governed; that whenever any form of government becomes destructive of these ends it is the right of the people to alter or abolish it and to institute a new government."

Because of this Western origin of human rights (e.g. the Habeas Corpus Act, the English Bill of Rights, the American Declaration of Independence, the French Declaration of the Rights of Man and the Citizen), An-Naim contends that the concept of human rights is inherently alien to the non-Western tradition of third world countries to which it is now being extended. He argues that a blanket application of Western principles to non-western conditions is unjustifiable.

Onuma observes critically on the universality of human rights that "in the discourse of universalism and cultural particularity, there is an implied assumption of the West signifying the universal and Asia signifying the particular. But universality is actually the Western approach in disguise." Does universality embody the "cultural imperialism" of the "decadent West", and does cultural relativism represent what Bull calls "the revolt against the West" by non-Western states? Should the West have more respect for other values and cultures?

HUMAN RIGHTS IN ASIA

The African Charter on Human and Peoples' Rights emphasizes the rights of collectivities such as "peoples." In Africa, the concept of human rights is based on the fact that "the group is more important than the individual; decisions are made by consensus rather than by competition." Second, rights are inseparable from the idea of duty because the African family is buttressed by powerful ideologies that stress loyalty to kinfolk and performance of duty (rather than assertion of rights). Article 29 of the African Charter stresses the individual's duty; to serve his national community; to preserve and strengthen social and national solidarity, as well as the national independence and the territorial integrity of his country and positive African cultural values; and to contribute to the promotion and achievement of African unity. Third, as for women, they have lacked all formal legally recognized rights throughout the four centuries of the colonial era.

Cohen observes that in Africa colonial rule destroyed traditional institutions that had constrained power and protected people, and introduced into Africa security police, prisons, and the practice of preventive detention. Colonial rule was replaced with authoritarian governments. As a result, Africans have had no real experience of living under democratic rule. After independence the African governments became members of the United Nations and accepted its principles, including the Universal Declaration of Human Rights. African governments' concentration on economic development and nation building has led to centralization of power in the hands of the state. M'Baye sums up human rights situations in Africa by saying that "governments have sacrificed rights and freedoms for the sake of economic development and political stability."

People in East Asia (Taiwan, Japan, China and the Koreas) are still instilled with Confucian values and habits. Confucianism has been so powerful and so pronounced that it has virtually ruled people's lives in East Asia. Confucius stresses submission to the hierarchical and patriarchal authority and the proper place for each person within the hierarchy. Confucius also emphasizes preservation of group harmony and discourages individualism. No man lives independently of other people or of his community. This idea is directly in contrast to Mill's notion that the "individual is sovereign."

Confucian societies are structured around duties, not rights. Lee Manwoo points out that East Asian society as a whole has preoccupied itself not with individual rights but with duties. The ruler had a duty towards Heaven rather than to the well-being of the people (the Mandate of Heaven). The well-being of the community (family bondage, communal peace, social harmony, etc) takes priority over that of the individual and conformity is stressed at the expense of individual expression; in this context the family is considered the building brick of society.

In Confucian tradition rights are granted, not inherent but granted by government to serve societal purposes. The ideal is not individual liberty, but order and harmony, not individual independence but cooperation, not the freedom of individual conscience but conformity to society. Confucius argues that to be effective, law must comply with the moral order inherent in society. He encourages the virtues of filiality, loyalty and social compassion. In Confucian society, the preferred mode of conflict resolution has been non-adversarial and non-judicial. This legacy has become the foundation of what Hsiung calls the "Oriental consensual model" and has often resulted in despotism. According to "Asian Values," (Asian concept of human rights, espoused by some leaders in the region), Asia has a unique set of values that provides a different understanding of human rights.

The "Asian Values," of which the principal philosophical foundation is the Confucian heritage, prescribe that, first, duties and discipline are more important than political liberty and civil rights; second, the collective good takes priority over an individual's rights; third, economic development must precede the advance of political and civil rights because political authoritarianism is helpful for economic growth. Thus, social and economic rights are more important than civil and political rights. This is sometimes called the "Lee thesis" (based on a contention of Lee Kuan Yew, the influential ex-Prime Minister of Singapore). Lee Kuan Yew stresses that Western-style democracy is not applicable to East Asia and defends "soft" authoritarianism by arguing that:

"As Prime Minister of Singapore, my first task was to lift my country out of the degradation that poverty, ignorance, and disease had wrought. Since it was dire poverty that made for such a low priority given to human life, all other things became secondary."

Tremewan, however, observes that Singapore holds its population in a political straitjacket. It has been argued that rights are not luxuries to be enjoyed only after a certain level of economic development has been achieved. In fact, there is no relationship between economic growth, the level of economic development, and overall protection of human rights.

Amartya Sen warns against the "Asian Values" contention by offering a penetrating observation that "no substantial famine has ever occurred in any country with a democratic form of government and a relatively free press." In the meantime, Sen recognizes human rights elements in Asian traditions that the treatment of elderly members of the family (such as aged parents) is more supportive in Asian countries. Asian values also hold that rights are a matter of national sovereignty; Ding defends China's human rights policy by arguing that no universal human rights override the laws of various countries.

Islam is the faith of nearly one-fifth of the world's population. There are neither monolithic Islamic cultural standards nor a single, definitive interpretation of Islamic rights principles. The term Islam means both "submission" and "peace." According to Monshipouri, Islam is a set of convictions, values, ideals, symbols, doctrines, institutions, and practice. On the interpretation, the purpose of the state in Islam is to enforce the principles of the Sharia (Islamic religious law). Abdullahi Ahmed El Naiem points out that Sharia does not recognize universal suffrage, organized political opposition, independence of the judiciary, separation of powers, or the rights of women. Islamic authority stems from the Koran (general ethical principles), Sunna (the practice of the prophet Muhammad) and Sharia.

Said explains that:

The essential characteristic of human rights in Islam is that they constitute obligations connected with the Divine. Human rights exist only in relation to human obligations. Individuals possess certain obligations toward God, fellow humans and nature, all of which are defined by Sharia. When individuals meet these obligations they acquire certain rights and freedoms.

In Islam the community comes before the individual because it is thought that the human personality is realized by action for the good of the collectivity through self-abnegation. Second, in Islam rights are subordinated to, and determined by duties because moral obligations to other persons and peoples take precedence over individual human rights. Donnelly comments, "in Islam what matters is duty rather than rights."

Khalid lists the following rights contemplated in the Koran:

1. Right to protection of life;
2. Right to justice;
3. Right to equality;
4. Duty to obey what is lawful, and right to disobey what is unlawful;
5. Right to participate in public life;
6. Right to freedom;
7. Right to freedom of conviction;
8. Right to freedom of expression;
9. Right of protection against persecution on the ground of difference;
10. Right to protection of honor and good name;
11. Right to privacy;
12. Economic rights;
13. Right to property;
14. Right to adequate remuneration and compensation.

Islam does not include the equal treatment of women and the freedom to change religion. The general rule of Sharia is that men are the guardians of women and as such have the license to discipline them to the extent of beating them "lightly" if they fear the women will become unruly. Whereas a man is entitled to marry up to four wives and divorce them at will, a woman is restricted to one husband and can only seek a judicial divorce on very limited and restricted grounds. Women receive only half a share of the man's inheritance, and less monetary compensation for criminal bodily harm (diya). Women are incompetent to testify in serious criminal cases; it takes two women to make a single witness. Muslim women may not hold any office involving exercise of authority over Muslim men.

Similarly, unbelievers are not allowed to live within an Islamic state except with a special permit of self-conduct (aman). Consequently non-Muslims are denied any public office, which would involve exercising such authority. Consequently, Islamic culture has been a breeding ground for authoritarian/patriarchal regimes.

CULTURAL RELATIVISM

Cultural relativism is defined as that culture is the source of the validity of moral rights and rules. The conceptual analysis of cultural relativism is provided by Nickel, who argues that cultural relativism means that all moral values, including human rights, are "culturally embedded" and thus are relative to the cultural context.

Crocker argues that moral relativism consists of three doctrines: (i) social descriptive relativism (i.e. cultural relativism) claims that different cultures, societies, or classes have significantly different positive social morality; (ii) social normative relativism (prescriptive relativism) prescribes to that one should follow the moral rules of one's group, since morality is relative; (iii) metaethical relativism (skeptical relativism) argues that moral judgments cannot be resolved rationally and both sides to the conflict are equally correct or justified.

Donnelly distinguishes three types of cultural relativism-radical, strong and weak. The differences between these relativist positions are that culture is the sole, principal or maybe an important source of the validity of moral rights or rule. Teson also proposes three types of relativism-descriptive, metaethical and normative-in order to analyze the moral status of relativism. For example, descriptive relativism asserts that different societies have different perceptions of right and wrong. According to cultural relativism, in view of the existence of diverse cultures, there is no universal culture therefore; no culture, tradition, ideology or religion can speak for all humankind. Thus, there exist no universal and transboundary legal or moral standards. Every society or culture recognizes certain values, mores, norms, and operational principles by which it seeks to approximate the ideas of human dignity.

Each country's human rights conditions are circumscribed by its historical, social, economic, and cultural conditions, and human rights reflect a country's stage of historical development. Non-relativists or Universalists argue that the Universal Declaration of Human Rights constitutes a common core of values to which all peoples and nations should aspire. However, what these rights mean in practice will differ from nation to nation and from culture to culture. Even if a body of substantive human rights norms does exist, its application varies substantially from culture to culture. For example, the European Court of Human Rights has developed the concept of the "margin of appreciation" when examining national legislation for compatibility with the European Convention of Human Rights, which enables the Court to permit a diversity of approaches within Europe.

In this context, relativists argue that certain human values such as equal protection or political participation are inappropriate in certain cultural or political contexts. For that reason, current international human rights standards are insensitive to or incompatible with various cultural, political, and social conditions. Mahbubani argues that the West has no right to give moral lectures to Asia. This line of argument may be used, however, for self-serving excuses for some governments' violations of human rights.

Western societies consider human rights to be individualistic, adversarial, just, and inalienable in contrast to social welfare, collective rights, consensual dispute resolution, economic development, and state interests in Asian, African and Islamic traditions. These have resulted in the contention that the concept of human rights is alien to non-Western cultures. Therefore, the contention has been made that the meaning and application of human rights should be dependent upon regional and national conditions. The Third World leaders may think that the human rights movement involves one more attempt by ethnocentric Europeans and Americans to impose their values on the rest of the world. They feel deeply about the importance of preserving their own traditions and cultures. In addition, the diversity of cultural traditions, political structures, and levels of economic development make it difficult to define a single distinctive and coherent human rights regime that can encompass vast regions.

These arguments lead to the notion that different societies have and should have different perceptions of right and wrong; "What is right or good for one individual or society is not right or good for another, even if the situations involved are similar." Then, they conclude: there is no one universally valid standard of human rights. In this context, human rights violations may have been condoned because they happen to be tolerated or sanctioned by the cultural tradition of the society or the community in question (e.g. female genital mutilation, child labor, and flogging).Furthermore, cultural relativists argues, human nature is to a considerable extent culturally determined, and if human rights are based on human nature, human rights themselves are culturally relative. The "Statement on Human Rights" prepared by the American Anthropological Association stated in 1947, in part:

1. The individual realizes his personality through his culture. Hence respect for individual differences entails a respect for cultural differences.
2. Standards and values are relative to the culture from which they derive.

The relativist position was strongly expressed in the Bangkok Government Declaration, which affirms a state-centric perspective based on respect for national sovereignty, and territorial integrity and noninterference in the internal affairs of states. The Declaration provides, in part:

Human rights must be considered in the context of the dynamic and evolving process of international norm-setting, bearing in mind the significance of national and regional particularities and various historical, cultural and religious backgrounds.

The strength of the relativists' argument stems from the fact that descriptive relativism captures much truth: there is diversity in norms. Their view reflects realities of contemporary international society. They demand that the concept of human rights should be modified by local cultural conditions. The Universalist position sometimes lacks local cultural sensitivity and destroys cultural diversity. The cultural relativity provides a legal ground for self-determination. It is an affirmation of "a right to be different."

Another feature of cultural relativism is that it inconsistently may advocate tolerance and call for respect for other cultures. Its cultural egalitarianism might reduce ethnocentrism in a multi-cultural world. But tolerance is a universally valid norm and it does not follow logically from diversity of values. Yet the negative aspect of relativism is that to uphold cultural pluralism is to argue that every culture is equally valid and that no external values should be allowed to influence them. Thus, oppressive governments have used the principle of nonintervention in the internal affairs of sovereign states as an defense of their human rights violations.

Relativists attack the Universalist position that the seemingly neutral title of international human rights law in fact favors widening and deepening the legitimacy of Western conceptions of human rights; the objections have ranged from accusations of "Western bias" to "cultural imperialism." Human rights are a "Western construct with limited applicability." Third World views on international human rights differ widely. Vincent makes the point that the international law of human rights is an export of the West to the rest of the world. In this respect, the Universal Declaration of Human Rights is the imposition of an alien value system-the universalization of Western values and aspirations.

UNIVERSALITY OF HUMAN RIGHTS

The Universalist position argues against the various forms of normative and metaethical relativism and affirms the existence of legitimate cross-cultural standards for evaluating human rights practices-even though some cultures may not yet accepts them. Li argues that there are three ways in which a value can be either universal or non-universal-origin, validity or implementation. Cranston affirms the "universality of validity" of human rights by arguing that a human right by definition is something which all men, everywhere, at all times ought to have, something of which no one may be deprived.

As for the validity of human rights, even if rights conceptions originated in the West (elements may have originated in the East), Universalists claim that there is a core of values that is valid for culture. All individuals solely by virtue of being human, that is, solely by virtue of potential ability to exercise rational choice, have moral rights which no society or state should deny. According to Shue, a moral right provides:

1. The rational basis for a justified demand;
2. The actual enjoyment of a substance;
3. Social guarantees against standard threats.

Likewise, for most of us, Donnelly argues, morality is inherently universalistic and egalitarian. All societies have underlying conceptions of human dignity and social justice. Furthermore, Li argues that an intercultural discourse has been taking place among people with different cultural assumptions, which has resulted in verifying the universal validity of human rights. Onuma argues that the *raison d'etre* of human rights must be grounded in a globally-legitimate inter-civilizational perspective.

There is a reasonable cross-cultural consensus on many of the values that today we seek to protect through human rights (e.g. life, protection from arbitrary rule, prohibition of inhuman and degrading treatment, slavery, genocide, and extrajudicial execution). This indicates the existence of the inherent validity of basic moral precepts even though some groups may not agree and may hold beliefs incompatible with human rights.

Individuals are entitled to basic rights (security, liberty and subsistence) regardless of contingent factors such as their cultural surroundings or the norms dominant in their societies. Basic rights represent "everyone's minimal reasonable demands upon the rest of humanity." Human rights apply for all human beings in every human society equally and in equal measure by virtue of their humanity; for every human being, regardless of gender or race, class or status, wealth or poverty, occupation, talent, merit, religion, ideology, or other commitment; in every society, regardless of geography, or history, culture or ideology, political or economic system, or stage of development.

One argument appeals to a human nature in which rights are independent of time, place, culture, ideology, or value systems. Human rights are claims made on society by individuals or groups on the basis of their humanity. They apply regardless of race, color, sex, or other distinctions and may not be withdrawn or denied by governments. Korea's Foreign Minister Han Sung-joo stresses that human rights cannot be altered according to circumstances. For that reason, the concept that human rights are alien to Asian culture is being challenged by Asian people themselves. It is the institutional implementation of human rights that differs between Asia and the West, not the concepts themselves.

As for the universality of the implementation of human rights a large number of international human rights agreements are in force today. They have been ratified by a substantial majority of the international community of states. The Universal Declaration of Human Rights, "Magna Carta of Mankind", proclaims that the Declaration is "a common standard of achievement for all peoples and all nations." It has been argued that the Declaration has become part of international customary law binding on all states without their express consent. The UN Charter (Article 1. stresses "respect for human rights and fundamental freedoms for all without distinction as to race, sex, language, religion." The Vienna Declaration and Programme of Action of 1993 stress that the "universal nature of these rights and freedoms is beyond question." and states that:

[A]ll human rights are universal, indivisible, and interdependent and interrelated. The international community must treat human rights globally in a fair and equal manner, on the same footing, and with the same emphasis.

Kofi Annan, UN General-Secretary, states that:

Human rights are African rights. They are also Asian rights, they are European rights. They are American rights. They belong to no government; they are limited to no continent, for they are fundamental to humankind itself.

While the codification efforts, which Donnelly calls "the convergence of cross-cultural human values," have been successful, the opposite is true with regard to implementation (e.g. the International Court of Human Rights).

As I have indicated so far, Africa, East Asia and Islam have distinctive traditions and outlooks on the concept of human rights. Current "internationally recognized human rights" may not be sufficiently universal because they lack legitimacy in major cultural traditions. The full idea of human rights is certainly Western-based. This is the root cause of the impediment to realizing universality of human rights.

However, even if there may not be a universal foundation in human nature, natural law, or existing normative beliefs for a concept of human rights, a global consensus could emerge because, as An-Naim argues, cultures are constantly changing and evolving internally. For example, the 1993 Bangkok NGO Declaration states, in part, that "We can learn from different cultures in a pluralistic perspective and draw lessons from the humanity of these cultures to deepen respect for human rights. There is emerging a new understanding of universalism... Universal human rights standards are rooted in many cultures."

In this context, Bielefeldt advocates that a serious international discourse on human rights through self-critical reevaluation is necessary to create a cross-cultural "overlapping consensus," which John Rawls defines this way:

Different groups, countries, religious communities, civilizations, while holding incompatible fundamental views on theology, metaphysics, human nature, etc., would come to an agreement on certain norms that ought to govern human behavior. Each would have its own way of justifying this from out of its profound background conception. We would agree on the norms, while disagreeing on why they were the right norms. And we would be content to live in this consensus, undisturbed by the difference of profound underlying belief.

The world has become increasingly interdependent. Interdependence implies that nations are sensitive or vulnerable in significant ways to developments taking place beyond their borders. Thus, governments become less the masters of what occurs within their countries, even though they continue to claim sovereignty. The concept of a right has been removed from the domain of domestic jurisdiction and has become a matter of treaty obligation. A state is thus obligated to incorporate international standards into its domestic system. The concern for human rights nullifies the principle of non-interference in domestic affairs. Rather, breaches of human rights, especially gross breaches, are increasingly removed from domestic jurisdiction and placed in international judicial processes, such as international criminal court.

Ghai argues that the national and international movement of rights is itself a product of globalization. Convergence is taking place across cultures, which results in a "cross-fertilization" that reinforces the global consensus on human rights. It promotes cosmopolitanism and respect for diversity. Taylor suggests an "unforced international consensus" that is defined as Agreement on norms, but a profound sense of difference, of unfamiliarity, in the ideals, the notions of human excellence, the rhetorical tropes and reference points by which these norms become objects of deep commitment for us.

I disagree with Marfording's argument that the universality versus cultural relativism debate has reached an impasse. Human rights are an evolving conception, expressing imperfectly the aspirations of many, if not all, peoples. It is my strong contention that human rights standards have been in a process of becoming universal because of modernization, which is a coherent process that produces a certain uniformity of economic and political institutions across different regions and cultures. Accordingly, in the last decade a majority of governments have either participated in the formulation process or subsequently ratified the relevant international human rights instruments. Thus, despite its largely Western origin, the concept of human rights has finally been in a process of becoming universally valid.

Moreover, it should be noted that universal human rights do not impose one thick cultural standard, rather one moral and legal standard of minimum protection necessary for human dignity.

Meanwhile, as Donoho argues, I must caution that a certain degree of cultural and political sensitivity with respect to implementation (not validity) is necessary in the interim to achieve human rights values in a diverse, pluralistic world. Human rights can be harmful if universalism is used to deny all aspects of diversity. To be denied are aspects of local culture that violate core rights. Pluralism is not merely healthy but necessary to any successful international human rights system. But pluralism must be constrained by universal rights and religious tolerance and freedom is one the rights. Based on an eclectic, cross-cultural approach to universal human rights, Schwartz contends that:

[E]very culture will have its distinctive ways of formulating and supporting human rights. Every society can learn from other societies more effective ways to implement human rights. While honoring the diversity of cultures, we can also build toward common principles that all can support. We are living at one of those junctures of history when a unique new culture is in the making. A global culture of human rights is an emerging world order, in Forsythe's phrase the "internationalization of human rights. Onuma advocates an "inter-civilizational approach to human rights" because it would liberate the human rights discourse from domination by Westcentrism; and second, it would expand and improve commitment to all human rights on a global scale.

Universal human rights are possible because of the emerging common culture of modernity and the global wave of democratization; Modernization involves industrialization, urbanization, increasing levels of education, literacy, wealth and social mobilization. Human rights are universal values to be defended and promoted. Human rights are a pillar of the UN Charter to which all states are bound. The Vienna Declaration pro vides that while the significance of national and regional particularities and various historical, cultural and religious backgrounds must be borne in mind, it is the duty of states, regardless of their political, economic and cultural systems, to promote and protect all human rights and fundamental freedoms.

Kofi Annan, General Secretary of the UN, provides a penetrating remark: "it was never the people who complained of the universality of human rights, nor did the people consider human rights as a Western imposition. It was often their leaders who did so." The global repudiation of normative and metaethical relativism and growing global acceptance of universality is a positive sign for establishing a regional human rights regime in East Asia. People in Asia are beginning to understand that it is necessary to have an implementation mechanism, albeit one with Asian traits based on universality of human rights in the region.

EXPANDING UNITED NATIONS HUMAN RIGHTS MECHANISMS

The acceptance of universality of human rights has resulted in codification of a large number of international human rights treaties, which have been signed and ratified by a majority of the international community. As a result, human rights laws occupy a major domain of international law today. Human rights promotion and protection mechanisms at the UN have been expanding rapidly to enforce international human rights standards and principles. According to functionalist analysis, this indicates the functional strategy of "consensus building." This globalization of human rights is a positive impetus for setting up a regional mechanism in East Asia.

International human rights standards and principles have been dramatically developed, especially since the end of the World War II, to promote and protect human rights in the world. The nucleus of international human rights treaties, in addition to the human rights provisions of the UN Charter, the International Bill of Rights, consists of the Universal Declaration of Human Rights; the International Covenant on Economic, Social and Cultural Rights; the International Covenant on Civil and Political Rights; and the Optional Protocols to the Covenant on Civil and Political Rights.

In 1948 the UN General Assembly adopted the Universal Declaration of Human Rights. The Universal Declaration is the first comprehensive human rights instrument and is ranked with the Magna Carta, the American Declaration of Independence, and the French Declaration of the Rights of Man and the Citizen. The Declaration, "a minimum response to the convergence of cross-cultural human values," is not a treaty, therefore, has no binding power but has a moral value. It serves as "a common standard of achievement for all peoples and all nations." French jurist Karel Vasak developed the notion of "three generations of human rights"; the first generation of civil and political rights (*liberte*), the second generation of economic, social and cultural rights (egalite), and the third generation of solidarity rights (*fraternite*) (e.g. the right to development, to peace, to democracy, to a healthy environment).

In 1948 the UN adopted the Genocide Convention. The Genocide Convention declares that genocide is a "crime under international law." The Convention defines genocide as the commission of acts "with intent to destroy, in whole or in part, a national, ethnic, racial or religious group (Art II)." The Convention does not have an implementation system. A dispute between state parties relating to the Convention may be brought to the International Court of Justice. The Tribunal does not have jurisdiction to try individuals for genocide. In 1965 the UN adopted the International Convention on the Elimination of All Forms of Racial Discrimination (CERD). The Convention prohibits "racial discrimination" which is defined as "any distinction, exclusion, restriction or preference based on race, color, descent, or national or ethnic origin" (Art. 1.. The state parties to the Convention have a legal obligation to eliminate racial discrimination in their territory by any person, group or organization.

In 1966 the UN General Assembly adopted the Covenants on Civil and Political Rights (ICCPR) and on Economic, Social and Cultural Rights (ICESCR). The Covenants created binding legal obligations for the state parties to them. Each Covenant establishes a distinct international enforcement system designed to insure that the state parties comply with their obligations. Each state party to the Covenants undertakes to respect and to ensure to all individuals within its territory and subject to its jurisdiction the rights recognized in the Covenant, without distinction of any kind. Whereas the obligations which a state party assumes by ratifying the Civil and Political Rights require immediate implementation, the Covenant on Economic, Social and Cultural Rights obligates state parties to achieve "progressively the full realization" of the rights enumerated in the Covenant.

The ICESCR Covenant does not establish any inter-state or individual complaint system. It only requires the state parties to submit reports on the measures, which they have adopted to realize the recognized rights. In 1979 the UN adopted the Convention on the Elimination of All Forms of Discrimination Against Women (CEDAW). That discrimination is defined as "any distinction, exclusion, or restriction made on the basis of sex." Article 5 of the Convention provides that State Parties shall take all appropriate measures:

(a) To modify the social and cultural patterns of conduct of men and women, with a view to achieving the elimination of prejudices and customary and all other practices which are based on the idea of the inferiority or the superiority of either of the sexes or on stereotyped roles for men and women.

The Convention is the first international treaty dealing with the rights of women in a global manner including provisions for a reporting system and review machinery. The Convention requires state parties to submit periodic reports relating to "the legislative, judicial, administrative or other measures they have adopted to give effect to the provisions of the Convention" (Art 18 [1]).

In 1984 the UN adopted the Convention Against Torture and Other Cruel, Inhuman or Degrading Treatment. This Convention is designed to prevent and punish torture, which is defined as "any act by which severe pain or suffering, whether physical or mental, is intentionally inflicted on a person" for the purpose of obtaining from him or a third person information or a confession (Art. 1[1]). The Torture Convention establishes a reporting system (Art. 19) as well as an optional inter-state complaint (Art. 21) and individual petition system (Art. 22).

Other relevant instruments preceding this Convention are: the Standard Minimum Rules for the Treatment of Prisoners (1955), the Code of Conduct for Law Enforcement Officers (1979), and the Principles of Medical Ethics (1982). In 1982 the United Nations established a Voluntary Fund for Victims of Torture.

In 1986 the Declaration of the Right to Development was adopted. The Declaration states that the right to development is an integral part of human rights and fundamental freedoms and aims at constant improvement of the well-being of the entire population, free and meaningful participation, and fair distribution of benefits. The Declaration postulates equality of opportunity as the main principle applicable to both nations and individuals.

In 1989 the UN adopted the Convention on the Rights of the Child (CRC). The Convention is the proposition that children are entitled to human rights in their own capacity. These international human rights treaties occupy a significant portion of international law today. These conventions connote an expanding human rights culture. As members of the international community the countries in East Asia have been influenced by this enlightenment. These treaties are the foundations for "internationally recognized human rights" upon which proposed East Asian human rights protection mechanisms would be based.

In Europe, the Council of Europe was established in 1949 by a group of ten states, which, as of 1995, expanded to include 34 states. The Council of Europe organized one of the most advanced human rights protection mechanisms. The Council supported the European Convention for the Protection of Human Rights and Fundamental Freedoms, which covers mainly civil and political rights, and was signed in 1950, as well as the European Social Charter, which recognizes economic and social rights, and was signed in 1961. In 1987 the European Convention for the Prevention of Torture and Inhuman or Degrading Treatment or Punishment was also adopted by the Council of Europe. The Convention established a Committee for the Prevention of Torture (CPT).

In 1948 the Organization of American States (OAS) was established and as of 1995 the OAS has 35 member states. The OAS adopted the American Declaration of the Rights and Duties of Man in 1948. The Declaration proclaims a list of twenty-seven rights and ten duties. The catalog of rights embraces civil and political as well as economic, social and cultural rights. The American Convention of Human Rights was opened for signature in 1969. In addition, the Inter-American Convention to Prevent and Punish Torture, the Inter-American Convention on the Forced Disappearance of Persons, and the Inter-American Convention on the Prevention, Punishment and Eradication of Violence Against Women were signed.

In 1963 the Organization of African Unity (OAU) was established and in 1981 the African Charter on Human and Peoples' Rights was adopted. As of 1995, forty-nine African states subscribed to the Charter. First, the Charter claims not only rights but also duties. Second, it codifies individual as well as peoples' rights. Third, it protects civil and political rights as well as economic, social and cultural rights. In 1975 at Helsinki, in the Final Act of the Conference on Security and Cooperation in Europe, 35 countries-all the sovereign states of Eastern and Western Europe with the single exception of Albania, as well as the United States and Canada, made a commitment to respect human rights. In 1994 the Council of the League of Arab States adopted the Arab Charter on Human Rights.

Let us examine the UN human rights mechanisms, which is the pragmatic and concrete expression of functional integration and interdependence. The expansion of UN mechanisms has contributed to globalization of human rights culture. However, as I will point out in due course, one of the drawbacks of the UN mechanisms are its weak enforcement. This is because the UN is comprised of nation-states. Accordingly under the UN mechanism, ultimate responsibility for human rights enforcement lies in the hands of nation-states. One *raison d'etre* of regional human rights regimes is its strong implementation mechanism compared to the UN arrangements.

This is one reason the East Asian regional human rights protection mechanism is justified and will be found useful. In 1997 Kofi Annan, Secretary-General, organized the work of the United Nations into five substantive fields-peace and security, economic and social affairs, development cooperation, humanitarian affairs and human rights. The UN employs a "two-track" approach in relation to human rights enforcement machinery, namely, the Charter-based organs (e.g. the Commission on Human Rights) and the treaty-based organs (e.g. the Human Rights Committee). According to Alston, the evolution of the United Nations human rights mechanism has gone through different phases of activity, that is, standard-setting, promotion, and protection (since 1967).

The United Nations human rights structure is a triptych of which one of the panels, the central panel is the Universal Declaration of Human Rights, while the two side panels could be formed by the various conventions and covenants on the one hand and the implementation measures on the other, the latter being the least developed. Boven observes that although the UN has developed a comprehensive set of international norms for the promotion and protection of human rights, its system of actual implementation and supervision is still rudimentary." Another criticism is made that the UN has given a high priority to peace and security and given a low priority to human rights. In fact, human rights get less than two percent of the UN budget. The United Nations human rights mechanism utilizes the following three methods to enforce protection of human rights.

THE REPORTING PROCEDURE

The reporting procedures envisage a system of international supervision, which obliges state parties to report on their implementation and enables supervisory bodies to evaluate their performance. The reporting procedures enable human rights bodies to determine national laws and practices which conform to the international standards, and to suggest necessary changes.

In this way governments submit their human rights records to international supervision. Reports are assessments of the situations of human rights by the government itself, a form of self-evaluation. Therefore, the weakness of the reporting system is dependent, to a large extent, upon the good faith of the states concerned. Tamasevski points out that an alarming number of overdue reports were noted by the General Assembly as early as 1985. Bayefsky summarizes the reporting system problems as follows:

In large numbers governments fail to produce timely reports, do not engage in reform activities in the course of producing reports, author inadequate reports, send uninformed representatives to the examination of reports by the treaty bodies, fail to respond to questions during the examinations, discourage greater media attention of the examination of reports, fail to disseminate reports and results of the examination within the state, elect non-independent/government employees to treaty body membership.

However, the positive aspect of reporting procedure is that it indicates the acceptance by governments concerned of the international community's right to scrutinize the observance of human rights.

A state party can claim that another state party is not fulfilling its obligations under the relevant treaty. The applicant state does not have to demonstrate any special interest in or relationship to the victim of the violation or in its subject matter. Inter-state complaints are not subject to the admissibility requirements prescribed for private petitions other than the obligation to exhaust domestic remedies. That some inter-state complaints have been politically motivated cannot be denied. Some cases, however, were compelled by humanitarian considerations.

An individual's interests are supposed to be protected by the state of which he is a national, and the individual has been considered to have no *locus standi* before international tribunes. However, individuals belonging to a state increasingly have in various ways come in contact with a foreign state in time of peace as well as of war. Various historical events have contributed to establish the individual as a subject of international law. For example, the Charter of the International Military Tribunals at Nuremberg and Tokyo rejected the view that states are the only subjects of international law and established the principle that the obligations of international law bind individuals directly, regardless of the law of their state and of any contrary order received from their superiors. The Tribunal states as follows:

"Crimes against international law are committed by men not by abstract entities, and only by punishing individuals who commit such crimes can the provisions of international law be enforced."

In 1948 the U.N. General Assembly declared that the right of petition is an essential human right. These historical events lead us to the conclusion that a rigid doctrine of absolute national sovereignty is incompatible with the concepts of fundamental human rights and duties.

The denial of human rights in one country has consequences that affect the affairs and interests of other countries. Only through an international mutuality of responsibility can individual liberty be preserved. Today it is widely held that a consideration of individual complaints would justify intervention in matters that are essentially within the domestic jurisdiction of states.

The Commission on Human Rights was established in 1946 as a subsidiary organ of ECOSOC. The 53 Commission members represent member states of the UN on the basis of "equitable geographical distribution and the representation of the different forms of civilization and the principal legal systems." Because the Commission is made up of governmental representatives, it is considered a highly political body.

Matthews and Pratt argue that the history of the Commission has been normative, promotional, and protection (1966-present). The main achievements of the Commission have been in standard setting, supervision and monitoring, and publicity. The Commission has played a critical role, especially in international human rights standard-setting, including drafting the Universal Declaration of Human Rights as one of its first acts. In recent years, the Commission has increasingly turned its attention to the promotion of economic, social and cultural rights, including the right to development.

The Resolution was adopted in 1967. It authorizes the Commission and its Sub-Commission on Prevention of Discrimination and Protection of Minorities to examine information relevant to "gross violations of human rights and fundamental freedoms." The 1235 procedure can be initiated by a member state, or group of states, or by the Sub-Commission.

The procedure is considered to be effective because the mere mention of a situation might embarrass a country ("mobilization of shame"), generate media coverage, or influence another country's foreign policy. Alston, however, points out that between 1975 and 1979 a succession of horror stories was presented to the Commission (e.g. Idi Amin's atrocities in Uganda, Pol Pot's genocidal regime in Democratic Kampuchea, the systematic disappearances and the widespread terror in Argentina and Uruguay, and the brutality of the military regime in Brazil). However, all these cases were ignored in the 1235 context.

Resolution 1503 was adopted by ECOSOC in 1970 and authorized the Commission and the Sub-Commission to examine the communications received by the UN, which "appear to reveal a consistent pattern of gross and reliably attested violations of human rights and fundamental freedoms."

Communications are examined by the Working Group on Situations, which makes recommendations as to how situations should be dealt with. The recommendations are then examined by the full Commission. The 1503 procedure is confidential until the Commission makes recommendations to the ECOSOC. The process is often criticized because of its painful slowness and vulnerability to political influence at many junctures. Amnesty International characterizes the confidentiality as not an instrument for promoting and protecting and exposing large-scale violations of human rights, but rather for concealing their occurrence.

Iain Guest observes, "Confidentiality has offered a useful refuge for repressive regimes." Alston points out that the 1503 procedure is not called a "petition-redress" procedure since it does not offer any redress to individual victims. He also points out that alleged violations of economic, social and cultural rights have never been examined and the Commission has responded to violations of only a limited range of civil and political rights. According to Nowak, resolution 1503 has played an important role for the development of protection mechanisms. Yet it has lost much of its importance and no longer responds to the present needs and is often misused by governments and should, therefore, be slowly abolished.

The Commission may at times establish a thematic mechanism (i.e. Working Group and Special Rapporteur) as opposed to country- linked supervisory activities. The thematic mechanism may use such methods as: 1. a request to governments for information on specific cases; 2. an urgent request that a government take immediate action to rectify a case; and 3. on-site visits for a more intensive examination of a case. Member states to the UN are obligated to co-operate in good faith with the thematic procedures.

The Commission has established the following Ad Hoc Working Groups of Experts: the Working Group on Enforced and Involuntary Disappearances, the Working Group on Indigenous Populations, and the Working Group on Arbitrary Detention, among others. The members of a Working Group act in an individual capacity.

A thematic rapporteur acts on his or her own initiative to address individual complaints, and investigates situations of widespread abuse and reports to the Commission. Special rapporteurs submit annual reports to the Commission on Human Rights. Special rapporteurs have dealt with such issues as torture, summary or arbitrary executions, religious intolerance, and sale of children, racism, and freedom of expression, internally displaced persons and mercenaries. Kamminga points out that the thematic procedures lack a firm legal framework, which has made the procedures vulnerable to outside pressure. However, the advantage of this has been that it provides a space to develop activities in a flexible way through trial and error.

This is the main subsidiary organ of the Commission on Human Rights. The Sub-Commission is composed of 26 experts who act in their personal capacity. Because the Sub-Commission is a subsidiary organ of the Commission on Human Rights composed of governmental representatives, the Sub-Commission has been dependent upon the "political will" of the governments concerned.

The subsidiary Working Groups of the Sub-Commission have been working on such themes as indigenous populations, contemporary forms of slavery, indigenous populations, minorities, administration of justice and transnational corporations. The Sub-Commission can also appoint a special rapporteur.

THE COMMISSION ON THE STATUS OF WOMEN

The Commission is the leading United Nations policy-making body concerned with women's rights and issues. The Commission prepares recommendations and reports to the ECOSOC on the promotion of women's rights. In 1982 the Commission established an individual complaint procedure. Reanda argues that the problem the Commission has been facing is that the question of equality for women has never become a priority issue for governments on the same level as racism and economic development.

The Commission was responsible for the International Women's Year in 1975 and the subsequent Women's Decade, which were "to intensify action to promote equality between men and women and to increase women's participation in national and international development." The Commission organized the World Conferences on Women being held in Mexico City (1975), Copenhagen (1980), Nairobi (1985) and Beijing (1990). The conferences were credited with laying the foundations for an international women's movement (e.g. the Mexico Declaration and Plan of Action, and the Copenhagen Programme of Action).

The Commission on Crime Prevention and Criminal Justice

This is the main United Nations policy-making body on criminal justice. It develops and monitors the United Nations program on crime prevention.

The United Nations High Commissioner for Human Rights

The High Commissioner for Human Rights was established in 1993 to coordinate the human rights work at the U.N. The mandates of the High Commissioner cover six areas, namely,

1. Promotion and protection of human rights throughout the world;
2. Reinforcement of international cooperation in the field of human rights;
3. The establishment of a dialogue with Governments with a view to ensuring respect for human rights;
4. The coordination of efforts made in this area by the different United Nations organs;
5. Adaptation of the United Nations machinery in this area to current and future needs; and
6. The supervision of the Center for Human Rights.

The High Commissioner would bring both moral and political stature to UN bodies seeking to ameliorate human rights abuses and ensure accountability. The Office of the High Commissioner for Human Rights (OHCHR) is located in Geneva with a liaison office at the New York headquarters, and serves as the focal point of the United Nations in the field of human rights, provides secretariat and substantive services to the United Nations organs concerned with human rights, including the General Assembly and ECOSOC and their subsidiary bodies. It also carries out research, administers the advisory services and technical assistance on human rights, coordinates with NGOs, and collects and disseminates information. The Office maintains a 24-hour fax "hot line" for reporting alleged human rights violations. Each year, it receives nearly 200,000 communications reporting violations.

THE HUMAN RIGHTS COMMITTEE

The Committee was established under the International Covenant on Civil and Political Rights and is described as "the most important UN's human rights body." The Committee's task is, first, to examine state reports, which are required to be submitted to the Committee every five years by member states. Second, the Committee hears inter-state complaints. Third, the Committee considers individual communications, alleging violations of the Covenant by a state party. The individual must have exhausted all available domestic remedies. The role of the Committee is considered to be a promoter, monitor and supervisory body.

The Committee on the Elimination of Racial Discrimination (CERD)

State parties to the International Convention on the Elimination of All Forms of Racial Discrimination (CERD) submit reports every two years to the Committee. The Committee makes annual reports to the General Assembly. The Committee also receives inter-state complaints and individual petitions.

The Committee Against Torture (CAT)

The Committee receives states' reports, inter-state complaints and hears individual communications. If the Committee receives "reliable evidence" that torture is being systematically practiced in the territory of a state party, it may invite the state in question to examine the evidence. The Committee will transmit the findings of the inquiry to the state, together with comments and suggestions.

The Committee on the Elimination of All Forms of Discrimination Against Women (CEDAW)

The Committee oversees the implementation of the Convention by examining state reports and submitting annual reports to the General Assembly. Jacobson points out that many states have been tardy in their submission of reports. The Committee does not have authority to receive individual petitions or inter-state complaints under the Convention.

The Committee on Economic, Social and Cultural Rights (CESCR)

The primary function of the Committee is to monitor the implementation of the Covenant by the state parties so that economic, social and cultural rights are effectively secured. The state parties are required to submit periodic reports outlining the legislative, judicial and other measures, which have been taken to ensure the enjoyment of the rights contained in the Covenant.

The problem stems from the fact that the Committee holds a single annual session of three weeks' duration for the consideration of state reports. Secondly, the breadth of subjects covered by the Covenant, combined with the lack of case law, means that significant importance has to be placed upon the Committee's "creative" or "interpretative" functions.

The Committee on the Rights of the Child

State parties are required to submit regular reports to the Committee on the measures they have taken to put the Convention into effect and on progress in the enjoyment of children's rights in their territories (Art. 44) There is no procedure for individual complaints. The Committee submits reports every two years to the General Assembly.

In conclusion, the six treaty bodies together have a membership of 97. A state party to all six treaties must submit six different reports to each Committee over a period of four to five years. In order to lessen the administrative burden for some states and make the UN mechanisms more cost effective, it has been suggested to have consolidated Committees, namely, the Committee on State Reports and the Committee on Communications and have single consolidated reporting.

The specialized agencies of the United Nations are functional intergovernmental organizations affiliated with the UN.

International Labor Organization (ILO)

The ILO was created in 1919 and has been in the vanguard of efforts to ensure the international protection of human rights. The ILO is composed of a unique tripartite structure representing governments, workers, and employers. The primary focus of ILO Conventions is in the field of labor and social justice (e.g. freedom of association, the right to organize trade unions, freedom from forced labor, freedom from discrimination in employment and equal remuneration) and the ILO utilizes such methods of compliance as reporting systems, complaint procedures, the Commission of Inquiry (guarantor of impartiality and objectivity), and direct contacts with government representatives.

The ILO has no procedure for receiving individual complaints. In addition, Leary points out that human rights NGOs have no easy means of participating in ILO activities. In sum, Cox observes that:

> The ILO emerged from World War II as a small staff with a high sense of commitment to building a new world order. The staff members were united by their efforts to survive the debacle of the League of Nations, by their conviction that they had a viewpoint on the issues of social policy.

The average number of ratification for the Asian countries is nineteen. As for East Asian countries, as of December 1998 PRC has ratified 19 ILO Conventions, Japan 42 Conventions, ROK 12 Conventions, Mongolia 12 Conventions.

The United Nations Educational, Scientific and Cultural Organization (UNESCO)

The first article of the UNESCO Constitution adopted in 1945 provides that the purpose of the organization is:

"To contribute to peace and security by promoting collaboration among the nations through education, science and culture in order to further universal respect for justice, for the rule of law and for the human rights and fundamental freedoms which are affirmed by the Charter of the United Nations."

In 1978 UNESCO adopted a decision by which it established a procedure to handle communications alleging violations of human rights. Weissbrodt and Farley point out that one of the strengths of the UNESCO procedure is its wide accessibility to individuals and NGOs. However, Marks points out that one of the drawbacks of the UNESCO procedure is its lack of strong investigatory mechanism. The following rights are covered by the procedure:

1. The right to education including the right of parents and guardians to ensure the religious and moral education of their children in conformity with their own convictions;

2. The right to share in scientific advancement and its benefits;
3. The right freely to participate in the cultural life of the community;
4. The right to hold opinions and to freedom of expression, including freedom to seek, receive, and impart information and ideas of all kinds;
5. The right to freedom of thought, conscience, and religion;
6. The right to protection of interests resulting from any scientific, literary, or artistic production;
7. The right to freedom of association including the right to form and join trade unions;
8. The right to every child, without discrimination, to such measures of protection as are required by his status as a minor;
9. The right of members of minority groups to enjoy their own culture, to profess and practice their own religion, or to use their own language.

In addition to the rights specified above, the procedure also deals with "massive, systematic or flagrant violations of human rights and fundamental freedoms." The Executive Board's Committee on Conventions and Recommendations makes a decision on the merits. The Committee tries to reach a "friendly solution to promote human rights." Under this procedure the Director-General has a role in seeking to strengthen the action of UNESCO in promoting human rights. UNESCO adopted the Convention against Discrimination in Education in 1960. The purpose of the Convention is to eliminate and prevent all discrimination and promote equal opportunity and treatment in education.

THE WORLD CONFERENCE ON HUMAN RIGHTS

The UN General Assembly designated 1968 as an International Year for Human Rights and in the same year an International Conference on Human Rights was held in Teheran. The goal of the Conference was to review the progress made in the 20 years since the adoption of the Universal Declaration, to identify obstacles to further progress, and to formulate a program for the future. The proclamation issued stated that "the primary aim of the United Nations in the sphere of human rights is the achievement of each individual of the maximum freedom and dignity" but acknowledged that "the widening gap between the economically developed and the developing countries impedes the realization of human rights in the international community."

The Second World Conference on Human Rights was held at Vienna in 1993. 171 states and approximately 1,500 NGOs participated in the Conference. The objectives of the Conference were:

1. To review and assess progress made in the field of human rights, since the adoption of the Universal Declaration in 1948;
2. To identify obstacles and ways in which they may be overcome;
3. To examine the link between development and the enjoyment of economic, social, cultural, civil and political rights;
4. To evaluate the effectiveness of the UN mechanisms;
5. To recommend ways to ensure adequate financial and other sources for UN human rights activities.

The Conference adopted the Vienna Declaration and Programme of Action, which stressed the principles of universality as well as indivisibility, interdependence and interrelatedness of human rights and urged the universal ratification of human rights treaties. It should be noted that the Universal Declaration of Human Rights was adopted with 48 states voting in favor of adoption, while the Vienna Declaration was adopted with 171 states' participation.

In conclusion a brief overview on the development of the UN human rights mechanisms since World War II had been presented. As pointed out earlier, the UN mechanisms lack strong enforcement procedures. This leads to legitimacy and justification of regional human rights mechanisms, including the one proposed in East Asia. It should be noted that the global mechanisms and regional mechanisms are mutually supporting and complementary.

Human rights diplomacy and development aid policy of the US, other developed countries, and international lending institutions have contributed to put human rights in a prominent place in international relations. Their policies have put pressure on human rights violating countries to comply with internationally recognized human rights standards. East Asian countries such as China have been feeling pressure from human rights diplomacy on the part of the US, the sole remaining superpower, to recognize that human rights have become the legitimate concern of the international community.

Article 2 (7) of the United Nations Charter provides that:

Nothing contained in the present Charter shall authorize the United Nations to intervene in matters which are essentially within the domestic jurisdiction.

However, the U.N. Charter requires the member states "to pledge themselves to take joint and separate action in cooperation with the Organization (Art.56)" in order "to promote universal respect for and observance of human rights and fundamental freedoms [Art.55(c)]." In this context, it has been widely accepted that no UN member state can claim that human rights as such are a matter within its domestic jurisdiction. In fact, it has been recognized that how a state treats its own subjects is now the legitimate concern of international law; especially serious violations of human rights are a matter of concern to the international community as a whole.

The argument has been made that there is "a right to intervene" when human rights are at stake. Eminent international lawyer H. Lauterpacht stated in the 1950s that:

"When a state renders itself guilty of cruelties against and persecution of its nationals in such a way as to deny their fundamental human rights and to shock the conscience of mankind, intervention in the interest of humanity is legally permissible."

Moving from permissibility to obligation, Murphy argues that the international community has a duty to intervene under customary international law to punish those states or individuals that commit "crimes against humanity" recognized by civilized nations.

Today there are few states that consider it inadmissible for another government to express concern about human rights issues in general; however, many accept that governments must sometimes express concern about the oppressive human rights situation in particular states. There is evidence that policies have been significantly altered because of hostile comment from elsewhere.

In human rights diplomacy, there are bilateral and multilateral efforts to deal with existing situations. Bilateral human rights diplomacy remains an important means for the promotion of human rights, though multilateral measures by like-minded states also should be undertaken against human rights violators. Mills supports human rights diplomacy by arguing that today it is necessary to reinvent conceptualization of sovereignty. He advocates "The New Sovereignty," which is based on the concept of individuals as humans rather than citizens of states, and as citizens of an emerging global community.

President Roosevelt outlined the "Four Freedoms" in his January 1941 State of the Union Message:

"We look forward to a world founded upon four essential freedoms, freedom of speech and expression, freedom of worship, freedom from want, and freedom from fear of aggression, and these freedoms are to prevail everywhere in the world."

In this message, he made clear that: 1. Human rights everywhere would be an American concern; 2. the rights to be served are civil, political, economic, and social; and 3. international peace and security is itself a human right.

In 1952 the California Court of Appeals in the Sei Fujii v. State case, held that the human rights provisions of the U.N. Charter were binding treaty obligations which superseded inconsistent state legislation by virtue of the supremacy clause. Article VI of the U.S. Constitution provides that "this Constitution...shall be the supreme Law of the Land." This provision has been interpreted to mean that federal statute and the treaties to which the US is a party have the same normative rank under the Constitution. In the event of a conflict between a federal statute and a self executing treaty provision, the latter prevails as far as the domestic law of the US is concerned. However, no treaty can override or conflict with the Constitution. The Constitution is paramount.

The Bricker Amendment was introduced between 1952 and 1957. The aims of the Amendment were: first, to make all international agreements non-self-executing under US law; second, to make international agreements subject under US law to those restraints of the Constitution that limit all powers of the federal government.

In 1961 the Foreign Assistance Act was adopted and Section 502B of the Act states that:

The United States shall, in accordance with its international obligations as set forth in the Charter of the United Nations...promote and encourage increased respect for human rights and fundamental freedoms throughout the world... Accordingly, a principal goal of the foreign policy of the United States shall be to promote the increased observance of internationally recognized human rights by all countries.

In 1967 and 1970 the United States joined the overwhelming votes for the ECOSOC Resolution 1235 and Resolution 1503 respectively.

Meanwhile, in the early 1970's, the Congress of the U.S. began a thorough assessment of international human rights issues and their foreign policy implications. In 1973, Donald Fraser, chair of the Subcommittee on International Organizations and Movements of the House Committee on Foreign Affairs, began extensive hearings on the subject. The hearings resulted, for example, in designating human rights officers in each of the State Department's five geographic bureaus and in creating an Office of Humanitarian Affairs.

Section 32 of the Foreign Assistance Act of 1973 and Section 46 of the Foreign Assistance Act of 1974 expressed the view that the President should reduce or terminate economic, military or security assistance in cases of a "consistent pattern of gross violations of internationally recognized human rights."

In 1975 the Final Act of the Conference on Security and Cooperation in Europe was signed in Helsinki by 33 Western and

Eastern European States as well as the United States and Canada. All of the signatories agreed to respect the human rights set forth in the document, thereby abandoning the argument that external scrutiny was an improper interference in their domestic affairs. The International Development and Food Assistance Act of 1975 became the first human rights legislation to adopt mandatory language, prohibiting aid to any government which grossly and consistently violates internationally recognized rights, unless such assistance will directly benefit the needy people of that country.

In 1975 Congress adopted Section 116 of the Foreign Assistance Act. The pertinent part of Section 116 reads:

No assistance may be provided to the government of any country which engages in a consistent pattern of gross violations of internationally recognized human rights, including torture or cruel, inhuman, or degrading treatment or punishment, prolonged detention without charges, or other flagrant denial of the right to life, liberty and the security of person, unless such assistance will directly benefit the needy people in such country.

The International Security Assistance and Arms Export Control Act of 1976 specify in part that "a principal goal of the foreign policy of the United States is to promote the increased observance of internationally recognized human rights by all countries." The Act also provides that "no security assistance may be provided to any country the government of which engages in a consistent pattern of gross violations of internationally recognized human rights."

The Act requires the Secretary of State to submit to Congress a statement on the status of human rights in the countries concerned; and Secretary is mandated to express an opinion as to whether US aid should be continued. Meanwhile, a proponent of "realpolitik," Kissinger advocated "quiet diplomacy" by arguing that US foreign policy must reflect fundamental national purposes, and the basic challenge of foreign policy is the perennial tension between morality and pragmatism. In 1976 Jimmy Carter was elected and in his inaugural address he stated that:

"Because we are free we can never be indifferent to the fate of freedom elsewhere. Our commitment to human rights must be absolute."

Speaking before the United Nations, Mr. Carter stated, "no member of the United Nations can claim that mistreatment of its citizens is solely its own business... All the signatories of the United Nations Charter have pledged themselves to observe and to respect basic human rights." He further stated, "in formulating security assistance programs, we will continue our efforts to promote and advance respect for human rights in recipient countries." Secretary of State Cyrus Vance articulated what the Carter Administration meant by human rights:

1. The right to be free from governmental violation of the integrity of the person: torture, cruel, inhuman, or degrading treatment or punishment, arbitrary arrest or imprisonment, denial of a fair, public trial, invasion of the home;
2. The right to the fulfillment of such vital needs as food, shelter, health care, and education;
3. The right to enjoy civil and political liberties: freedom of thought, religion, assembly, speech, press, movement both within and outside one's own country, and freedom to take part in government.

Under Carter, human rights concerns became more institutionalized and accepted as a high priority interest of the administration. For example, the State Department established a Bureau of Human Rights and Humanitarian Affairs in 1977, and established the first Country Reports requiring, for each country proposed for security assistance, that an annual report on human rights practices be submitted to Congress.

The Harkin Amendment of 1976 required the American representatives at the Inter-American Development Bank, the African Development Fund and other international lending institutions to vote against loans to governments who engage "in a consistent pattern of gross violations of internationally recognized human rights." The 1976 Amendment to Section 502B of the Foreign Assistance Act of 1961 states:

1. The promotion of internationally recognized human rights as a principal goal of U.S. foreign policy;
2. No security assistance is to be provided for any country whose government engages in a consistent pattern of gross violations of internationally recognized human rights;

3. International security assistance programs are so formulated as to promote and advance human rights.

In 1984, USAID, the agency of the US State Department responsible for official development assistance, recommended the guideline for policy determination as to development aid, that includes strengthening awareness of civil and political rights, of a legal order based on the rule of law, promotion of free and democratic election systems, development of democratic principles and institutions which promote human rights, establishment of human rights NGOs and better access for women and ethnic groups to justice and the political process.

Thus, since the end of World War II, the US has gradually improved human rights provisions of pertinent foreign policy legislation. It has been pointed out, however, that the problem of the US human rights policy is the selective application of human rights criteria in the punitive approach. The US has overlooked the poor human rights record of friendly repressive authoritarian regimes provided that they were opposed to the totalitarian states of communism, in Kirkpatrick's term "moderate autocrats friendly to American interests with less friendly autocrats of extreme persuasion." The lack of consistency of the US human rights policy has resulted in being criticized as a "double standard." However, two years earlier Moynihan defended this by saying that human rights are a political component of American foreign policy, not a humanitarian program.

Furthermore, historically, the US has had ideological limitations towards human rights by focusing solely on civil and political rights and overlooking economic, social and cultural rights. Third, the U.S. has an extremely poor record, when it comes to the ratification of human rights treaties, be they universal or regional in character.

In conclusion, the Lawyers Committee for Human Rights advocate that it should be in the US national interest for human rights issues to be afforded a higher priority and given greater attention in the foreign policy decision-making process.

In Netherlands, the criteria for development aid originally included human rights in 1975 and were further developed in the ensuing years. The Netherlands considers human rights an important component of development assistance and apprises civil and political and economic, social and cultural rights situations of receiving countries based on three criteria:

1. A pluralist, representative democracy supported by human rights;
2. A market economy organized and regulated by an active government;
3. Public services and a safety net for the promotion of equal opportunities as a guarantee against poverty.

Thus, the relevance of the human rights policy of the recipient government is explicitly recognized as an aid criterion because the Netherlands considers democracy, good governance and respect for human rights are essential for the achievement of international order and conflict management. The Permanent Commission on Human Rights gives advice to the Foreign Minister on development aid. The Netherlands considers human rights as a matter of realizing "internationally recognized universal values and norms". The Netherlands and Norway, followed by Sweden and Denmark, have been in competition for many years over who gives the largest percentage of GNP for development aid.

The main criteria for the allocation of aid are: aid needs (that is, the priority for the poorest countries); the socio-economic policy pursued by the recipient government; and respect for human rights. Contrary to the punitive American approach, Dutch development aid aims to create conditions for the realization of human rights because the Dutch policy affirms that development assistance ought to be guided by the needs of the people, rather than by the conduct of their government.

Norway initiated its official development aid (ODA) in 1952 and published the first White Paper "Norway and the Protection of International Human Rights" in 1977. The Ministry of Foreign Affairs began publishing "Annual Report on Norway's Efforts to Promote Human Rights." In 1998 the government presented a Bill on the incorporation of the three human rights conventions into Norwegian law, namely, the European Convention on

Human Rights, the UN Covenants on Civil and Political Rights (CCPR) and Economic, Social and Cultural Rights (CESCR).

The Norwegian Agency for Development Corporation (NORAD) and the Norwegian Institute for Human Rights cooperate to implement projects relating to human rights and democracy (e.g. the China Project). Norway protested against human rights violations in international fora and in bilateral contacts with such countries as Burma, China and Turkey. The Ministry of International Development and Human Rights evaluates the human rights situations in the recipient countries of Norwegian development assistance and publishes an Annual Human Rights Review. Kjekhus stresses that using aid to strive for improvements in human rights is not exporting myopic Eurocentric values.

Canada considers development aid as a vital instrument of foreign policy and is overseen by the Canadian International Development Agency (CIDA). The purpose of such aid is to:

"Support sustainable development in developing countries in order to reduce poverty and to contribute to a more secure, equitable and prosperous world."

The priorities of development aid are given to basic human needs, women in development, infrastructure services, human rights, democracy, good governance, private sector development and environment. As for human rights, development aid policy is "to increase respect for human rights to promote democracy and better governance and to strengthen civil society."

By 1979, linking aid with human rights became accepted Canadian foreign policy. Criteria for granting aid include assessment of the recipient's policies to promote human rights because Canadian aid policy is based on the premise that "respect for human rights is one of the most important conditions for a true development process."

Development aid is considered essential in contributing to an improved respect for human rights in developing countries. Canada was the first donor whose aid policy required recipient governments to adhere to international human rights treaties and implement their human rights obligations, that is, the ratification of human rights treaties and/or the incorporation of international human rights standards into national law. The policy stresses that human rights criteria must be applied in a universal, consistent and transparent manner. Gross, systematic and continuous violations of human rights are recognized as an obstacle to Canadian aid.

The development policy of Germany is overseen by the Ministry for Economic Cooperation and Development. The aims of the development policy of Germany are to:

1. Promote social justice all over the world, alleviate poverty, and support respect for human rights and democratic principles;
2. Contribute to the peaceful resolution and management of conflicts;
3. Protect the environment and limit population growth; and
4. Help to shape economic development in our partner countries.

The guiding principle of their development policy is to contribute to globally sustainable development, that is, productive economic growth, social justice and ecological sustainability. The criteria which influence development cooperation are:

1. Respect for human rights;
2. The rule of law and the certainty of the law;
3. Introduction of a social market economy; and
4. The development commitment of the partner government (e.g. consideration of excessive arms expenditure).

The development cooperation is carried out through the European Union, the European Development Fund, the World Bank and the UN. One of the characteristics of the development policy of Germany is that development cooperation is carried out by NGOs, who have many years of experience in cooperation with their partners abroad because some of NGOs have considerable expertise in the areas of education, poverty alleviation, environment and development, human rights, emergency relief, crisis prevention and conflict resolution.

Japan has been the largest aid donor in the world since 1989. Japanese foreign aid is equivalent to approximately one fifth of all worldwide foreign aid. The Japanese Official Development Aid (ODA) Charter was first adopted in 1991 and the 1992 ODA Charter attempted to blend a diversity of objectives, ranging from environmental concerns and women in development, to democratization and attention to military spending. Japan has considered ODA as an important tool of diplomacy, especially in Asia. For example, in 1993, approximately two-thirds of ODA was given to Asian countries such as Indonesia, China, India, the Philippines, and Thailand. The basic rationales of the ODA Charter are a) humanitarianism, and b) interdependence, among others. The Charter states, in part, that:

Full attention should be paid to the efforts for promoting democratization and introduction of a market-oriented economy, and the situation regarding the securing of basic human rights and freedoms in the recipient country.

In spite of this provision, Japan lacks strict implementation of the ODA policy (e.g. China and Burma). Japanese aid has been intended to serve its own mercantilist interests, by promoting Japanese exports and securing imports of natural resources. Japanese foreign aid is a legitimate arm of industrial policy for Japan's model of guided capitalism. The ODA policy has been formulated as a result of consensus-building between the following governmental bodies:

1. Ministry of Foreign Affairs (MOFA)
2. Japan International Co-operation Agency (JICA) (Foreign policy related economic co-operation, including grant aid and technical assistance)
3. Ministry of Finance (MOF) (Public finance and international monetary policy)
4. Ministry of International Trade and Industry (MITI) (Economic co-operation related to trade)
5. Economic Planning Agency (EPA)
6. The Overseas Economic Co-operation Fund (OECF) (Formulation of basic policies on economic co-operation, including loan aid)

Yasutomo argues that Japan's bureaucratic policy process makes it impossible to develop a comprehensive aid philosophy. ODA has a role to play as a diplomatic tool that combines Japan's national strengths-finance, technology, knowledge, and human resources. Lehmann sums up Japanese foreign aid that Japan's aid is business for Japanese business although Japan has had opportunities to improve human rights situations of recipient countries. Critics argue that ODA requires Diet oversight, consideration of recipient people's interests, and greater transparency and centralization of the aid policy apparatus and process.

WORLD BANK

The Bank is a specialized agency of the United Nations, and the specialized agencies are the main pillars of the UN, which ought to promote universal respect for and observance of human rights. The World Bank is a group of four multilateral financial institutions: 1. the International Bank for Reconstruction and Development (IBRD); 2. the International Development Association (IDA); 3. the International Finance Corporation (IFC); and 4. the Multilateral Investment Guarantee Agency (MIGA). The World Bank is the largest single source of lending for development, with significant influence on the political and economic fate of Third World countries. The Bank applies its own constitutional rules, contained in its Articles of Agreement and follows its own policies. The Bank's role encompasses three different functions: lending, policy advice and co-ordination of development aid.

The World Bank's development aid reflects the following contemporary trends:

1. The normative global appeal of human rights and democratic governance;
2. An erosion of the principles of sovereignty and non-intervention;
3. The demonstrative effect of bilateral donors linking human rights and foreign aid;
4. The addition of human rights and democracy to the charter of the European Bank for Reconstruction and Development.

The "conditionality of aid" is viewed as a legitimate intervention by aid donors in the domestic affairs of borrowing countries to maintain the sustainable development of recipient countries. The conditionality of the World Bank is based on the concept of "good governance" that entails accountability of the government, rule of law, an independent and effective judiciary, transparency of decision-making and freedom of information, institutional pluralism and freedom of association and participation.

The World Bank also insists on the release of political prisoners, the establishment of national and independent human rights commissions, access by international human rights monitors, action to improve government accountability and transparency, dismantling of legislation circumscribing the role of NGOs, freedom of the press and of association. However, it has been pointed out that in practice the World Bank hardly ever addresses civil and political rights in its development aid mandate except in rare circumstances, because civil and political rights are considered political interference and the Bank should be "neutral" politically.

As for NGOs, the World Bank recognizes the expanding role and influence of NGOs, as well as benefits NGO involvement brings to its operations. Capacity building for NGOs is encouraged. The World Bank maintains a consultative committee comprising World Bank staff and NGO representatives.

Gillies suggest five guiding principles to international donors such as the World Bank;

1. State sovereignty is not sacrosanct. True sovereignty resides in the will of the people. As the Universal Declaration of Human Rights puts it: "The will of the people shall be the basis of the authority of government [Art. 21(3)."
2. Respect for fundamental human rights is a sine qua non of legitimate governance.
3. State sovereignty is abused and loses its legitimacy when it seeks to shield gross violations of human rights or grievous and deliberate human suffering.

4. The principle of non-intervention cannot be used to prohibit legitimate international action to protect human rights.
5. The international community has a duty to act for the relief of human suffering and to end the gross violation of human rights.

ASIAN DEVELOPMENT BANK (ADB)

ADB, a multilateral development finance institution, was established in 1966. The purpose of ADB is, among others, to:

1. Extend loans and equity investments;
2. Provide technical assistance and advisory services;

ADB, located in Manila, Philippines, currently has 58 members including ROK, Japan, ROC, PRC and Mongolia. ADB's work with regard to human rights is that lately ADB has been working on harmonization of laws in the region. The project involves codification, unification and standard setting of trade, commerce, banking and financial transaction. The models for harmonization are the Hague Conference on Private International Law (UNCITRAL) and the Uniform Commercial Code (UCC) in the US. The development of legal regime in the region contributes to underpin market-driven economic development. The consistent legal system and institutions are indispensable for economic development because market exchange cannot be affected in the absence of a reasonable expectation that market agreement will be performed and enforced. ADB's efforts in this field would consequently create environment to set up a regional human rights protection mechanism.

Secondly, the Bank's 1987 policy paper "The Bank's Cooperation with Non-Governmental Organization" established a broad framework for cooperation between the Bank and NGOs. NGOs have been sources of information on local conditions and implementing agencies. The emergence of NGOs is becoming apparent in a number of countries in Asia and there has been steadily increasing NGO involvement in Bank operations in a variety of fields. As NGO capacity develops, it is likely that new occasions for such cooperation will emerge. This Bank's work indicates a good example of cooperation between IGO and NGOs.

It also indicates NGOs' participation in regional governance and contribution to regional integration.

Humanitarian intervention is considered international enforcement of human rights and thus contributes to growing globalization of human rights. Henkin defines humanitarian intervention as "coercive intervention by states, singly or collectively, through economic sanctions or by use of military force, in response to widespread deprivation of internationally recognized human rights." Vincent contends that the doctrine of humanitarian intervention obliges a response from outsiders if a state by its conduct shocks the "conscience of mankind."

The legal basis for collective intervention is based on Article 1 of the UN, which provides that:

To maintain international peace and security, and to that end to take effective collective measures for the prevention and removal of threats to the peace, and for suppression of acts of aggression or other breaches of the peace, and to bring about by peaceful means...adjustments or settlements of international disputes or situations that might lead to a breach of the peace.

However, it is important to note that military intervention must be a measure of last resort. The Article 2(4.)of the UN Charter states that:

All members shall refrain in their international relations from the threat or use of force against the territorial integrity or political independence of any state, or in any other manner inconsistent with the purposes of the United Nations.

The principal sources of humanitarian intervention law are the four Geneva Conventions of 1949 and the two 1977 Additional Protocols to those treaties. The four Geneva Conventions are:

1. The Geneva Convention for the Amelioration of the Condition of the Wounded and Sick in Armed Forces in the Field;
2. The Geneva Convention for the Amelioration of the Condition of Wounded, Sick and Shipwrecked Members of Armed Forces at Sea;
3. The Geneva Convention Relative to the Treatment of Prisoners of War; and

4. The Geneva Convention Relative to the Protection of Civilian Persons in Time of War.

These Conventions were formed considering that the First World War was responsible for 10 million deaths, the Second for 50 million; this included 26 million combatants and 24 million civilians. To ensure that the state parties comply with their obligations, the Geneva Conventions provide for a system of supervision that is administered by Protecting Powers. Each state party to the Convention has the right to designate a neutral country to serve as its Protecting Power. The role of Protecting Power may also be performed by the International Red Cross or another comparable impartial humanitarian organization (Art. 10 of Geneva Convention I, II and III and Art. 11 of Geneva Convention IV). Protocol I of 1977 provides for an International Fact-Finding Commission for competence to inquire into grave breaches of the Geneva Conventions (Article 85 of Protocol I of 1977). The Conventions do not, however, establish a mandatory system for the arbitration or adjudication of disputes.

What have been attempted to set forth in this chapter is that the globalization of human rights has increasingly crossed cultures since the dawn of the human rights century. The steady convergence of cross-cultural human values has resulted in the global consensus on human rights that is called the universality of human rights. Human rights, many now believe, apply to all human beings in every human society, equally, by virtue of their humanity. The overwhelming majority of states and organizations in the international community have accepted the universality of human rights. The ratification of international human rights treaties by a large number of countries indicates precisely the globalization of human rights.

Moreover, as indicated in this chapter, international human rights standards have been codified in rapid succession since World War II, beginning with the Universal Declaration of Human Rights in 1948. The codification efforts have not only taken place at the global level but also at regional and national levels. The treaty system constitutes the cornerstone of human rights endeavors and represents the globalization of human rights.

At the UN, human rights endeavors have gone through three different phases- standard-setting, promotion, and currently the protection stage. In the process the UN has created and developed numerous mechanisms and procedures within the UN structure to promote and protect human rights (e.g. Working Group, Special Rapporteur, a High Commissioner for Human Rights, etc). At the same time, the UN has devised and employed various methods such as reporting procedures, inter-state procedures and individual communications to enforce protection of human rights.

The UN human rights mechanism has been in a process of evolution, mechanism and procedure that has strengths and weaknesses. The overall shortcoming of the UN mechanism is that it depends to a great extent upon the good will of member states. It will be necessary to develop the procedures based on the concept of individuals as citizen of an emerging global community rather than merely as citizens of a state.

In addition, globalization of human rights has also been achieved by human rights diplomacy and the development aid policy of the US, major countries and international lending institutions. Democracy, good governance, and respect for human rights are essential for maintaining international peace and security. Human rights diplomacy is an expression of the internationalization of human rights. Based on global consciousness and responsibility, humanitarian intervention and proposal for a permanent international criminal court are good examples of the globalization of human rights. These trends represent a likely step toward establishing a regional human rights regime in East Asia.

2

Conflict in Sri Lanka
Considerations

Coming to Sri Lanka with some training in classical philosophy, East and West found that Sri Lankan experiences involving religious-political struggles often contradicted naive, uninformed preconceptions and expectations. For example, many influential Sinhalese Buddhists - monks, scholars, politicians, and others - citing the authority of the Buddha and his dhamma (teaching, doctrine) to explain and justify their commitments and policies what had always understood to be basic teachings emphasizing tolerance, cooperation, compassion, loving-kindness, and nonviolence were being used to legitimate intolerance, hatred, repression, and violence.

Most of the leading peace and justice activist scholars in Sri Lanka were in great despair. Part of this despair arose from a sense of frustration and confusion. Their historical research, political and economic analyses, and rational arguments seemed irrelevant to those caught up in the hatred, racism, ethnic chauvinism, repression, and violence. This chapter is an attempt at making some sense of religious-political conflicts in Sri Lanka and other parts of South Asia. The focus will be on Sinhala Buddhism as the dominant Sri Lankan ideology. As a vehicle for getting at some of the philosophical issues, we shall consider a number of views of the self at the foundation of economic, political, and cultural orientations: classical Western views, as seen in the Cartesian orientation, and then classical Buddhist alternative views. Our classical formulations disclose rather abstract, general, often idealized positions.

My background is in philosophy, and some of my philosophical considerations may get at dimensions of the religious-political conflict usually omitted by empiricists, historians, anthropologists, and other specialists. At the same time, it is important to recognize that my more general philosophical approach does not focus on what other authors have emphasized: recent changes in modes of production, uneven development and increasing inequality and poverty, destruction of traditional gender relations and other social bonds, and other specific variables and transformations defining much of life in Sri Lanka and other parts of South Asia.

Therefore, it is important to keep in mind that one cannot understand actual evolving concepts of the self and key super structural developments without understanding the omitted specific historical, economic, cultural, social, moral, and aesthetic phenomena and contexts within which such general concepts and structures are constituted and verified philosophically and experientially. At the same time, we must avoid any crude or total reductionism of the following symbolic, mythic, and philosophical structures and meanings to an analysis of specific economic, political, and cultural variables in contemporary Sri Lanka.

After presenting these classical positions, we shall consider a contemporary Sinhala-Buddhist Sri Lankan "reality" that seems to contradict the abstract analysis as expressed in the teachings of the Buddha. We shall then try to make some sense of these contradictions by considering the complex, often contradictory nature of myth and then the dynamic complex relations between abstract analysis and concrete historical developments. Finally, in challenging not only those who maximize and exploit the political-religious conflicts, but also those progressives proposing a radically pluralistic framework, we shall suggest the need to do justice to both commonality and differences, unity and diversity.

Examination of the nature of the self has been one of the key philosophical concerns, both East and West. With a few significant exceptions, such as the teachings of the Buddha or various forms of relativism and scepticism, traditional philosophers have argued for some view of an ahistoric, objective, universal, "true" or authentic self. Traditional philosophers could not avoid recognizing that various concepts of the self were historically and culturally constituted; but typically these alternative formulations were then analyzed as subjective, superficial, illusory, and inadequate perspectives, veiling or distorting the deeper, underlying, objective view of the self that transcended such historical and cultural expressions.

Modern Western views of the self can be seen as arising from the orientation of the "father of modern philosophy," René Descartes, for whom a correct analysis of the self constituted the foundation of his entire philosophy. This modern Western philosophical tradition was developed through the key contributions of such formative philosophers as Thomas Hobbes, John Locke, and David Hume. Even though these philosophers often disagreed with each other, to the extent that a Humean critique raised doubt as to whether "the self" had any objective status, they all assumed a general, shared orientation, expressing highly atomistic, individualistic, essentially nonsocial, egoistic views of the self, and that has defined most of "modern philosophy."

It may be objected that much of contemporary Western philosophy on the self has been anti-Cartesian. There has, for example, been a proliferation of books in British and U.S. analytic philosophy focusing on the problem of "personal identity." But such philosophical analysis is almost totally irrelevant to our project. These analytic philosophers usually focus on a technical epistemological problem of memory and personal identity, largely derived from Locke, and really tells us nothing about actual Western views of the self. We are concerned here with modern philosophical views of the self that are assumed and shape our economic, political, legal, and cultural institutions, religious ideologies, assumptions about human nature, and so forth. It is such views that have been imposed on, resisted by, and adopted within the lives of millions of Sri Lankans.

What comes to mind when we think of our own "self" or of some other "person"? Those of us in the modern industrial and technological societies of the West have tended to assume, both for our own self and for other selves, some view of a person as a separate, independent, autonomous, I-me individual or ego. Most of our modern Western concepts of the self have had Cartesian epistemological roots.

In the Meditations, Descartes attempted to analyze the self not through the more faith-oriented Medieval approaches but rather through the modern acceptance of critical, completely autonomous, rational thought. Through his radical methodological procedure of logical doubt, Descartes finally arrived at his absolute certain, philosophical starting point: "I am, I exist." I can be absolutely certain that at the moment I am thinking (perceiving, imagining, doubting, etc.), I must exist. To the objection that a Buddhist or Humean might offer, that one has established only that thinking or doubting is taking place, Descartes responded that "it is certain that no thought can exist apart from a thing that thinks." Therefore, the essential nature of I or self, according to this Cartesian account, is that of an autonomous, individual, "thinking thing."

Similarly, modern Western social and political philosophers, often with Hobbesian and Lockean roots, have usually started with some assumed condition of rather isolated and insulated separate individuals, existing in some "state of nature," and then postulated how these atomistic selves could come together through some "social contract" to establish a legitimate state. The influential capitalist political economists, such as Adam Smith and David Ricardo, also assumed a human condition of separate I-me individuals and then theorized how these atomistic selves could interact to establish a rationally ordered economy.

Those of us in the West have been socialized to accept, usually without any explicit recognition, variations of the concept of the separate, I-me, individual self, the autonomous individual, as an integral part of our educational, political, legal, cultural, and economic systems. We incorrectly tend to assume that our view of the self or person is not socially, culturally, and historically constituted but rather is essentially "natural," ahistorical, nonpolitical, rational, ethical, and universal. Whether we examine an economic system in which individuals sell their separate labor power for a separate wage or are bombarded with endless commercials presenting models of separate individual "success" by maximizing separate ego possession and consumption of commodities, we carry within ourselves variations of the autonomous individual self as inseparable from what it is to be a true person. And such assumptions and patterns of socialization have increasingly dominated Sri Lankan economic, political, and cultural life.

When missionaries (including contemporary political and economic "missionaries" in Washington and elsewhere), anthropologists, philosophers, and other Westerners encountered various South Asian, African, Latin American, Native American, and other views of the self (including, as revealed in recent feminist studies, female views of the self in the West), they often dismissed or devalued these other views, which seemed to lack a separate, independent, I-me self, as "pre-modern," backward, subjective, irrational, immoral, and at a lower evolutionary stage of development.

The fact that so many modern Western philosophers have assumed that their concepts of the self were not socially, culturally, and historically constituted may seem to have some common-sense basis. Each of us does have a separate body, a separate nervous system, a separate physical identity. But this sense of a separate biological or physical identity does not in itself provide some ahistoric and universal concept of the self or person. Such concepts always involve a filling in, a completion, an interpretation, a constitution. Even the concept of the self as the separate, atomistic, private, autonomous individual has been constituted by specific and complex social, economic, historical, cultural, and psychological relations.

We have presented a part of the dominant, modern, Western model with its hegemonic claims toward ahistoric objectivity and universality. It is our position that such a modern, Western self-claim to ahistoric rationality and universal objectivity is not only philosophically inadequate but has also served colonial and imperial goals of domination. This Western orientation has had a tremendous impact on Sri Lankan life: first, through the economic, political, and educational domination of Sri Lanka by British colonialism; and since independence, by outside Western economic and cultural influences and the modern Western-oriented commitments of the urbanized Sri Lankan elite. Even the Buddhist revivalists of the late nineteenth and twentieth centuries, who reacted so strongly against "foreign" British colonial and Christian domination, were themselves strongly influenced by the modern Western orientation, with its primacy of separate autonomous individuals, in their reformulated Sinhala Buddhism.

THE BUDDHA'S TEACHING OF ANATTA

Perhaps more than any other major figure in the history of philosophy and religion, Siddhartha Gautama, the Buddha, emphasized that our concepts of the self or ego are illusory, that an ego-constructed world is essential to our ignorance and suffering, and that freedom or liberation (nirvâna, nibbâna) entails self transcendence, or, since there is no substantial self, transcendence of the illusion of the self. Many interpreters simply define Buddhism as a philosophy of "noself." We shall briefly consider the Buddha's foundational teaching of no-self (anatta, anâtma) in terms of which concepts of the self/ego are analyzed as illusory constructions essential to our suffering and mode of being in the world of samòsâra (cycle of existence). What makes the Buddha's teaching of anatta especially relevant to the religious-political situation today is the fact that contemporary Sinhala Theravâdins insist that they are the protectors - at times claiming to be the only true protectors - of the "original," "pure" Buddhism, now being threatened by outside, primarily Hindu Tamil, forces.

In "the three characteristics" ("marks," "signata," "signs of being") of all finite, limited, imperfect phenomena in the cycles of existence, the Buddha states: "It remains a fact and the fixed and necessary constitution of being, that all its elements are lacking in an ego." Representative of the frequent critiques of the self or ego found in the Canonical literature on no-self (anatta) is the following: The Buddha does not consider it fitting to consider any of the five aggregates of attachment - the body, feeling, perception, the predispositions/impressions, and consciousness - "which are impermanent, painful, and subject to change" as "this is mine, this am I, this is my ego (soul, self)."

According to the "characteristic" of anicca, everything is "impermanent"; in the continuous becoming of lived experience, we find no permanent, unchanging, everlasting entity such as a self or soul. That which we tend to call an ego or self or person is merely a combination of the ever changing physical and mental states. The composite constructed self or person creates the illusion of a permanent individual self, thus preventing us from experiencing the flow of continuous becoming. This imaginary false belief in an independent separate self is essential to the generation of our selfish desires, greed, craving, hatred, and ego-attachments.

We could extend this analysis of anatta by examining the Buddha's other foundational teachings such as the "doctrine of dependent origination or conditioned genesis" (pratîtya-samutpâda; patòicca-samuppâda) and the "four noble truths." All factors in the chain or circle of dependent origination including "consciousness" (especially of an "I") are conditioned and conditioning, relative and interdependent. Therefore, the constructed self is not some permanent, abiding, Cartesian or other independent entity. Tanhâ (thirst, craving, desire) conditions upâdâna (attachment, clinging), and the Buddha focuses on this "weak link" as a place to decondition and eventually break the chain of samòsâra by transcending such egoistic desires.

In the Buddha's teachings of the four noble truths, we find that the aggregates of attachment, which create the illusion of the "individual" or "I," are dukkha (suffering, impermanence, the human condition); that tanhâ (craving, desiring), as the immediate cause of dukkha, has at its center of attachment (upâdâna) the false concept of a self; and that the overcoming of dukkha, by eliminating tanòhâ, consists in the extinction of the illusory concept of an individual self. The experiential realization of reality is denoted in Pali texts as ñânòa-dassana: insight, "seeing with wisdom," "seeing things as they really are."

According to the Buddha's teachings, our imaginary false belief in a self/ego is not some harmless epistemological error but "produces harmful thoughts of 'me' and 'mine', selfish desire, craving, attachment, hatred, ill-will, conceit, pride, egoism, and other defilements, impurities and problems. It is the source of all the troubles in the world from personal conflicts to wars between nations. In short, to this false view can be traced all the evil in the world." To summarize, according to the Buddha's analysis, our views of the self, including our modern concepts of separate egoistic individuals, are illusory, temporal and historical constructions of the world of samòsâra; such ego constructed worlds are essential to our ignorance and suffering, creating conditions of bondage and illusion through the generation of ego-desires and attachments; concepts of the false self, structured by the skandhas (khandas, the five aggregates), disguise the basic flow of continuous becoming of lived experience and the organic interrelatedness of all life; and freedom and enlightenment finally involve the transcendence of the illusion that there is some reality corresponding to the belief in a permanent isolated individual self or ego.

We may note that although these classical Buddhist critiques of the construction of the individual separate self maintain that such self-concepts are historically and culturally constituted, they remain on a very general and abstract level of analysis and reflect what essentially an ahistorical approach is. The analysis of the illusory concepts of the self really transcends any specific historical and cultural conditions and expresses the general human condition within the context of the finite, spatial, temporal world of samòsâra.

It may be objected that our brief presentation of the Buddha's scriptural teachings and universal analysis of anatta does not do justice to the full range of Buddhist views of the self. In recent years there have been many studies challenging such an unqualified scriptural interpretation: they maintain that such traditional interpretations reflect the hegemonic social position of the Buddhist monkhood with its interlocking power relations with the privileged classes of society and ignore the very different religious orientations of mass or popular Buddhism.

In Selfless Persons, Steven Collins convincingly demonstrates through detailed textual analysis that traditional Theravâda Buddhism recognized distinctions between "actual" Buddhism versus anatta Buddhism, between "popular" versus "specialist" Buddhism, between "conventional" versus "ultimate" truth; that the strict Canonical analysis of "no-self" was intended only for the elite monks or spiritual specialists, not for those preoccupied with worldly affairs, and that Buddhism itself always made provision for other interpretations of the self.

Nevertheless, our brief formulation of anatta is precisely the kind of presentation one finds in the writings of most monks and scholars in Sri Lanka writing about "original," "true," "pure," or "real" Buddhism. This is true, for example, of numerous "Wheel Publications" of the Buddhist Publication Society of Kandy on the Buddhist analysis of the self. This is even true of a number of Sinhalese Buddhist monk-scholars, who are not forest hermits or otherwise removed from socioeconomic and political issues and whose writings often depart from contemporary Sinhala-Buddhist nationalistic ideology.

For example, Philosophy Professor Dharmasiri Gunapala, a former Sinhalese Buddhist monk, freely acknowledges that many Marxist criticisms of contemporary Sinhala Buddhism are justified. But he distinguishes between the corrupt and degenerate "popular Buddhism" and "early Buddhism," consisting of anatta and other original teachings of the Buddha found in the Pali Canon. He then argues that the defects of Sinhala Buddhism can be remedied on the basis of the Buddha's original teachings.

To provide another illustration, Walpola Rahula, probably Sri Lanka's internationally best known Sinhala-Buddhist monk-scholar has been a frequent critic of the violence and other aspects of the political-religious conflict. But his writings are full of claims that such Sinhala-Buddhist manifestations are not "real Buddhism." "Buddhism is not an ethnocentric religion"; "it transcends any ethnic, tribal or national boundaries and limits." The freedom of thought, tolerance, and sympathetic understanding taught by the Buddha are truly astonishing and may be the most important lesson the world can learn from

Buddhism. Certainly there have been wars for political and economic reasons, but Rahula's true Buddhism is so abstracted and idealized that he claims "not a single example of persecution or the shedding of blood in order to convert people to Buddhism, or to propagate it" has occurred during the past 2,500 years!

Since our primary topic is the political-religious conflict in Sri Lanka, where close to 75 percent of the population are Sinhalese, we shall focus on a dominant form of Sinhala Buddhism that has defined so much contemporary life. In particular, we shall point to some of the Sinhala Buddhism that blatantly contradicts the essential teachings of the Buddha. What are some of the religious political features of that dominant Sri Lankan "reality," with its specific Sinhala Buddhist self-identity and self-consciousness?

In briefly describing some of this complex Sri Lankan reality, we note two important qualifications. First, there is not one, homogeneous Sinhala-Buddhist reality. As opposed to earlier uncritical, sweeping generalizations and claims for uniformities, many recent studies have correctly emphasized significant differences between "popular Buddhism" and the doctrinal/scriptural Buddhism of the spiritual elite; differences between traditional rural Buddhism and more modern, Western-influenced, urban, "revivalist," and other Buddhist manifestations; and the indispensable recognition of class, caste, gender, and other relations in defining radically different forms of Buddhism. We shall ignore this rich diversity and pluralism of Sinhala-Buddhist realities and focus instead on a dominant contemporary reality as articulated especially by the most powerful monks and political figures.

Secondly, we do not intend to present a comprehensive accurate account of what is actually occurring in religious-political conflicts. Indeed, much of our analysis in the following sections is intended to make some sense of discrepancies between this Sinhala-Buddhist reality and a more rational, critical, and accurate historical account. Our formulations of this Sinhala-Buddhist reality, with its unique forms of self-identity, present some of the key features of the dominant religious-political perspective: the ideological framework used by politicians, monks, and scholars to legitimate contemporary policies and actions, especially those directed against Tamil Hindus. Such a Sinhala-Buddhist perspective, with its metaphysical and theological framework, claims to get at a deeper level of truth, a deeper reality, than what appears on the more superficial level investigated by many "objective," empirical, secular, modern historians and social scientists.

This unique Sinhala-Buddhist self-identity and consciousness has been constituted through a synthesis of ancient and medieval traditional claims (especially in the Sri Lankan "chronicles") with late nineteenth-century and early twentieth century revivalist developments (especially associated with Anagârika Dharmapâla) and influenced by twentieth-century, especially post independence changes (capitalist transformations, destruction of traditional economic, social, and cultural life, new economic and political competition with "Sinhala only" slogans and other narrow ethnic appeals). One finds many Sinhalese myths and many Buddhist myths increasingly overlapping, intersecting, and mutually reinforcing to form a personal, group, and national Sinhala-Buddhist identity. Such a constructed reality combines religious and historical myths, legends, other imaginary creations, and empirical data and interpretations of changes in the "real" economic, political, and historical world.

In simplest terms, this Sinhala-Buddhist reality equates ethnic community (Sinhalese Buddhists), religion (Theravâda Buddhism), language (Sinhala), race (Aryan Sinhalese), and nation (Sri Lanka). In this reality, the island nation of Sri Lanka is the land of the Sinhalese, a Buddhist nation of Sinhala-speaking people of the Aryan race. "The Sinhalese nationalist ideology is a peculiar combination of a nativized Theravâda Buddhism, the self-understanding of a 'superior' (Aryan) and 'chosen' race, and a near-apocalyptic fear of being overrun by Dravidian Tamils."

The legendary Prince/ King Vijaya came to Sri Lanka in the sixth century B.C.E., arriving on the day of the Buddha's death to fulfill the Buddha's death bed wish that the island be the home of his true doctrine and its inhabitants the defenders of his pure

Buddhism. Vijaya was a North Indian Aryan from the Buddha's Sakya clan, thus establishing the racial and religious origin and identity of his Sinhalese descendents.

As with so many fundamentalists and other religious revivalists in South Asia and throughout the world, there is often a belief in some pre-modern "golden age"; in this case, a peaceful, prosperous, and spiritually superior civilization created by Aryan Sinhala Buddhists, centered at Anuradhapura, and later destroyed by inferior non-Aryan, non-Buddhist invaders from South India. Dravidian Tamils continue to pose an "outside" threat to Sinhala-Buddhist identity and to the very survival of Sinhalese and Buddhism on the island. Often paradigmatic for contemporary Sinhala Buddhists have been accounts in the Chronicles of the defeat of the Tamil Hindu king Elòâra by the Sinhala-Buddhist king Duhòugämunòu in 161 B.C.E., thus legitimating the use of violence by Sinhalese to protect or further the cause of Sinhala-Buddhist nationalism.

Unlike many recent studies, it is not our purpose to analyze the economic, political, and cultural foundation of this Sinhala-Buddhist ideology. Also, unlike many recent studies, it is not our purpose to provide a detailed evaluation of the empirical, scientific, and historical adequacy of such mythic claims. We may simply indicate that some of the major claims have no historical basis. For example, Vijaya, who was not a Buddhist (Mahinda, son of King Asoka of India, brought Buddhism to Sri Lanka three centuries later through King Devânamòpiyatissa), did not establish some pure, homogeneous, North Indian Sinhalese group. Properly speaking, Sinhala and Tamil are linguistic terms, the former related to its Indo-European Sanskritic roots and the latter to the Dravidian family of languages. As a social classification, Sinhala originally referred only to the king and his immediate kin group. Its identification with a large ethnic group of Sinhalese was a much later historical development.

The continual references to Sinhalese and Tamil "races" have no historical basis. From the beginning, Sinhala speakers and Sinhalese kings mixed with others and the term "race" was not even part of Sinhala and Tamil vocabularies. The Sinhalese-Buddhist-Aryan racial identification was a nineteenth- and twentieth-century innovation. Aryan also was primarily a linguistic term, played a part in Indian history, was proposed and then rejected as a racial term by Max Müller in the nineteenth century, and was promoted as a racial term primarily by German racist nationalists and then incorporated by Dharmapâla and other Sinhala-Buddhist revivalists, exclusivists, and chauvinists in claiming racial superiority.

It is not even clear what contemporary Sri Lankans mean when they collapse language into race and continually refer to (Aryan) Sinhala versus (non-Aryan, Dravidian) Tamil "races" ı ecall a conversation at the Universit y of Peradeniya in which an influential Sinhala-Buddhist philosophy professor, who in physical appearance seemed to me indistinguishable from Tamil Hindus, kept referring to the different Sinhala and Tamil races, pointed to his colleagues and asked him if he could distinguish between Sinhalese and Tamils. He paused and then replied that he could - once he heard them speak! Sinhala and Tamil may have meaning as overlapping and opposing ways of constituting ethnic and religious consciousness, and Sinhalese and Tamils generally speak different languages and identify with different religions, but there is no racial basis for their differentiation.

Other parts of the Sinhala-Buddhist consciousness and self-identity have some historical basis but have been embellished and imaginatively reconstructed. For example, there really have been "outside" invasions from South India, and Sinhalese Buddhists, especially under British colonial rule, really were at a religious, economic, educational, political, and linguistic disadvantage. Still other Sinhala-Buddhist claims are unresolved sources of much scholarly debate. For example, it is not clear whether Sinhalese or Tamils came first to Sri Lanka (not that either was the original inhabitants of the island). This debate over who came first occupies much scholarly, political, and religious attention and often exacerbates religious-political conflict. Why such historical claims should have any relevance for issues about present-day national composition and Sri Lankan identity is not obvious.

Our main point is that little, if any, of the key claims in this Sinhala-Buddhist consciousness and identity can be found in the teachings of the Buddha, as presented in the scriptural Pali Canon and other primary ethical and philosophical texts or in the popular Jâtaka tales. Indeed, there is often a clear contradiction between the teachings of the Buddha and this Sinhala-Buddhist ideology. One way of making some sense of these bewildering claims and contradictions is to analyze the Sinhala-Buddhist consciousness as disclosing mythic structures and fulfilling mythic functions.

The history of philosophy and religion reveal two diametrically opposed meanings of "myth": as something "untrue," but also as a "sacred" and "true" story. Plato and especially Aristotle introduced to Western philosophy a common meaning of myth as something untrue. To label, and usually dismiss, something as a myth, as "merely" a myth, is to regard it as a fictitious, imaginary creation that may be believed by some but is irrational, does not correspond to factual and historical evidence, and is false. For many philosophers and scientists, myth represented an earlier, subjective, non-reflective, and uncritical stage of human development. Today, much of our ordinary language reflects this meaning of "myth" versus "reality."

This meaning of myth as "untrue" sheds considerable light on Sinhalese and other Sri Lankan responses to religious-political conflicts. In the present atmosphere of narrow ethnic allegiances, heightened passions, group intimidation and manipulation, fear, hatred, scapegoat, vindictiveness, and violence, there are very few politicians, religious leaders, or members of the establishment mass media willing to reflect on the basic causes, consequences, and lessons of the conflict. Sinhalese Buddhists with political power aligned with a number of the more powerful Buddhist religious figures and aided by servile functionaries at scholarly institutions and in the media, have constructed an effective "mythology" of the ethnic conflict and civil war.

In recent years, there have been impressive historical, archaeological, and other studies by Sri Lankan scholars associated with the Social Scientists' Association, the Committee for Rational Development, and the International Centre for Ethnic Studies, as well as research by other critics of the political-religious conflict. These critics, often writing about Sinhalese and Buddhist (or Tamil and Hindu) myths, have attempted to expose, debunk, and counter ethnic, nationalist, neocolonialist, racist, classist, sexist, and other contemporary ideological constructions. In a Sri Lankan context of relative economic, political, and religious powerlessness, these critics have often been most effective in analyzing Sinhala Buddhist ideological/mythic obfuscations and falsifications. This process of demythologization, at its best, exposes the reality of violence, repression, domination, and injustice.

In analyzing this Sinhala-Buddhist mythic construction, why isn't it sufficient simply to analyze myth as something that is factually and historically false, functioning ideologically to legitimate dominant Sri Lankan economic and political interests? Why is it necessary to consider the traditional use of myth by those who believe and "live" myths? Because after providing the necessary historical, economic, political, cultural, psychological, and media explanations, one has the feeling that one hasn't made sense of the whole story. Something else, something more, is also going on that perplexes, frustrates, and is often ignored by some of the interpreters and critics of the present conflict.

This is most clear when noting the resistance to refutations on the part of those perpetuating and accepting the Sinhala-Buddhist myths. One might assume that counterfactual evidence, exposing internal inconsistencies, showing the unscientific and non-historical nature of key assertions, and other forms of refutation would make a significant difference; that those who accept the myths would feel compelled to defend, modify, or discard their beliefs when confronted by critical evidence and arguments. But within the contemporary ethnic situation of religious-political conflict, this rarely seems to happen. Simply to dismiss Sinhalese Buddhists (or Tamil Hindus) as pre-modern, superstitious, unscientific, and irrational - as so many Western colonialists and imperialists have done - is too easy. The second sense of myth may help us to understand better this resistance to refutations.

The other meaning of myth, much older than classical Greek or Buddhist philosophy, reflects the views of religious people who believe the myths, "live" the myths, and are "mythic people." For such Sinhalese Buddhists, their myths are special narratives, "true" stories of sacred or transcendent realities; they are to be told and retold, are reenacted through rituals and other practices, and provide an essential foundation for their lived world. These symbolic sacred narratives involve the disclosure of ultimate meanings that to most modern people seem non-rational, if not irrational. The mythic truths allow today's Sinhalese Buddhist believers to make sense of their extreme existential crises (poverty, suffering, destruction of traditional social networks and bonds, disorienting migrations, meaninglessness and hopelessness, death), to bring a structured order out of new forms of socioeconomic and cultural (as well as traditional cosmic/ontological) chaos, and to integrate themselves within a coherent, meaningful mythic/religious world.

Myths as sacred histories are historical texts and are historically significant: They arise out of and are experientially verified or legitimated in terms of specific historical, economic, and social contexts; are sources of historical data, sometimes not otherwise available; and they can be revalorized or even "die," in the sense of losing their mythic power, with changes in historical conditions.

But such myths, although they often seem to make historical and scientific claims, always function, at least partially, on an imaginary level, revealing transhistorical meanings and significances for mythic people. Therefore, to attack these Sinhala-Buddhist myths as non-historical and unscientific is, to some extent, to miss the very point of their mythic nature, structure, and function. Indeed, attempts at modern scientific and historical refutation may produce the opposite effect. Millions of Sinhalese who have accepted and clung to new forms of Sinhala-Buddhist mythology may have done this as a rejection of modern scientific, political, and economic models and explanations. These modern developments were experienced as disorienting, threatening, and often producing increased inequality and misery. Such attempted refutations may reinforce the very mythic positions they are intended to refute.

We do not intend to minimize the importance of historical, scientific and other scholarly studies by those attempting to get at the truths and realities. In an atmosphere of political and religious demagoguery and cynical manipulation and exploitation of ethnic discontent, it is essential to expose and oppose the ideological constructions that legitimize the widespread repression, torture, and death. The first sense of myth, the creation and perpetuation of untruths, helps us to get at economic, political, ideological, psychological, military, and media dimensions of Sinhala-Buddhist responses to religious-political conflicts. The first sense of creating and popularizing fictitious accounts and other untruths is also often related to the second sense of myth. The construction and perpetuation of recent Sinhala-Buddhist mythic consciousness, ideology, and self-identity is fueled by historically and factually false accounts. But, as we have noted, countering the untruths does not necessarily remove the believed myths or mythic behavior.

Indeed, dismissing Sinhala-Buddhist mythic idealization as "false consciousness" may sometimes be narrow-minded, a rigid and inadequate approach to reality and even counterproductive if we are concerned with radical social transformation. A demythologization of Sinhala-Buddhist consciousness might even leave most Sri Lankans in a hopeless situation of poverty, dehumanization, and suffering, not getting at the basic causes of oppression and exploitation.

Sinhala-Buddhist and other Sri Lankan constructions of mythic consciousness, in their exemplary models and imaginative idealization, may reveal important truths about difficult realities of existence in Sri Lanka today; they may also symbolically disclose, often in disguised or distorted forms, transhistorical truths about our human condition, our mode of being in the world, our need for community, and our relation to nature and the cosmos.

What may be needed, in addition to exposing dangerous mythic untruths, is the imaginative creation of new narratives growing out of and relevant to the present economic and historical situation and symbolically expressing ideals of loving-kindness, compassion, justice, ego-transcendence, cooperation, mutuality, and even integrating positive aspects of Buddhist mythic consciousness. One could argue that those rare secular socialist and communist movements, which historically won over the allegiance of masses of peasants and workers, created, often unintentionally, deep mythic structures, self-identities, and ideologies.

We began by noting a bewildering discrepancy, an often blatant contradiction, between what has traditionally been upheld in classical Buddhist philosophy as the essential, universal, foundational teachings of the Buddha and recent Sinhalese-Buddhist responses to the religious-political conflict. We then briefly formulated two general concepts or analyses of the self: a Cartesian, ego-oriented, Western orientation increasingly prevalent in contemporary Sri Lankan socioeconomic and cultural life, and the Buddha's deconstruction of claims to a separate permanent ego/self and his project of ego-transcendence.

We then focused on a dominant contemporary Sinhala-Buddhist "reality": key features in the construction of a consciousness and self-identity that are used to legitimize commitments, policies, and actions seemingly at odds with the Buddha's teachings. Finally, we pointed to two opposing, general views of myth in attempting to make some sense of the contradictions related to religious-political conflicts.

It is important to emphasize that our formulations have tended to be on a very general and abstract level of analysis, and there are great dangers in this method of abstraction. Any approach to political-religious conflict remaining on this level of abstraction is doomed to confusion and misinterpretation. We cannot make sense of present political-religious conflicts by uncritically applying the abstract analysis to more specific, concrete, historical and cultural contexts. In understanding these historically specific, Sri Lankan contexts, which are far more complex than formulations of general foundational teachings of the Buddha, one must become aware of all sorts of particular economic, political, social, cultural, and religious variables.

In the dynamic specific contexts of religious-political conflicts, all sorts of unexpected contradictions, not apparent on the level of highest abstraction, do in fact emerge. What may at first appear from some perspective of "true" or "real" Buddhism to be unethical, unspiritual (even "non-Buddhist") aberrations may become the dominant contradictions defining the present

Sinhala-Buddhist context; and what may appear from the universal idealized perspective as acknowledged but secondary manifestations of particular contradictions may become the primary aspects most defining religious-political contradictions within specific Sri Lankan contexts.

Recall our formulation of the Buddha's key analysis of anatta. As one considers only the general teachings of the Buddha in the Pali Canon and other primary ethical and philosophical sources, the central emphasis on egolessness would seem to lead to more openness to experiences of others and more cooperative human relations, greater compassion and tolerance, than would an egoistic orientation, with its ego-insecurities, defense mechanisms, and attachments. As part of the world of samòsâra, selfishness, greed, and intolerance are not denied or ignored, but they are viewed as less ethical and less spiritual karmic (kammic) manifestations, which Buddhists strive to decondition and extinguish.

What one finds instead in present Sinhalese-Buddhist contexts is that what might have been assumed to be secondary contradictions and secondary aspects of contradictions, far from being deconditioned and extinguished, are maximized and exploited. Selfishness, intolerance, repression, and even ideological justifications for violence often appear as the dominant aspects of a Sinhala-Buddhist exclusivistic, chauvinistic nationalism. Within such a complex Sinhala-Buddhist nationalistic context, general Buddhist values, even appeals to egolessness, are used by politicians and monks as mythic and ideological justifications for the oppression of Hindu Tamils. And as we know from many twentieth-century economic and political precedents, appeals to ego transcendence, to extinguishing social boundaries and rights of individual egos, can be intended not for spiritual enlightenment and freedom but instead to impose the most inhumane forms of fascism.

The same dangers in uncritically applying the Buddha's teachings on anatta are true of one's naive expectations regarding violence, nationalism, and other aspects of contemporary Sinhalese Buddhism. Many commentators, examining only the Pali Canon and other basic ethical and philosophical foundations, have maintained that Buddhism, probably more than any other world religion, is a philosophy of nonviolence or benevolent harmlessness. Similarly, it has often been maintained that the Buddha's teachings do not lend themselves to political nationalism; that Buddhism, perhaps more than any other world religion, tends to be cosmopolitan, transhistorical, universal, freeing the individual from any specific social and political conditionings, and even potentially subversive of any nationalistic manifestations.

Only those refusing to examine Buddhist history beyond the foundational texts could maintain such views of Buddhist reality. Whatever the apparent contradictions, the Mahâvamòa and other Chronicles, as well as economic, political, and cultural variables in Sri Lankan history, have provided unique, often dominant, Sinhala-Buddhist ideological justifications for various forms of violence. Whatever the apparent contradictions, an examination of the history of kings and their expanding kingdoms, their relation to the sangha, feudal relations, and many modern developments reveals ideological justifications for a unique, often dominant, Sinhala-Buddhist nationalism. Another dimension of this dialectical complexity can be seen in the different contradictions that appear when situating the abstract analysis of egolessness or other scriptural teachings within different historical contexts. What is progressive and liberating in one context may be reactionary and regressive in another.

A Buddhist emphasis on egolessness may be progressive in mobilizing and unifying resistance to ego-oriented imperialist domination and in countering the excesses, inequalities, and sufferings caused by ego-oriented capitalist development; but it may also assume reactionary forms, exacerbating or even creating internal divisions and oppressions, as we have seen with repressive forms of a Sinhala Buddhist ideology. The same is true of Sri Lankan and other nationalisms, which may be progressive in anti-colonial and anti-imperialist struggles for independence, self-determination, and social development, but may also be regressive when exploiting ethnic hatred and fear, racism, and religious fanaticism, and legitimating violence, denial of human rights, and unnecessary suffering.

We may offer a few additional observations pointing to the confusions and dangers of uncritically applying abstract analysis from traditional Buddhist texts to contemporary political-religious conflicts. First, we may note that the attempt, in the name of the Buddha and his doctrine, to justify later contradictory policies and actions has been present throughout Buddhist history. Traditional and contemporary interpretations and applications of Sinhala-Buddhist King Dutòugämunòu's defeat of Tamil-Hindu King Elòâra, usually establishing this not as a violation of the Buddha's teachings but as a noble Buddhist precedent, are analyzed in this volume by Professor Obeyesekere.

We may cite the illustration of Anagârika Dharmapâla, who, in leading the Sinhala-Buddhist revival, upheld an abstract, doctrinal, philosophical, traditional Buddhism; but as part of uplifting the consciousness of Sinhalese Buddhists, he constituted a unique Sinhala-Buddhist identity by opposing it to Christian, Hindu, Muslim, and other non-Sinhala-Buddhist identities. Much of the post-independence, militant, political use of Sinhala-Buddhist ideology was strongly influenced by Dharmapâla's abstract, doctrinal, and oppositional Buddhist revivalism.

Next we may point to confusion and dangers in remaining on the level of general formulations, whether on the level of the Buddha's teachings or a constituted Sinhalese-Buddhist "reality," without taking into consideration class, caste, gender, and other specific variables. During my stay in Sri Lanka, then President J. R. Jayawardena, in appealing to and politically exploiting the grievances, fears, and aspirations of peasants and workers, continually spoke of the "historical" examples of Prince Vijaya, founder of the Sinhala race in Sri Lanka, and other figures and episodes from Sinhalese-Buddhist "history." At the same time, Jayawardena was a modern, privileged, Western-oriented pro-capitalist, whose United National Party (UNP) government took drastic steps that destroyed traditional socioeconomic and religious structures of the Sinhalese-Buddhist masses. It would be a serious mistake to remain on the level of some abstract ideology and to assume that the intentionality, consciousness, life-world, and identity of J. R. Jayawardena's articulated Sinhala

Buddhism were identical with Sinhala-Buddhist identities and realities even of peasants and workers attracted to his message.

Finally, we may cite several contemporary political-religious considerations further complicating relations between abstract teachings and concrete historical situations. As we have seen, recent scholars have distinguished the abstract (elitist, specialist) doctrine from popular Buddhism and refused to identify the former as the only "real" Buddhism. Rather than devaluing or dismissing popular Buddhism, Obeyesekere goes so far as to claim that the doctrinal teachings of the Buddha lack a sufficient basis for ethical behavior in this world and that this was provided by the Jâtaka tales and other texts of popular Buddhism.

In addition, we must be careful when interpreting the frequent exhortations about the abstract teachings of the Buddha by earlier Western-educated and influenced Sinhalese-Buddhist revivalists or contemporary urban-based, Western-oriented politicians. It would also be a mistake uncritically to overextend the influences of a militant Sinhala-Buddhist "reality" and minimize the force of more traditional, rural-based Theravâda in taking more seriously some of the teachings of the Buddha and in resisting, subverting, and redefining previously discussed Sinhala-Buddhist consciousness and identity.

At this point, an obvious question may be why we should pay any attention to the abstract Buddhist analysis. In terms of the political-religious conflict, why not resolve contradictions by accepting that the Buddha's universal teachings are substantially irrelevant, that they are simply cited by Sinhalese leaders to manipulate the masses and ideologically legitimate their actions? In understanding the conflicts, why not ignore any transhistorical truth claims of the original doctrine and focus all of our analysis on the specific, concrete, economic, historical, social, and cultural variables defining present conflicts?

The problem is that historically and empirically based specialization, which ignores or is unaware of classical texts and a larger philosophical, spiritual, and cultural framework of interpretation, also tends to produce confusion, misinterpretation, and limited understanding. There are countless highly specialized studies that accumulate impressive quantities of "objective" data, but remain superficial in their analysis and interpretations. Indeed, the particular qua particular is unintelligible. Even narrowly oriented historicists and empirically based specialists necessarily make assumptions and value judgments and assume a methodological approach and interpretative framework. Without some understanding of the Buddhist Pali Canon and the history of Sinhalese Buddhism, their very principles of selectivity, classification, and interpretation of empirical data defining present conflicts are open to question. Indeed, without this more abstract and general framework, their specialized studies remain superficial and they fail to grasp the deeper issues constituting the basis of religious-political conflict.

In addition, it is not the case that general religious and political structures and abstract universal teachings are not present or of great force in determining specific contexts of religious-political conflict. Sinhalese Buddhists are not born into a void that is then filled with discrete, particular economic, social, political, and religious data. They are born into and socialized within a structured world not of their own creation - a complex world of significances and meanings already structured by their patterns of linguistic acquisition, scriptural teachings, modes of production, class and caste and gender and ethnic relations, and so forth. Scholars uncover these religious and political structures through methods of abstraction. They abstract from the accumulated data in order to decipher and analyze general patterns of meaning, determine ways to arrange specific variables so as to evaluate levels of significance, and direct our attention to the most profound imaginary idealizations and essential mythic and symbolic structures.

But interpretation on this level of high abstraction and general analysis does not by itself adequately get at any Sinhalese Buddhist "realities." That is why claims about the universal scriptural teachings of the Buddha as the "true" or "real" Buddhism are not very helpful in making sense of present religious political conflicts. Sinhalese Buddhists do live within worlds of general religious and political structures and patterns of meanings; but Sinhala-Buddhist realities are constituted by what real flesh-and-blood, productive, conscious, suffering, creating Sri Lankans do with those abstract truths and general structures. And to make sense of that dialectical process we must do justice to specific historical variables defining political-religious conflicts. Various economic and social variables help us to make sense of why abstract teachings on egolessness or loving kindness are reinforced, redefined, manipulated, distorted, or rejected.

In short, various abstract teachings, traditional idealizations, and essential mythic and symbolic structures get at some of the foundation or "givenness" defining much of a Buddhist life-world; particular historical, economic, cultural, and religious variables determine much of the new manifestations of Sinhala Buddhism; and it is only by doing justice to the complex relations between abstract analysis and specific historical conditions, by approaching religious-political conflicts as "constituted givens," constituted by living subjects, not static abstractions, but within a context of general structures of significance and meaning, that we can make sense of Sinhala-Buddhist, Hindu-Tamil, and other Sri Lankan realities.

UNITY WITH DIVERSITY

Because our topic has been religious-political conflict, we have tended to focus on differences - on how a Sinhala-Buddhist consciousness and identity has been constituted in opposition to non-Sinhalese, non-Buddhist differences. But to leave any impression that Sri Lankan history consists only of religious, ethnic, and other Sinhala-Tamil and Buddhist-Hindu conflicts and differences would be far from the truth.

We have already observed the mythic untruths of modern racial differentiations: Sinhalese Buddhists and Tamil Hindus (as well as Muslim and other Tamils) are racially indistinguishable. What is even more remarkable is that clear Buddhist and Hindu abstract religious differences are often difficult to maintain. The initial visits to the oldest, highly revered Buddhist temples and shrines in the Kandy area and being astonished to find featured deities and practices I had previously been taught to classify as Hindu and non-Buddhist. Deities, such as the gods Visnòu, Nâtha, Saman, Vibhisanòa, and Kataragama and the goddess

Pattinî, demons, and the manipulation of supernatural powers have long been a part of Sinhala Buddhism. Hebniyam, Kâlî, and especially Kataragama have gained increasing prominence in recent Sinhala Buddhism.

One observes profound Tamil-Hindu influences on Sinhala religion and the Sinhalicization of Tamil-Hindu tantra and bhakti, highly emotional and devotional and so different from the dispassionate awareness and control of desires and emotions generally associated with the abstract teachings of the Buddha. Simply to dismiss such central features of traditional and contemporary Sinhala-Buddhist life as non-Buddhist is not very helpful for understanding religious-political conflicts.

We must not forget that almost all Sinhalese and Buddhists first came to Sri Lanka from South India. The process of transformation that allowed them to become Sinhalese Buddhists was made possible, not so much through inquisitions and crusades and forced conversions, but more through the class, caste, cultural, and religious similarities with their Tamil-Hindu and other pre-Sinhala Buddhist identities.

Focusing only on differences is not only inadequate for Sri Lankan historical and cultural understanding. There is much to be said for the emphasis on differences, diversity, and pluralism in deconstructionism, postmodernism, pragmatism, and other recent philosophical developments, as well as in organizations established to protect the rights and greater self-determination of women and oppressed minorities. But the exclusive emphasis on the historical and cultural constitutions of diverse concepts of the self can lead not only to a critique of modern Western self-claims to universal ahistoric objectivity, or to a critique of Sinhala-Buddhist ideological claims to be the only "real" Sri Lankan self-identity.

It also can lead to a rejection of all claims by constituted concepts of the self to any sort of commonality, generality, or universality; to an extreme relativism denying any objectivity or relation to reality. At its best, such an extreme anti-essentialism rejects the imposition of dominant Sinhala-Buddhist philosophical, political, and religious models denying the rich plurality of "other"-ness and insists on the significance of traditionally neglected concepts of other selves (non-Sinhalese, non-Buddhist, and within Sinhala Buddhism itself) outside the dominant relations of power. But such positions may also have unintended disastrous consequences when dealing with present religious-political conflicts.

While granting that much can be said for such contemporary positions in resisting the exclusive hegemonic claims of a militant Sinhala-Buddhist racist nationalism, an opposite extreme emphasis on differences and plurality can be self-defeating. As with so much contemporary Western philosophy, one can deconstruct oneself into an intellectually attractive position of powerlessness and irrelevance. For those concerned with the real historical, economic, and cultural constitution of Sinhala-Buddhist self-identities and how certain specific models of Sinhala-Buddhist reality reflect dominant power relations that must be resisted, an emphasis on differences and diversity may lead to a kind of conceptual tolerance and even eclecticism; but it may prove inadequate for real struggles against general interlocking structures of concentrated power at the heart of exploitation and oppression.

Indeed, in a paradoxical manner, it is the real, profound, human desire and need for community, social integration, and unity that has led to much of the exploitation of differences in Sri Lanka's political-religious conflicts. A significant aspect of our commonality and universality can be seen in historically, politically, economically, technologically, and ecologically real evolving structures of interconnectedness and interdependencies. But it is a significant paradox of much contemporary life that while pre-modern, pre-capitalist, rather isolated, largely agrarian human beings tended to conceive of themselves in terms of transparently social, interrelated, and interdependent communities, modern, urbanized people, objectively dependent on others for their food, clothing, transportation, information, recreation, and culture, conceive of themselves as isolated, atomistic, nonsocial, egoistic, alienated individuals.

Much of the resurgence of religious and political fundamentalism in Sri Lanka, other parts of South Asia, and throughout the world, especially in recent decades, can be interpreted as a resistance to modern Western concepts of the self and their constituted worlds of significance and meaning. This resurgence can be seen as an attempt, at least partially, to reconstitute essential structures of a pre-modern, more communal self and a more coherent and unified reality. Political-religious leaders exploit racist, sexist, ethnic, and other differences. But this should not obscure the objective reality of destroyed communities, increased dehumanization and suffering, and the human need for meaningful coherent social identity.

We have maintained that abstract general analysis, as with foundational teachings of the Buddha or constituted Sinhala-Buddhist realities, is indispensable for making sense of religious-political conflicts and contradictions, but only if such abstraction is then situated within specific Sri Lankan contexts. This means that our approach, including the application of general concepts and truth claims about commonality and unity, must be flexible. What may be progressive when contextualized with specific Sinhala-Buddhist variables may be reactionary when situated within different contexts defining religious-political conflicts.

In many contemporary contexts of religious-political conflict, abstract appeals to universal teachings of the Buddha may be irrelevant or even oppressive and this point to the dangers of the application of decontextualized abstractions. To take an analogy from many recent feminist studies, altruism and caring have often been presented as absolute, eternal goods. But within specific contexts of relative powerlessness, socialized roles of women as altruistic wives and mothers, caring for the welfare of others, have often reinforced woman's status as "other," and denied her the capacity for self-definition as a self-transcending empowered subject.

Altruism and caring are good human qualities but only when contextualized within more symmetrical relations of power allowing for genuine mutuality and reciprocity in the dynamic process of human development. Similarly, even the Buddha's abstract teachings about loving-kindness and egolessness, when situated within exclusivistic nationalistic Sinhala-Buddhists contexts, may contribute to the fear, racism, hatred, and violence. Within such contexts of torture and killings, a modern, post-Enlightenment, Western framework of separate autonomous egos, each with fundamental rights and freedoms, may be the most effective mechanism for exposing and resisting the repression and making demands for basic civil and human rights. In other words, in a Sri Lankan contradiction between a dominant chauvinistic, Sinhala Buddhist ideology and constituted reality and a secondary modern, ego-oriented, general framework of individual rights and freedoms, the modern secular political framework may become a form of resistance to oppression and slaughter.

At the same time, when one is struggling with issues of religious-political conflict but is relating to progressive monks and scholars and to masses of Sinhalese-Buddhist peasants and workers who do not have an objective vested interest in repressing Tamil Hindus and other non-Buddhists, it may be possible to contextualize appeals to ideals of love, compassion, cooperation, tolerance, and the transcendence of the ego. This is precisely what many dedicated Sinhalese Buddhists are doing: using such approaches to expose contradictions between certain general and foundational Buddhist values and what is being upheld by some under a banner of Sinhala-Buddhist nationalism, to counter the hatred and violence, and to revalorize those progressive features of Sinhala Buddhism into new models of economic and social development and ethical and spiritual liberation.

3

Manifold Challenge and Human Rights

The concept of "the international community", if it is to have practical meaning and encapsulate the notion of "solidarity without borders" instead of being an empty slogan, must come to terms with the multitude and gravity of the challenges confronting the peoples and nations of South Asia (Bangladesh, Bhutan, India, Maldives, Nepal, Pakistan and Sri Lanka). The scale of the problems faced in the region and the numbers of people involved are so huge that success or failure in South Asia pose defining challenges to the core mandates of the United Nations as the global arena for problem-solving. South Asia by itself accounts for one-fifth of "We the peoples of the United Nations".

Developments in South Asia cut across the major fault lines of the UN system with respect to the challenges of economic development, environmental protection, food and water security, democratic governance and human rights, nuclear war and peace, inter-state and internal conflicts, and new security issues such as AIDS (acquired immune deficiency syndrome) and international terrorism. What happens in South Asia will surely shape the contours of the global community in the decades ahead. Two of the central purposes of the United Nations as expressed in the UN Charter – to maintain international peace and security and to promote social and economic advancement – make it imperative for the organization to address these issues in South Asia.

The United Nations University (UNU), in collaboration with the UN agencies in Japan, organized an international conference in May 2002 on "The United Nations and South Asia". UNU in Tokyo is particularly well suited as a forum for discussing these issues as the major UN agencies are located in its headquarters building in Tokyo, "UN House". The South Asian embassies in Japan offered their support for the conference and collaborated in its organization. The conference was well timed in that 2002 marked the fiftieth anniversary of the establishment of diplomatic relations with Japan by India, Pakistan and Sri Lanka. But it was ill timed in that on that date India and Pakistan were in the middle of the biggest and most tense mobilization of their full military mights along the full length of their border.

Yet, by presenting a forum for communication between different actors within the various sectors, the conference helped to alleviate the substantial lack of interaction and thus contributed to improved efforts at addressing the problems in South Asia. Their emphasis is on discussing issues of particular relevance to the region and exploring the potential for improvement in both domestic and international efforts at alleviating the problems of South Asia. If and where appropriate, the role that the United Nations can play in this respect is also underscored.

One of the more interesting features of this volume is the divergence of cultures and writing styles of the scholars and the practitioners (officials, politicians, generals). Academics are addicted to notes, whereas practitioners are allergic to them. Many academic shave to be reined in so that their contributions form chapters in a book instead of mini-tomes in themselves, whereas some practitioners have to be coaxed into extending their brief vignettes to a length and intellectual weight suitable for publication by a university press. Two of the UNU's five mandated tasks are to serve as a bridge between the normally isolated worlds of scholarship and policy and to serve as a platform for dialogue. This volume is testimony to the need for dialogue not only between participants from the different nations and societies of a deeply divided region of the world, but also between the different professional cultures in the modern world.

Former prime minister of India, I. K. Gujral, expresses the hope that the recent international interest in South Asia is not temporary and based solely on the threat of terrorism and nuclearization, but rather reflects a realization that the world community cannot be safe or happy unless it involves the billion-plus people of South Asia in the critical decisions regarding peace, security and development. According to Gujral, the most serious current challenge facing South Asia is terrorism. But the fight against terrorism cannot be won by force alone. It is of course necessary to fight the jihadi culture. But, even without jihad, there would still be manifestations of terrorism in all South Asian countries in the form of insurgency movements.

Therefore there is an urgent need to address the root causes of terrorism, such as lack of good governance, low levels of human development, and new threats such as drug trafficking and the spread of AIDS. Although the main responsibility for the problems and their resolution lies with the South Asian countries, the region has not been brought into the global developmental mainstream by the international community. The international community needs a peaceful, cooperative and dynamic South Asia; it is in its interest to facilitate this. Gujral sees great potential for development in South Asia in the fields of science and technology, as well as in traditional industries such as chemicals, pharmaceuticals, heavy industries, steel and electronics. For this potential to be realized, however, regional cooperation is necessary. India, as the leading power, can afford to be accommodative to promote such cooperation.

Sartaj Aziz, while calling for a comprehensive programme to reduce poverty in South Asia, also asks for UN action to reduce tension between the region's two nuclear powers. There is an urgent need to accelerate the pace of economic and social progress in the region and to meet the challenges of globalization. The United Nations must assume and discharge its responsibility to focus on the inequalities of the globalization process and regain a leadership role in providing a level playing field. Nor can the international community continue to overlook the security problems in the region. International assistance is needed to fight terrorism and extremism in the region as well as to stabilize Afghanistan. At the same time, Aziz calls for the United Nations to curb "liberal imperialism", that is, the notion that the so-called "postmodern" world can use force, pre-emptive attack or even deception to violate international boundaries with impunity.

PEACE AND SECURITY

An immediate concern of the international community is the region's impact on international peace and security. South Asia poses many potential threats to regional and global peace and security: it has two nuclear powers engaged in a major territorial dispute; there are several dominant insurgency conflicts here; terrorism is pronounced; and the refugee situation has the potential to be deeply destabilizing. There are also significant cross-regional linkages with respect to relations with China (one of the five permanent members of the UN Security Council), Central Asia (and Russia beyond), the Middle East and South-East Asia. How can domestic and international efforts at resolving conflicts in the region be improved?

INTER-STATE CONFLICT

Since the end of the Cold War, the global pattern of conflict has shifted from inter-state to intra-state conflicts (many of which have transnational regional links), yet one of the remaining potential inter-state conflicts is found in South Asia. The situation is aggravated by the fact that the two potential belligerents are armed with nuclear-armed weapons. Whereas the stability of the nuclear deterrence between the superpowers during the Cold War was itself somewhat suspect, the relationship between Pakistan and India is qualitatively different and even more volatile. The two countries share a long border, which allows little time to decide whether to "use or lose" nuclear weapons in response to a perceived threat. Furthermore, Pakistan and India are involved in a territorial dispute over Kashmir. This dispute has already resulted in two wars between the countries and the possibility of armed conflict has not yet been eliminated.

Neither country has second-strike retaliatory capability, which makes both of them more vulnerable to a pre-emptive strike than was the case between the superpowers during the Cold War. South Asia's relationship with and ties to neighbouring countries also have implications for the involvement of the international community in the region. A complicating element is India's disputed border with China, a third nuclear power with tangible interests in the region. Resurgence of Islamic fundamentalism in the region is also a cause for concern for regional stability. The disruptive nature of this potential conflict is exacerbated by domestic political volatility in all South Asian countries. It is imperative for the United Nations to contribute to a de-escalation of this conflict in order to maintain international peace and security.

Stephen Cohen cautions that, in light of the failure of past predictions, it is impossible to predict future use of nuclear weapons by India and Pakistan with any confidence. It is likely that the future will look much like the current situation – a stable relationship between China and India and a rocky one between India and Pakistan, but with innate common sense or external mediation preventing an outbreak of nuclear conflict. However, Cohen also acknowledges the large number of political and military variables that might affect possible outcomes with regard to the nuclear future of South Asia, only some of which can be influenced or controlled by outside powers. He offers two suggestions: the international community should assist in managing crises; and security planners in the region should avoid overconfidence in deterrence and keep their arsenals low so as to reduce the scale of the catastrophe if there should be a regional war.

Echoing many of the same themes, Christophe Carle emphasizes that the future security of South Asia depends on the relationship between Pakistan and India; the other security threats of the region pale in comparison. He points to the elements of instability in the subcontinent's nuclear deterrence. Contiguity undermines the development of effective and reliable command and control systems and, with ballistic missiles, decision-making time may be reduced to 5–10 minutes. The nuclearization of South Asia and the inherent volatility of the nuclear equation in the region mean that external actors, particularly the United States, have become increasingly important. Thus South Asian (in) security has been internationalized.

INTRA-STATE CONFLICT AND TRANSNATIONAL LINKAGES

Most of the countries in South Asia have insurgency movements. The level of violence is variable, but several of these conflicts have been classified as high intensity. The separatist Tamil Tiger movement in Sri Lanka is one example, where an ethnic group seeks territorial withdrawal from the state entity. The Kashmir dispute feeds on and exacerbates political instability in both India and Pakistan. India faces further challenges in its north-eastern regions. The Maoist movement in Nepal impedes effective government in a similar way, and over the past few years commentators have expressed concern about the possible Talibanization of Pakistan. With these threats to political stability and territorial integrity, South Asia remains a region with a high potential for violence and conflict. How can the international community contribute to the peaceful settlement of these disputes? And what can be done domestically to defuse these conflicts?

Nepal has been much in the news in the past couple of years or so, in part because of the palace massacre of the royal family, but mainly because of the ferocity and intractability of the Maoist insurgency. He points to the transnational elements of the conflict in Nepal, noting that India is often dragged into domestic issues in Nepal, a landlocked Himalayan kingdom sandwiched between two Asian giants with porous and open borders. Weakened states and enfeebled political institutions and leaderships are increasingly incapable of dealing with domestic crises in South Asia, which, in turn, breed inter-state conflicts.

Cross-country migration and refugee flows, as well as the issue of treatment of one's own nationals in neighbouring countries, have the potential to trigger inter-state conflict. Conflicts occur over the exploitation of natural resources such as Nepal's water, and over transit rights for a poor and small country seeking an outlet to the sea for its products. There are also challenges with respect to new security issues such as trafficking in drugs and women. The insurgency in Sri Lanka has been going on for much longer and is also more ferocious: it is the Tamil Tigers, after all, who introduced and perfected the gruesome art of suicide terrorism. Kingsley de Silva notes that South Asia's record of violence in public life is unusual even compared with other post-colonial states. One special feature is the high number of public figures assassinated. Rajiv Gandhi was killed on Indian soil but in the context of Sri Lanka's bitter civil war.

The Kashmir conflict has clearer external factors in its origin than Sri Lanka's but, once the conflict in Sri Lanka erupted and persisted; it was prolonged largely because of Indian intervention. In the Kashmir conflict, terrorism became a distinctive factor in the mid-1980s. The two principal protagonists remain inflexibly resistant to any change in their attitude on this issue. In Sri Lanka the Tamil movement was transformed from a relatively peaceful one until the 1960s into an extraordinarily violent struggle with regional ramifications in the 1980s. Assassinations and suicide bombings became central means of terror. Once terrorism becomes a major factor in the political struggle, de Silva notes, the prospects of negotiating a settlement become all the more difficult. A similar central trait is the marginalization of the so-called moderates.

It is argued by some that the major locus of international terrorism has shifted to South Asia. Terrorist acts are committed in relation to both internal and inter-state conflicts, and the level of violence is alarming. Allegations are also frequently made that governments may support cross-border terrorism to undermine neighbouring states. The phrase "aid, abet and harbour" terrorists has entered the international policymaking agenda since 11 September 2001. How can terrorism be curbed; how can domestic and international actors work to decrease terrorist violence? Is terrorism a purely security problem with no significant political dimensions? Can the challenge of "political terrorism" be met without addressing the fundamental political issues that may underlie it?

PEACEKEEPING

If South Asia poses a challenge to international peace and security, it is also true that the region contributes strongly to the

UN efforts at peacekeeping. Of the total of 44,715 military observers, civilian police and military troops involved in UN peacekeeping operations (PKOs) in July 2001, 12,590 (28 per cent) were from South Asian countries.

As of March 2002, Bangladesh was the biggest contributor to UN PKOs, Pakistan was in second place, India third and Nepal eleventh. What accounts for their continued commitment to UN peace operations in the light of the marked reluctance of some Western countries to accept the burden of UN peacekeeping? South Asian countries contribute with unique and useful skills, for example the Indian army's experience in counter-insurgency operations. Are there wider lessons to be drawn from their experience in peacekeeping operations? One might be improved cooperation on training and perhaps institutional cooperation in the future.

In the light of the contributions by South Asia to the United Nations and the size and importance of the region, one may ask also if South Asia has gained the influence in international forums that it ought to have. The generals call for adherence to recommendations from the Brahimi Report on UN Peace Operations, especially that troop contributing countries must be involved in decision-making on mandates for missions. In addition, though, should South Asia have permanent representation on the Security Council?

SOCIAL AND ECONOMIC ADVANCEMENT

South Asia is home to about a quarter of the world's population, but has 43 per cent of the world's poor and accounts for only 2 per cent of the world's gross domestic product. The region is characterized by poverty, illiteracy and low life expectancy. It does not compare well even by developing-country standards, let alone global benchmarks. The region has experienced improvement in all the main indicators, but with large geographical differences. What can the United Nations and the respective governments do, and how can efforts both domestically and internationally be improved to foster growth and development? How can population control be practiced in a humane and ethical way and in conformity with religious beliefs, precepts and practices?

Hafiz Pasha points out that the absolute number of poor in South Asia has remained stable at about 400 million, despite economic growth in the region. He calls therefore for pro-poor policies to ensure "growth with equity" as the way to achieve poverty reduction in South Asia. From a UN point of view, further economic growth in South Asia is necessary in order to achieve the Millennium Development Goals of reducing the incidence of global poverty by half the 1990s level by 2015. Poverty reduction hinges on reducing inequality through targeted pro-poor policies. However, economic growth is necessary but not by itself sufficient to implement such policies.

An improved level of governance would facilitate the adoption of such policies by helping to protect the general public's interests rather than being hostage to vested interests. To achieve the targets for poverty reduction in South Asia, pro-poor policies will have to be implemented at all levels: global (Official Development Assistance targeted at South Asia, and trade restrictions relaxed), regional (regional cooperation for peace, growth of trade and development of infrastructure), national (reconciliation processes, improved investment climate, better governance) and local (governance reforms, social mobilization). Nevertheless, a word of caution may be in order. Decades of supposedly pro-poor policies in India produced outcomes of rapid poverty multiplication, not poverty eradication. How do we distinguish rhetoric from substance in pro-poor policies, taking care to eschew one while promoting the other?

East Asia has often been held up as providing examples of successful state-directed or managed development. By contrast, South Asia has been a notable example of the failures of dirigisme. Now, in part under the influence of the "Washington consensus" on economic orthodoxy, even South Asian countries are trying to embrace the market and engage with the international economy. At the same time, and in the opposite direction, they face pressures to adjust to the reality of globalization even as it has come under attack from critics. The benefits or penalties of globalization raise further questions of how to alleviate poverty and promote rapid growth in South Asia. How can the need to liberalize in a global market be balanced with the need to protect economic sovereignty and policy autonomy, safeguard vulnerable industrial/manufacturing sectors, or quarantine cultural icons from baleful external influences?

Farooq Sobhan and Riffat Zaman point out that an immense opportunity exists in South Asia for a leap towards higher growth and welfare through expansion in trade and investment. But the countries of the region are constrained by inadequate access to finance for investment, a huge debt burden and current account deficits. Their share of official international trade is small, and trade among South Asian countries is still more meager.

They suffer from an increasing trade deficit. They need to focus on trade, investment and technology. The role of the South Asian Association for Regional Cooperation (SAARC) will be crucial in the liberalization of intra-regional trade. SAARC cannot be an efficient organization unless and until all its members participate with full vigour on the same wavelength. In order to facilitate South Asian cooperation, a development mechanism needs to be in operation with effective regulatory bodies, well-functioning infrastructure and the determination of governments and civil society to carry forward a coordinated development strategy. In this context the utilization of power, water resources, transport and communications, pan-Asian highways, ports, capital markets, financial intermediaries and so on could promote trade and investment for development in South Asia.

DEMOCRATIZATION, GOVERNANCE AND HUMAN RIGHTS

When addressing these problems, the system of government is an integral part of the debate. South Asia has been central to the worldwide debate on bread versus liberty, and indeed on whether the choice is a false dichotomy. Arguments against the efficacy of democracy as a vehicle for sustainable growth within a framework of good governance in impoverished nations have been made for decades. In the South Asian context, there are two schools: one that holds that democracy in a liberal sense is not appropriate for South Asia, while the other (notably from the West) holds that democracy is not viable in unstable societies.

India is the world's largest democracy, but is this necessarily the most efficient form of government for dealing with the low level of development in South Asia? Similarly, to meet the challenges posed by the ethnically heterogeneous South Asian states, does a strong central government or a decentralized political structure allow for more self-government? Is a secular state or a state asserting a religious identity better suited to face the problems of this region? Given experience elsewhere in the world, and given the size of the countries in South Asia, will the establishment and consolidation of institutions for protecting human rights in the countries of the region be a threat to or a safeguard for national integration?

Gautam Adhikari evaluates democracy in four states: Afghanistan (which has no democratic tradition and will depend on external assistance and security presence), Bangladesh (which is firmly on a democratic path but suffers from a lack of resources and should be externally supported), Pakistan (which because of prolonged and repeated spells of military rule has never had a sustained opportunity to develop democracy) and India (which is a democracy but ought to improve transparency and accountability and decentralize). Afghanistan and Pakistan should be subjected to international pressure for incremental democratic nation building; India and Bangladesh are democratic but need to improve their governance. Both Bangladesh and India are liberalizing their economies and decentralizing the polity. Adhikari argues that the international community should support transitions instead of dismissing democracy as irrelevant for stability with growth.

Paikiasothy Saravanamuttu believes that the problem of governance in South Asia stems in large measure from the failure to acknowledge social diversity and embed it in political and constitutional structures. This gives rise to and sustains a crisis of state legitimacy. Applying this to Sri Lanka specifically, he endorses the federal solution proposed in the peace talks in Sri Lanka as a tool for stability within social diversity. This has to be buttressed by an overarching political culture, as well as protection and strengthening of the electoral process, the media, multi-party democracy, the role and responsibility of civil society, and checks and balances on the exercise of authority. Perhaps most importantly, in order to substitute politics for violence, there is a need to provide effective political channels for articulating social grievances.

The economic development of South Asia can be closely linked to concerns about the degree of environmental degradation. Three major drivers behind this can be readily identified: a very high population growth rate, coupled with a lack of appropriate infrastructure; somewhat unfettered industrial growth without due environmental considerations; and major demographic shifts, including intense urbanization. Other factors, in particular poverty and lack of education, further exacerbate the impacts on the environment. Not without coincidence, these environmental impacts also adversely affect livelihoods and the availability of natural resources, forming a vicious cycle of destruction.

Examples include exploitation of fisheries beyond the rate of replenishment, destruction of mangrove forests and the natural bounty contained therein, and pollution of river systems by urban and industrial wastes. In addition to affecting ecosystems and economic infrastructure, adverse environmental impacts also have very serious consequences for the health of people living in this region. The number of people suffering from poisoning by arsenic and fluoride is staggering. Air pollution in South Asia's congested cities is cited as a major cause of respiratory and cancer-related diseases. Access to clean drinking water remains a major challenge for this region.

Zafar Adeel and Awais Piracha review the current situation of human and economic development in South Asia, which is critically linked to the stresses on and depletion of environmental resources. With the help of a case-study of Punjab Province in Pakistan, they demonstrate that the environmental problems faced by the region are a result not of high levels of resource use or industrialization but of population pressure. They provide a summary of the available policy perspectives and set the stage for Adil Najam's discussion of environmental security issues. Najam draws five lessons from South Asia:

1. Environment and security are best conceptualized within the context of sustainable development;

2. The challenge of environment and security in South Asia is principally a challenge at the domestic, even local, level, but it is a challenge common to the region;
3. Institutions and governance are a bigger problem than resource endowments or geography;
4. The prospects of inter-state violence in South Asia over environmental issues are slim, but they can add to tensions and perpetuate distrust;
5. There is a small potential for a new generation of security relations in the region emerging around the nexus of environment and security that is based on the principles of mutual trust, harmony and cooperation rather than on legacies of distrust and dispute.

In fact the last point is taken up by Ashok Swain, who argues that, as a result of human-induced environmental destruction, the world is witnessing a sharp reduction in the availability of arable land, forests, fresh water, clean air and fisheries. The adverse effect of pollution on these scarce resources is worsened by the growing demand for them. The unequal distribution of these resources further complicates the situation. The outcome can be conflict. Nevertheless new research is pointing out that in some cases environmental scarcity might result in cooperation.

Swain examines this with respect to two case-studies: the Indus River agreement of 1960 between India and Pakistan; and the Ganges River agreement of 1996 between India and Bangladesh. In both cases, despite volatile relationships between the countries, agreements on water-sharing have worked. The positive spillover effects of environmental cooperation are possible only if the state institutions are prepared and willing to take advantage of it. A democratically elected legitimate political authority will be more likely to provide a conducive atmosphere for the spread and sustenance of cooperation originating from environmental issues. This accounts for the success of the Ganges Agreement and the failure of the Indus Treaty.

REFUGEES

Of a total of more than 21 million "refugees and others of concern to UNHCR", South Asia have 3,030,562, or 14 per cent.

In view of current developments, this number may increase significantly. Neighbouring regions have similar or worse refugee situations, which may in turn exacerbate the problem in South Asia. Refugee flows are a destabilizing trait domestically, and since the 1990s the problem has increasingly been considered a threat to international peace and security and as such of particular interest to the United Nations. Similarly, there have been disputes over migration, such as when India tried to limit migration from Bangladesh. How do the United Nations and the respective states address refugee issues in South Asia, and how can this be done in a constructive and stabilizing way?

REGIONAL COOPERATION

Another facet of these problems is the implications for regional security. As natural resources are over-exploited, increasing population pressures may lead to transboundary conflicts. This is most obvious for the sharing of water resources, and inter alia energy resources, in this region. The challenge for international organizations remains how to solve these problems in an integrated manner while promoting economic growth and development.

South Asia needs a regional identity and rationality. Niaz Naik laments the fact that South Asia remains mired in conflicts and tension. He lists the varied sources of instability: inter-state conflict, internal instability, terrorism, drug trafficking, clandestine arms sale, migration, trafficking in women and children, and the spread of HIV/AIDS. Regional cooperation is necessary to face the multidimensional threat to security in South Asia. Since the Male Summit in 1997, the South Asian Association for Regional Cooperation (SAARC) has addressed pivotal issues such as fostering mutual trust, conflict resolution, promoting good-neighbourly relations and confidence-building.

But, in light of the experience of other regional organizations, Naik concludes that the absence of an institutionalized security mechanism has hindered South Asian regional stability. He warns that South Asia is at a crossroads: "either it can pursue a path of purposeful cooperation based on peace, development and reconciliation, or it can sink deeper into the abyss of hopeless poverty, deprivation, disease and illiteracy, resulting in the gradual erosion of the very core of our ancient societies."

Nihal Rodrigo acknowledges the existence of two extreme views of SAARC: it is ineffectual and incapable of responding to the challenges facing South Asia: or, as the only functioning intergovernmental organization in South Asia, it can contribute to peace and stability in the region and help cooperation among its member states. A realistic assessment falls somewhere between these extremes, he believes. Although criticized and unable to accomplish much in the three years preceding the Kathmandu Summit in 2002, the institutional framework of SAARC has facilitated closer South Asian interaction in a number of arenas. And Rodrigo notes that closer relations among the seven South Asian countries and effective regional cooperation are bound together symbiotically.

HUMAN INSECURITY IN SOUTH ASIA

In many ways, environmental pressures and refugees stand at the intersection of national and human security (as shown, for example, by the sudden flare-up of tension between India and Bangladesh in February 2003 over the subject of "illegal immigrants"). Regional cooperation within the SAARC framework has proven problematical within traditional, state-based and territorially grounded "national security"; it may fare better with respect to de-territorialized and de-nationalized "human security".

Manzoor Ahmed discusses the concept of human security from the perspective of children and women in South Asia. South Asia scores badly on human development indicators, even compared with developing countries. The situation is especially grave for women and children with respect to education, health care, access to clean water and sanitation, and basic protection from threats to human existence.

To improve the situation, effective and accountable governance and a redistribution of resources are required. For example, at present India spends 70 per cent more on defence and debt service than on the social sector. Ahmed recommends a prioritization of women and children politically, partnerships between different actors for social and development services, decentralization to improve governance, greater use of the legal system to promote the rights of the disadvantaged, higher priority to education, and regional cooperation. He also identifies possible roles for the United Nations in this process - as the forum for international consensus on goals for children and women, for raising awareness and for setting moral and legal norms; cooperation with countries on plans and action; and promotion of the role of civil society.

Santosh Mehrotra takes up in a more focused way the question of whether the worst malnutrition is linked to the worst gender discrimination in the world. Half of the world's malnourished children are to be found in just three countries: Bangladesh, India and Pakistan. Child malnutrition cannot be reversed as the child grows, and it is both a symptom and a cause of poverty. South Asia has the worst record on all three indices of malnutrition: under-weight, stunting and wasting. In developing countries, on average 29 per cent of children are under-weight; in South Asia the figure is 49 per cent.

The record is similarly bad for women, as indicated by lower height and body mass index. To counteract this, Mehrotra suggests that public distribution networks for food must be improved and loss through spoilage in warehouse storage reduced. Also, given the skewed food allocation within households, which discriminates against women and children, school feeding programmes must be set up and health care for pregnant women and infants must be improved.

Taking up the same theme, Rekha Datta identifies child labour and the lack of rights for self-employed women as major human security threats in South Asia. Non-governmental organizations (NGOs) are the primary agencies addressing issues of human security. She elaborates on a case study of the Self-Employed Women's Association (SEWA), a trade union movement of sorts providing access to resources, capital, knowledge- and skill-building, use of technology, health care, and savings for capital and for security, and literacy.

SEWA has been at the forefront of NGO efforts for human security, silently changing women's lives. It has also had considerable policy impact – for instance, the Gujarat government recognized self-employed women as labourers – and, on an international level, SEWA has cooperated with the International Labour Organization (ILO). Datta concludes that, to improve human security, grass-roots activism must be integrated with policy-making on national, regional and global levels.

9/11, AFGHANISTAN AND SOUTH ASIA

Afghanistan has been a historical gateway to South Asia and a playing-cum-killing field for imperialistic great games in the region. Its security problems demonstrate only too graphically and tragically how national and human insecurity can in fact intersect and feed off each other. The terrorist attacks on US targets on 11 September 2001 ("9/11") provoked a massive US-led attack on the Taliban regime of Afghanistan. In discussing the implications of that, Samina Ahmed argues that continued conflict in Afghanistan will destabilize South Asia. Conversely, a pacified Afghanistan will promote regional stability, reduce the threat of terrorism in the region and create trade opportunities with Central Asian neighbours. Although the US-led coalition overthrew the Taliban, it has found it difficult to achieve the follow-up goal of eradicating the threat of terrorism through political, economic and social reconstruction.

Afghanistan's Transitional Administration faces multiple challenges: alienated ethnic actors contest its legitimacy; warlords still control their territories; infighting prevails over rule of law; and the slow pace of reconstruction is hampering reconciliation. National and regional security is threatened by the reluctance of international forces to expand their security presence beyond Kabul. As a consequence, the peace is fragile and, if conflict resumes, terrorism will return with it. Also, the unchecked war economy (involving drugs and arms trade) strengthens warlords and militias compared with the central government. India and Pakistan must refrain from interfering in Afghanistan's reconstruction to promote their own agendas, Ahmed urges. It is in the security interest of both to lobby for greater international reconstruction assistance. Non-intervention by neighbours in Afghanistan's affairs would enhance the prospects for peace and deprive extremists of support.

Mohammed Ayoob argues that, in its war on terrorism, Washington has attempted to untie the knot of Islamic extremism that has been at the centre of Pakistani–Afghan relations for years. It has recorded two modest successes: the establishment of an interim Afghan government with a moderate leader, and General Pervez Musharraf's pledge to break Pakistani-based terror groups and pull away from the theocratic state. But South-West Asia is still threatened by instability. Further conflict and fragmentation in Afghanistan could have ripple effects.

Moreover, Afghan stability looks elusive: the government does not have control beyond Kabul; the strategic interests of external neighbours are at odds and they have different favourite clients; the warlords are benefiting from strife; the government has less resources and it is also unpopular because of the ban on poppy cultivation and the drug trade. With Afghanistan and Pakistan in unrest, Ayoob concludes that the United States needs support from India and Iran as the only responsible powers with capabilities and interest in South-West Asia's stability.

The Taliban and al-Qaida have been replaced by a US-supported coalition, Pakistan has switched sides to join the United States, India has upped the ante with Pakistan over "cross border terrorism" in the light of the US war on terror, Afghanistan and the Central Asian republics have been transformed into US footholds, Iran is encircled by US forces, and political Islam has been put on the defensive. In this fluid situation the United States and its allies have to choose either to remain fully engaged in Afghanistan for 5–10 years or to risk its falling into renewed fragmentation.

The United States is ambivalent about engaging in nation-building in Afghanistan, Pakistan and Central Asia. Yet this is necessary to stabilize Central, West and South Asia. The United States will need to adopt multilateralism in order to do this.

The volume ends with two possible roadmaps for a better, more prosperous and peaceful South Asia. The pivot is the historic animosity between India and Pakistan. Samina Yasmeen postulates that the negative mythology of "the other" provides the context for perceptions and decision-making between India and Pakistan. This has permeated the relationship since independence, and has been aggravated by three wars and the continuing rivalry over Kashmir. The symmetrical negative imagery pervades the two civil societies as well. Education (for example, history books), the media and cultural elements such as movies contribute to a "shared consciousness" that rests upon and fuels the demonization of the other.

Yasmeen distinguishes between hawkish/orthodox and moderate schools of thought in both countries, and identifies the moderate tendencies throughout the turbulent relationship. Nevertheless, the orthodox perception of the relationship as a zero-sum conflict has influenced decision-making on the process of nuclearization as well as the missile race. Hawkish leaders in both countries have used the other country's difficulties and problems to tilt the balance in their favour. While recommending continuing efforts for moderation within and between the two countries, such as the Gujral Doctrine and Lahore agreement, Yasmeen suggests that, among external actors, the United States is better placed to play a short-term role as the facilitating superpower, while the United Nations should play a longer-term part, addressing the root causes of instability such as poverty, population growth rates, environmental degradation and the AIDS epidemic.

India's former High Commissioner (ambassador) to Pakistan, Gopalaswami Parthasarathy, reminds us that the conflict in Afghanistan has spilled over into Pakistan, the Taliban and its supporters have not been eliminated, and the Indian and Pakistani armies are still facing each other in Kashmir. But he argues that the nuclear dimension is exaggerated, being less threatening than the West thinks. For practical purposes, the two defence forces have known of each other's nuclear capability for a decade. Despite the persistent volatility, there are positive trends in the relationship between India and Pakistan, including the Lahore Summit and progress towards economic integration.

It is now necessary to create the conditions for moving from conflict to cooperation. Parthasarathy compares the situation to that of Ireland and the United Kingdom over Northern Ireland, conciliated in part because they are both members of the European Union. He hopes that the vision statement from Lahore – of an economic union in South Asia by 2020 – will be implemented, because economic links and integration will facilitate conflict resolution. Mistrust must be reduced in populations – by people-to-people contact (tourism and exchange programmes), the media, trade and the promotion of cultural understanding – and also between governments, for example through agreements on a set of confidence-building measures for both nuclear and conventional weapons.

It is important to create a climate conducive to bilateral dialogue. The SAARC summits in Lahore and Kathmandu show that positive development is possible, and that neither party gains by remaining hostage to the mistrust and animosity of the past. In sum, the facts of geography have given the seven countries of South Asia a shared history and will ensure a common destiny. Neither enmity nor friendship, neither poverty nor prosperity, is predestined. With mutual and international goodwill, with the mustering of the necessary political will, and with the adoption of mutually conciliatory, market friendly and pro-growth policies, the peoples and governments of South Asia could as yet take their fate back into their own hands and rediscover the greatness and the glory that once were theirs.

4

Threat to Global Peace

The continuing inability of the United Nations to solve the Kashmir problem is the single most important cause of many other problems in South Asia. If the leaders of India and Pakistan had found a reasonable solution of the Kashmir problem in the 1950s, the per capita income of South Asia would have been at least twice the present level and the South Asian Association for Regional Cooperation (SAARC) would by now be a functioning common market. Instead, Pakistan - after three wars with India, the loss of its eastern wing in 1971 and a disproportionately large burden of defence expenditure - is facing a formidable military stand-off with a country seven times its size.

The stand-off started in January 2002 with the deployment of half a million Indian troops along the Pakistan border, the highest level of mobilization in 30 years. This is a very dangerous situation. The well-known Indian writer Arundhati Roy, in an article on state terrorism in Gujarat, wrote in Outlook India: "The buzz is that engineering a war against Pakistan is going to be the BJP's strategy to swing the vote in the next general elections". In an article under the title "The Kashmir Time Bomb", the Washington Post said, "the sub-continent is the only part of the world where nuclear war is today a serious possibility".

The central purpose of the United Nations, under the UN Charter, is to maintain peace and security. The United Nations and its important members cannot therefore continue their present policy of indifference towards one of the two most serious threats to global peace (the other being the Middle East). There is a need for bold and fresh thinking. The Secretary-General of the United Nations should consider launching a joint initiative through the five permanent members of the Security Council to promote durable peace in South Asia, by focusing, inter alia, on the following measures:

- Persuade India and Pakistan to withdraw their forces from the border and to defuse the prevailing tensions through military de-escalation;
- Request both countries to implement, in letter and in spirit, the Memorandum of Understanding signed during the visit of India's prime minister Vajpayee to Lahore on 21 February 1999, for confidence-building in the nuclear and conventional fields aimed at avoidance of conflict; in this context, it is important for both countries not to deploy nuclear weapons;
- Encourage both countries to resume serious negotiations on Kashmir and other issues and to recognize that relations between India and Pakistan cannot improve unless they find a just and acceptable solution to the Kashmir problem.

In taking the initiative for promoting durable peace in this volatile region, the international community should also evolve a common view of the problem and narrow the options to specific guidelines for serious negotiations between the two countries. The world has changed in the past few years, with both countries becoming nuclear powers in May 1998 and both now being partners in the international campaign against terrorism after the events of 11 September 2001.

In responding to such a peace initiative, India has to face the stark reality of the Kashmir problem, rather than insist that it is only a problem of cross-border terrorism. If Kashmir is really a part of India, as India claims, then it should allow observers from the Commonwealth or the European Union to monitor the forthcoming elections in the Kashmir Valley, and to verify the percentage of voters actually taking part in these elections. (In the past few elections, the percentage of Muslim voters in Kashmir Valley, despite rigging, never rose above 5 per cent.)

Even on the issue of cross-border terrorism, Pakistan has taken unprecedented steps since January 2002 to curb extremist and militant organizations within Pakistan, but Pakistan cannot restrain the activities of freedom fighters within Kashmir, who are fighting for their right of self determination, promised to them by the United Nations in the 1950s. They can be persuaded only by serious negotiations to find a solution acceptable to the Kashmiri people.

The growth of extremism and Islamic fundamentalism in Afghanistan and their spillover into neighbouring Pakistan are a direct legacy of the proxy war between the United States and Russia, which started in 1979 with the Russian invasion of Afghanistan. The United States launched a major counter-operation in close cooperation with Pakistan to recruit, train and fund thousands of Islamic volunteers or "mujahidin" to fight and eventually defeat a superpower over the next 10 years.

But the United States and its allies walked away from Afghanistan soon after the Russian forces were withdrawn, leaving Pakistan to deal with the grave consequences of the decade-long conflict: 3 million refugees, an unprecedented influx of guns and drugs, and a formidable network of madrasas and training camps – some in Pakistan, some in Afghanistan – training thousands of volunteers every year. In the absence of any large-scale assistance for the rehabilitation of Afghanistan and in the face of conflicting claims by various warlords, who had superseded the traditional tribal leadership, a prolonged civil war further ravaged Afghanistan throughout the 1990s. The resultant disorder and chaos provided a very good safe haven for Osama bin Laden and his network to establish them in Afghanistan.

The tragic events of 11 September 2001 have set into motion another chain of events in the region, whose final consequences are difficult to predict at this stage. A concerted international coalition against terrorism was launched within days, with a focus on Islamic countries. The faceless enemies who had destroyed the Twin Towers were given the face of Osama bin Laden and his al-Qaida network, and the Taliban regime was bracketed with the enemy because it had given shelter to Osama bin Laden.

That provided the justification for launching a ferocious war on Afghanistan in which thousands of innocent lives have been lost but without capturing Osama bin Laden and Mullah Omar and without bringing peace and stability to Afghanistan. Pakistan joined the international campaign against terrorism soon after it was launched in September 2001, and, after reversing its policy of supporting the Taliban regime, offered its airfields and other logistical support for air attacks on Afghanistan. It also took unprecedented measures to clamp down on extremist and militant organizations within Pakistan by banning many of them and freezing their accounts and other facilities.

Apart from the Indo-Pakistan tensions over the Kashmir dispute, there are high-intensity conflicts within most countries of South Asia. These include the Tamil Tiger movement in Sri Lanka, the Maoist insurgency in Nepal, sectarian and ethnic tensions in Pakistan, the continuing insurgency in the north-east of India and recent communal riots in Gujarat. These conflicts, which illustrate the structural problems inherent in heterogeneous societies, are serious obstacles to the establishment of sustainable political systems and viable institutions of good governance. South Asia will not be able to achieve peace and stability unless the governments concerned can successfully overcome these obstacles.

The objective of curbing extremism in South Asia will be possible if there is peace and stability in Afghanistan. This, in turn, will require (i) extending the role of multinational forces from Kabul to at least four other cities: Herat, Mazar-e Sharif, Kandahar and Jalalabad; (ii) full support of the UN role in implementing the Bonn Agreement in letter and spirit and ensuring a truly broad-based Loya Jirga (traditional tribal Grand Council), leading to a more balanced transitional government; and (iii) converting the pledges of US $4.5 billion made in Tokyo in January 2002 for the reconstruction of Afghanistan into actual resource flows. The international coalition is spending US $1 billion a month on military operations in Afghanistan but cannot provide even US $50 million a month regularly to the interim administration so that it can pay the salaries of all its teachers, doctors and security personnel.

Another global fault line whose long shadows continue to fall on Pakistan is the unending and tragic saga in the Middle East. Al-Qaida and many other organizations that have been operating in Pakistan's neighbourhood trace their roots and desperate acts to the continuing occupation of Palestine and other Arab lands. Instead of the underlying causes being dealt with justly, these people and their sympathizers are now being pushed further to the wall. Encouraged by the unilateral decision to attack Afghanistan to counter terrorism, Israel launched a ferocious onslaught on the West Bank, killing countless innocent civilians.

In fact, any country can now assume the right to act unilaterally against any other country, even on suspicion or allegation of terrorism, without presenting any evidence to the UN Security Council or the International Criminal Court. The United Nations must act to restore the sanctity of international law by prescribing a proper system to deal with such complaints and allegations, and it must also define terrorism to, inter alia, and distinguish freedom fighters from terrorists.

Underlying the happenings in Afghanistan and the Middle East is a new and dangerous philosophy, which has been called "liberal imperialism". This is the doctrine of a new world order in which the powerful "postmodern states" no longer give paramount importance to the concept of a nation-state, exercising sovereignty within a well-defined geographical jurisdiction. In the name of human rights, curbing terrorism or global economic interests (such as safeguarding the flow of oil), the "postmodern" world can use "force, pre-emptive attack or even deception" to violate the international boundaries of pre-modern or modern states with impunity. The United Nations must assert its collective authority to curb this "liberal imperialism" before it is too late.

REALIZING THE DEVELOPMENT POTENTIAL

South Asia, despite its enormous human and physical resources, has become the most deprived region of the world. Its per capita income (US $460, or US $2,260 in terms of purchasing power parity) is lower than that in any other region; its adult literacy rate of 47 per cent is also the lowest in the world; it is the most malnourished region of the world, with half its children being under-weight, compared with 30 per cent in Sub-Saharan Africa. It is the least gender-sensitive region and it has the highest human deprivation, in terms of access to health facilities, safe drinking water, sanitation facilities and opportunities for work and leisure. At the same time, South Asia is the most militarized region in the developing world, with the highest percentage of GDP going to military expenditures.

Is there a greater challenge facing the leaders of South Asia to change these priorities and grasp the opportunities for economic and social progress that the twenty-first century offers? There are many positive elements in South Asia today, such as the progress in information technology, self-sufficiency in food, much greater emphasis on the development of human resources and a wide-ranging consensus on strategies to reduce poverty. However, the obstacles to realizing the full development potential of South Asia are formidable. There are many internal obstacles, such as recurrent political instability, internal insurgencies and poor governance, but the international obstacles seem even more daunting.

Each country must assume primary responsibility for improving the living standards of its people. But in this task it needs, as a minimum, a level playing field and a fair share of global public goods. That unfortunately has not been forthcoming. The global economic system has always been more favourable for the rich and powerful countries, and the system of globalization that has been evolving for the past two decades has added to the chronic difficulties. This should be clear from the following examples of distortions and inequities:

- The global trading system works against the longer-term interest of low-income countries and poor people and does not provide a level playing field or a truly competitive environment. The World Trade Organization's policy of liberalizing trade concentrates on high-tech products largely of interest to developed countries, a few middle-income developing countries and multinational companies. Simple manufactures such as textiles and leather goods, which are of greater interest to low-income developing countries, are still subject to quotas and protectionist policies. Movement of labour, which is an important factor in the production cycle, is also seriously restricted.

- The developed countries provide subsidies totalling US $350 billion a year to their agriculture sectors, which is almost six times the total Official Development Assistance provided to developing countries. The developing countries, which primarily depend on agricultural exports, cannot compete in international markets with these subsidized agricultural exports from the developed countries. This has not only reduced the share of developing countries in global agricultural trade but also weakened their incentive system for increasing domestic production.
- The world monetary system creates excess liquidity every year by transferring purchasing power to the richest country in the world because the US dollar has been the main reserve currency. All attempts to establish a global system of liquidity creation by the International Monetary Fund (IMF), for example, which could distribute the resultant resources more equitably, have been turned down. Now, belatedly, the European Union is trying to secure a share in this liquidity through the use of the euro as a reserve currency, but it is facing serious difficulties.
- The flow of Official Development Assistance, which was partly a compensation for the inequities of the global system, instead of moving towards the internationally accepted target of 0.7 per cent of GDP, declined from US $87 billion to US $61 billion in the 1990s. The latest report from the OECD's Development Assistance Committee (OECD-DAC, 2002. shows the figure fell further to US $51 billion in 2001. This was only 0.22 per cent of OECD countries' GDP (the United States provided only 0.11 percent). At the UN Conference on Financing for Development in Monterrey, Mexico, in March 2002, the United States and the European Union pledged to increase development assistance significantly in the next few years. But the projected increase is linked to much vague conditionality such as "good governance", which may not be easy for many low-income countries to meet.
- The globalization package being offered to developing countries by the international financial institutions is not confined to liberalizing the economy but involves a new

development philosophy that greatly restricts the role of the state in economic and social activity and imposes a standard "one size fits all" adjustment policy devised by the IMF/ World Bank. The main emphasis of this policy is to achieve macroeconomic stability by reducing government spending, raising utility charges and eliminating all subsidies. In the process, the growth rate slows down, unemployment goes up, poverty increases and poor farmers become more vulnerable in a volatile and highly subsidized market. Even in terms of economic objectives, openness alone is not enough to attract investment. There are many other factors, including non-economic factors, some of which are outside the control of the country concerned.

The United Nations has a major responsibility to draw attention to these severe inequities of the globalization process and to regain the leadership role it abandoned in the early 1980s to the World Bank/IMF in providing a level playing field and in creating a more favourable global environment for developing countries. As explained in the next section, major rethinking is required if the millennium goals, particularly that of halving poverty by 2015, are to be achieved.

REDUCING POVERTY IN SOUTH ASIA

A report by the Mahbub ul Haq Human Development Centre (2001. in Islamabad has presented some revealing but grim findings on the impact of globalization on the poor people of South Asia:

- Half a billion people in South Asia, or 40 per cent of its population, have experienced a decline in their income, despite a 5.4 per cent increase in the South Asian GDP during the 1990s.
- Under the influence of stabilization policies imposed by the World Bank/IMF demanding the elimination of subsidies and price support measures, and the resultant squeeze on the fiscal space, the provision of social safety nets has been weakened in the region.

- Globalization has not been accompanied by a reduction in poverty or improvement in human development since most South Asian countries have failed to maintain a balance between economic and social development policies. For most South Asians, the outcome of the globalization process has been higher prices, fewer employment opportunities, increased disparities in income and a higher incidence of poverty.
- South Asia suffers from an additional disadvantage in the globalization process because of the worldwide movement towards regional trading blocs. In South Asia, however, SAARC is facing serious political obstacles, and intraregional trade therefore remains low in comparison with such trade in other regional groups.

These conclusions, in the context of South Asia, fully support the strong consensus at the global level about the negative aspects of globalization and the recognition that the globalization process cannot deal effectively with the problems of poverty and the insecurities that arise from poverty.

It should not be difficult to comprehend why economic liberalization would not automatically benefit the poor. The concept of globalization is based on the principles of competition and, by definition, poor people and poor countries are on the lowest rung of the competitive ladder. The inherent inadequacies of an unregulated market system and the need to protect the poor are fully understood in the more advanced societies. That is why they have created laws and institutions against monopolies and malpractices to protect the consumer and small businesses; they have also developed elaborate systems of taxation, social security and welfare programmes to meet the basic needs of the poor in their societies. Unfortunately, at the global level they refuse to recognize the impact of globalization on poor countries and poor people and do not agree to similar taxation and social security policies at the global level.

The greatest threat to security today is poverty, but very few recognize the complex causes of chronic poverty and the policies and changes needed to address them. A determined attack on poverty will require a new development paradigm that recognizes the role of the state in protecting the rights of the weaker and poorer segments of the population and in meeting their basic needs. In articulating this new paradigm, we have to recognize:

- That balanced social development is a basic and essential prerequisite for sustainable development and that social problems are not simply the "inevitable costs" of structural adjustment;
- That sustainable development does not mean "development with environment" but involves a pattern of development that is meaningful for a large majority of the population;
- That social development cannot be financed merely from the residual financial resources spared by the adjustment process and that the policies that restrict demand and thereby increase poverty and unemployment must be modified by providing either a longer time-frame or additional external resources on soft terms; and
- That market-oriented economic policies are necessary for economic growth, attracting investment and improving competitiveness in international markets, but the pace of liberalization should not be faster than a country's institutional structure can cope with. Before large scale liberalization is undertaken, effective regulatory mechanisms to deal with the growing volatility of the capital and foreign exchange markets need to be created.

A meeting of the SAARC countries' finance and planning ministers in Pakistan in April 2002 adopted a comprehensive Action Plan for poverty alleviation. The plan covers the internal policies and external support considered necessary for achieving balanced and sustainable development. The external agenda of the Action Plan may be more difficult to realize than the internal policies. The World Bank president, James Wolfensohn, during his visits to Pakistan in mid-May 2002, said, "The India–Pakistan conflict was the single most important hurdle in the way of poverty alleviation in the region".

In recent years, there have been seven high-profile UN conferences at the level of heads of state and government – on

Children, Environment, Population, Social Development, Women and Food, culminating in the Millennium Summit held in New York in September 2000. But very limited progress has been made in moving towards the goals adopted by these summits. The United Nations must evolve an effective institutional mechanism that can regularly monitor such progress and bring the results, including the causes of inaction, to the notice of the heads of state who actually attended these summits and made those commitments.

5

Conflict Resolution in South Asia

Conflict resolution as a specific area of study was developed in the 1950s and 1960s as a response to the Cold War phenomenon. The word "conflict" has been broadly defined as the pursuit of incompatible goals by different parties or groups. The comprehensive term "conflict resolution" is defined as addressing and resolving deep-rooted sources of conflict so that behaviour is no longer violent, attitudes are no longer hostile and the structure of conflicts has been changed. In fact, many academics prefer the more specific and commonly used terms "conflict settlement" - reaching an agreement between two groups, enabling them to end armed conflict - or "conflict management" - which refers to the limitation, mitigation and containment of violent conflict. Nowhere is the need for conflict resolution greater than in South Asia.

The region remains mired in conflicts and tension. The two principal actors - India and Pakistan - have fought three wars without resolving the core issue of Jammu and Kashmir. The nuclear tests in May 1998 by India and Pakistan evoked global concern about Kashmir becoming a "nuclear flash-point". The horrendous terrorist's attacks of 11 September 2001 in New York and Washington were a watershed in international security, redefining the concept of terrorism and possibly sparking future armed conflict. The current stand-off between India and Pakistan and the deployment of nearly 1 million troops by both countries on the Line of Control in Kashmir and the international border have brought India and Pakistan perilously close to yet another devastating conflict.

At the same time, other conflicts in South Asia are equally explosive. In Nepal, the Maoist rebellion has already shaken the peace and stability of this Himalayan kingdom. The Maoists are determined to overthrow the monarchy and establish a communist regime in Nepal. The unresolved issue of over 100,000 refugees of Bhutanese origin has the potential of destabilizing Bhutan and Nepal. The separatist insurgencies in north-east India and similar separatist movements in other parts of India pose constant threats to stability in South Asia. The Chittagong Hill Tracts in Bangladesh also tend to flare up at regular intervals.

Sri Lanka has suffered bloodshed and instability owing to the long unresolved separatist struggle of the Liberation Tigers of Tamil Eelam (LTTE). This has resulted in hundreds of casualties and, according to the latest estimates, the conflict has cost nearly 1,443 billion Sri Lankan rupees, including the increase in defence expenditure, the cost of damage and reconstruction, and the loss of economic output and of tourism. There is currently a ray of hope that, with active diplomatic efforts by Norway, the violent situation may end, ushering in an era of reconciliation among the warring segments of the Sri Lankan population.

Maldives is confronted with serious challenges to its survival as a result of global warming. Several islands have already been submerged under the rising oceans and the remaining islands face the same predicament in coming years. In contrast to other regions, South Asia is beset with multidimensional threats. Terrorism, drug trafficking, arms smuggling, rising illegal immigration, including trafficking in women and children, and the spread of HIV/AIDS and other communicable diseases are eroding the social and moral fabric of South Asian societies.

Moreover, the region has failed to reap the peace dividends of the end of the Cold War. Comprising over one-fifth of the world's population, South Asia is one of the poorest, most illiterate and most malnourished regions of the world. Yet it is heavily and lethally armed with nuclear missiles and other weapons of mass destruction. The stark reality is that South Asia stands marginalized in a highly competitive and efficient globalized world. In fact, a new pattern of conflicts has emerged, calling for a different response. The focus used to be on international wars; now it is on asymmetrical conflicts, especially in South Asia, given its size, its massive population, its huge resources and one of the largest military machines in the contemporary era. South Asia has yet to find a solution to this problem.

A PROCESS OF INFORMAL POLITICAL CONSULTATION

South Asia has a greater need as well as justification for regional integration than almost any other part of the world. But this can be realized only by fostering mutual trust, resolving conflicts, promoting good neighbourly relations and building confidence. The leaders of the seven countries of the South Asian Association for Regional Cooperation (SAARC) recognized this fundamental requirement at the ninth SAARC summit held in Male in 1997. They agreed that a process of informal political consultations would prove useful in this regard. There is, of course, no formal institutionalized process for the discussion of bilateral political disputes among member states within the existing framework of SAARC. The SAARC Charter very clearly precludes discussion of what the Charter describes as bilateral and contentious issues.

However, political discussions do take place, including on some bilateral issues, but this is between the countries directly concerned, informally and on the fringes of summits and council meetings. These discussions are, of course, not part of the agenda of SAARC meetings and collective debate on these issues by all member states do not take place. For example, the understanding reached at the tenth SAARC summit between the prime ministers of India and Pakistan to resume official-level dialogue greatly reduced tensions between the two countries. This process resulted in further promoting goodwill and trust and facilitated the signing of the Lahore Declaration in February 1999.

The Male Summit established a Group of Eminent Persons (GEP) with the mandate to undertake a comprehensive appraisal of SAARC and to identify measures that could further vitalize and enhance the effectiveness of the association in achieving its objectives. In addition the GEP was mandated to define a long-term vision for SAARC and to identify the elements of a plan of action, including a SAARC Agenda for 2000 and beyond. The GEP submitted its report, including a set of recommended actions, to the tenth SAARC summit in Colombo in 1998.

Due to lack of time the GEP Report could not be considered by the 1998 Colombo Summit and its consideration was deferred to the next summit, which did not take place until 2002. None the less, it is relevant that the GEP Report welcomed the practice of holding informal political consultations initiated at the ninth SAARC summit and unanimously recommended that the process should be continued and operationalized so as to achieve the Charter objectives of fostering mutual trust, understanding and friendly relations among the member states.

A REDEFINITION OF PEACE, SECURITY AND DEVELOPMENT

In the wake of the rapidly changing global strategic and economic environment, the concepts of peace, security and development have been radically redefined. Peace no longer means peace on the battlefield. It means peace where we live, where we work and where we worship; in other words, peace in the entire civil society. Security is no longer measured only in military terms. It includes economic security, human security and, indeed, comprehensive security.

The 1994 United Nations Conference on Human Rights in Vienna proclaimed the right to development as a fundamental human right. The object of development is the individual and not the government. The right to development includes political, economic, social and cultural rights. These rights are interrelated, indivisible and universal. They are best exercised by an individual in a participatory democracy in which all segments of civil society – men, women, young people and minorities – have a role to play.

SOME MODELS OF EXISTING SECURITY MECHANISMS

The globalization of security issues has enhanced the importance of multilateral cooperation. Many of these issues can be tackled more intensively on a regional scale, because regional actors have political interests in common and because there is economic interdependence, close neighbourhood interaction and cultural affinities among the partners. Over time, various frameworks of regional cooperation have emerged worldwide, more or less comprehensive, more or less binding.

In the changed post–Cold War era, the content of regional and international security has changed and expanded. As a result of the rapid development of globalization, members of the international community are now more interdependent. The security of a country is not confined to its own, but is related with others and indispensable from others. Cooperative security must be based on the equality of members and the security mechanisms must fully respect the sovereignty and territorial integrity of all partners. It should give full play to the United Nations and other international organizations. It must promise mutual benefits and common prosperity. South Asia can learn from the experience of existing and emerging models.

CSCE / OSCE

The idea for creating a comprehensive pan-European security system was initiated by the Finnish government in 1972. Invited by the Finnish government to draft a conceptual framework, all European states except Albania participated in the meeting along with the United States and Canada. The setting-up phase ended with the signing of the final Act of the Conference on Security and Co-operation in Europe (CSCE) in Helsinki in August 1975. The final Act of Helsinki comprised 10 founding principles, which formed the normative basis for promoting cooperation among the participating states of the CSCE. These principles were:

- Sovereign equality, respect for the rights inherent in sovereignty;

- Refraining from the threat or use of force;
- Inviolability of frontiers;
- Territorial integrity of states;
- Peaceful settlement of disputes;
- Non-intervention in internal affairs;
- Respect for human rights and fundamental freedoms, including freedom of thought, conscience, religion or belief;
- Equal rights and self-determination of peoples;
- Cooperation among states; and
- Fulfillment in good faith of obligations under international law.

The CSCE was characterized by remarkable innovations. First, it had a wide and inclusive membership – all the states of a region were involved. Each participating state took part in its sovereign and independent capacity. Secondly, in contrast to a piecemeal, mainly military, approach to security, the CSCE endorsed a comprehensive perspective. Security was explicitly understood in an extended way, thereby including not only military but also political, economic, social, cultural and humanitarian issues.

Thirdly, decisions were taken by consensus, thus often making the decision-making as important as the decision itself. Fourthly, the CSCE had no institutional structures until 1994; as a result, the very impetus needed to keep the process going was an end in itself. The CSCE being comprehensive and inclusive was based on equality and flexibility, on political will and consensus of all participating states. The comprehensive CSCE agenda was prospective. It not only provided a wide range of fields for cooperation, but created a long-term vision for this cooperation. More than 20 years passed by before the CSCE took stock of the profound changes ushered in by the end of the Cold War and the opening of a new era. It was realized that, to acquire more operational capability, the CSCE had to transform itself from a low-level institutionalized conference into a proactive organization. This realization was reflected in the Charter of Paris of August 1991 and materialized at the Budapest Summit meeting on 5 and 6 December 1994.

Though neither the character of commitments and the principles nor the status of institutions became altered significantly, by renaming the major decision-making bodies, the participating states expressed their political will to provide a new impetus and dynamic to the CSCE as the primary instrument for early warning, conflict prevention and crisis management. The CSCE was renamed Organization for Security and Co-operation in Europe (OSCE). At the Istanbul Summit in November 1999, the participating states agreed to elaborate a model for the common and comprehensive security of a Europe of the twenty-first century. The OSCE has become a pan-European organization, whose 55 participating states span the geographical area from Vancouver to Vladivostock, and it has been recognized as a regional arrangement under Chapter VIII of the UN Charter.

The OSCE has established several bodies for decision-making and operational activities, the most important of which are summits, review conferences, the Ministerial Council, the Permanent Council, the Senior Council and the Forum for Security Cooperation. The operational activities of the OSCE are controlled by the Chairman-in-Office, the Secretary General and the OSCE Secretariat. The OSCE has other important institutions such as the Office for Democratic Institutions and Human Rights in Warsaw, the High Commissioner on National Minorities in The Hague, the OSCE Parliamentary Assembly in Copenhagen, the Court of Conciliation and Arbitration and the Representative on Freedom of the Media in Berlin. Among its operational activities, the most important have been OSCE's field missions as an instrument for supporting the translation of principles into reality.

REGIONAL FORUM OF THE ASSOCIATION OF SOUTH EAST ASIAN NATIONS

In 1994 the ASEAN Regional Forum (ARF) was instituted with the aim of evolving a broad security framework. The concept of cooperative security and comprehensive security was used for designing the basic objectives of this forum. These objectives were to foster constructive dialogue and consultation on political and security issues of common interest and concern, and to make a significant contribution to efforts towards confidence-building and preventive diplomacy in the region.

The ARF's activities are based on several fundamental principles, including:

- Mutual respect for the independence, sovereignty, equality, territorial integrity and national identity of all participating nations;
- The right of every state to lead its national existence free from external interference, subversion or coercion;
- Non-interference in the internal affairs of one another;
- Settlement of differences or disputes by peaceful means;
- Renunciation of the threat or use of force.

The ARF developed certain criteria for participation by its dialogue partners, stressing that all new participants must be committed to the ARF goals and its three-stage process for creating an environment conductive to peace and stability in the region. The three-stage process consists of confidence-building measures, preventive diplomacy and conflict resolution. These principles were translated into specific agreements such as the Declaration on the Zone of Peace, Freedom and Neutrality. This Declaration committed all ASEAN members to making an effort to secure the recognition of and respect for South-East Asia as a Zone of Peace free from any interference by outside powers. The Declaration called on all members to broaden the area of cooperation, which would contribute to their strength, solidarity and closer relationship.

The Bali Summit changed ASEAN's vision and future course. Some important agreements were signed, including the forward-looking Declaration of ASEAN Concord and the Treaty of Amity and Cooperation. At the Bangkok Summit, the ASEAN leaders signed the Treaty on the South East Asian Nuclear Weapon Free Zone, stressing their determination to contribute towards general and complete disarmament and the promotion of international peace and security. The Treaty also aimed at protecting the region from environmental pollution and the hazards caused by radioactive waste and other toxic materials. The ARF has made steady progress over the years and enjoys a high reputation as an effective mechanism for safeguarding peace and stability in the area.

SHANGHAI COOPERATION ORGANIZATION

In 1996, five states - China, Kazakhstan, Kyrgyztan, Tajikistan and Russia - signed the Treaty of Deepening Military Trust in Border Regions in Shanghai. The "Shanghai Five" evolved over a number of years. The signing of the Treaty on Reduction of Military Forces in Border Regions followed in Moscow in 1997. Subsequent summit meetings in Almaty in 1998, Bishkek in 1999 and Dushanbe (Tajikistan) in 2000 made significant contributions to regional peace, security and cooperation. Against the backdrop of political multi-polarization and economic and information globalization in the twenty-first century, the five countries agreed to transform the "Shanghai Five" mechanism into a higher level of cooperation to share opportunities and deal with new challenges and threats more effectively.

They invited Uzbekistan to join and the group was officially named the Shanghai Cooperation Organization (SCO) in June 2001, with the aim of strengthening mutual trust and good-neighbourly and friendly relations among the member states, thus jointly ensuring regional peace, security and stability.

The SCO agreed to abide strictly by the principles of the UN Charter: to respect each other's independence, sovereignty and territorial integrity; not to interfere in each other's internal affairs; not to use force or threaten to use force; to achieve equality and mutual benefit; to solve all issues through consultation; and never to try to gain military superiority over neighbouring countries. The SCO attaches special importance to making every effort to ensure regional security. All members States are to cooperate closely with each other in implementing the Shanghai Treaty on the Crackdown on Terrorism, Separatism and Extremism, including the establishment of the SCO anti-terrorism centre in Bishkek, Kyrgyztan. The member states will also work out instruments to curb illegal arms smuggling, drug trafficking, illegal migration and other criminal activities.

The SCO has established a Council of Coordinators to coordinate comprehensive cooperation among the member states. The Council has been charged with the task of drafting an SCO Charter on the basis of the declarations and other documents signed by the heads of state of the "Shanghai Five". The Charter will expound the principles, purposes and tasks of the SCO's future cooperation, the principles and procedures for accepting new members, the legal effect of the organization's decisions, and means of cooperation between the SCO and other international organizations.

CONFIDENCE BUILDING MEASURES IN ASIA

A 16-member Conference on Interaction and Confidence Building Measures in Asia (CICA) was held on 4–5 June 2002 in Almaty, Kazakhstan. The participating states were Afghanistan, Azerbaijan, China, Egypt, India, Iran, Israel, Kazakhstan, Kyrgyztan, Mongolia, Pakistan, the Palestinian National Authority, Russia, Tajikistan, Turkey and Uzbekistan.

The first significant aspect of CICA is its membership. The 16 members are together home to nearly half of the world's population, i.e. 3.5 billion people. They account for 55 per cent of the world's GNP and 40 per cent of world trade. Moreover, six of its members - China, Russia, Kazakhstan, Uzbekistan, Tajikistan and Kyrgyztan - are also members of the SCO. The composition of CICA is interesting in another way. Two major trouble spots of the world find representation in CICA through the presence of the protagonists. As well as India and Pakistan, which are the key actors in the war drama being played out in South Asia, Palestine and Israel have also been brought in. CICA intends to take its role seriously as a forum for dialogue envisaged for the Conference by its founding members.

This was evident from the important Almaty Declaration issued at the conclusion of the conference on 5 June 2002. Recognizing that profound changes were taking place in Asia and the world, the summit leaders set out their vision of security in Asia and their resolve to enhance their capabilities for cooperation on issues of peace, security and stability in Asia and the rest of the world. They declared their determination to form in Asia a common and indivisible area of security where all states peacefully coexist and their peoples live in conditions of peace, freedom and prosperity. They also expressed their confidence that full, equal and comprehensive implementation and observance of the principles, provisions and commitments enshrined in the Almaty Act would create the conditions for cooperation among the CICA members.

The Almaty Declaration identified measures concerning security and cooperation through multilateral approaches to promoting peace, security and stability in Asia. These include the pacific settlement of disputes in conformity with the principles of the UN Charter, respect for human rights and fundamental freedoms; humanitarian issues, natural disasters and refugees flows; arms control, disarmament and nuclear-free zones; the right to self-determination of peoples under foreign occupation; and the global coalition against terrorism. CICA will be developed as a forum for dialogue, consultation and the adoption of decisions and measures on the basis of consensus on security issues in Asia. CICA will evolve a variety of confidence-building measures.

In June 2002, Asian politicians from 17 countries met in Thailand to form a new forum called the Asian Cooperation Dialogue (ACD). The initiative was taken by the prime minister of Thailand, Thaksin Shinawatra. Foreign ministers from 13 Asian countries and other ministers from the remaining 4 countries attended the ministerial-level meeting. The ACD will be exclusively Asian and will discuss social and economic issues against the backdrop of a security environment profoundly changed by the terrorist attacks of 11 September 2001 in the United States. The ACD is still in its preliminary stages but it does represent a promising step towards evolving a comprehensive set of principles and objectives to strengthen peace and development through cooperative security in Asia.

From the foregoing, it is clear that the absence of an institutionalized security mechanism in South Asia has severely hindered progress towards building the trust and confidence that are so essential for accelerating regional integration and stability. The rapidly changing global security and strategic environment warrants the early establishment of a formal security mechanism in South Asia. The seeds of such a mechanism were sown with the initiation of the process of informal political consultations held on the fringes of SAARC summits and the unanimous recommendation by the Group of Eminent Persons that this process be operationalized. This security mechanism could be called the "Security Organization for South Asia" (SOSA).

The proposed South Asian Peace and Security Forum could conduct its activities on the basis of universally accepted principles of inter-state relations as enshrined in the Charter of the United Nations. The Five Principles of Peaceful Coexistence, which are fully consistent with the UN Charter and have been observed by Asian countries, could also provide a useful framework. To respond to multidimensional security challenges and threats, the SOSA may evolve its own functional instruments. These might include fact-finding missions, special envoys, monitors to deter human rights violations, problem-solving workshops for disputants, and efforts at capacity building for mediation, community-based peace initiatives, and media mobilization.

Without a doubt, South Asia is at a crossroads today. Whereas the rest of the world is moving rapidly in the direction of peace, stability and development, the region continues to be gravely threatened by conflicts and multiple security threats. Poverty, terrorism, the flow of arms, drug trafficking, the smuggling of people, and the spread of diseases such as HIV/ AIDS are threats that are not solvable by individual governments; they require collective and cooperative action by all countries of the region.

The choice for South Asia is simple: either it can pursue a path of purposeful cooperation based on peace, development and reconciliation; or it can sink deeper into the abyss of hopeless poverty, deprivation, disease and illiteracy, resulting in the gradual erosion of the very core of its ancient societies. By getting together, moving together and acting together through the proposed security organization, South Asia has much to gain.

SOLUTION TO CONFLICT IN SOUTH ASIA

In the summer of 1947, following the withdrawal of the British India colonial administration, South Asia was torn asunder. The political and ethnic forces that led to the partition of India resulted in dreadful massacres and incomprehensible human suffering as 15 million people scrambled to cross the borders. The number of people affected will never be known, but the estimates are that 7.4 million Hindus moved from Pakistan to India, and 7.2 million Muslims moved from India to Pakistan during the months following Independence. Several million persons were killed in the mad scramble for the new countries. The most severely affected places were in the Punjab, which found itself bisected by the drawing of the new boundary between Pakistan and India, and in East Pakistan, where Bengal state was split between Hindu and Muslim control. East Pakistan later became independent Bangladesh in 1971, after another regional liberation struggle, this time with West Pakistan.

With the exception of Sri Lanka, where the indigenous Sinhalese people and the immigrant Tamils were in conflict, the other South Asian countries were spared much of the ethnic violence inflicted upon India and Pakistan during the months following partition. Bhutan and Nepal had maintained their independence during the British period, and their relative isolation in the Himalaya provided them with some sanctuary from the tumultuous events unfolding in the southern plains. But in the fifty years since Independence, communal unrest has grown throughout the subcontinent. All the South Asian countries include ethnic constituencies with very different linguistic, religious, caste, and territorial aspirations. To the extent that the government policies fail to assimilate that diversity into a national unity, the prospect for ethnicity-based violence is great. Today, sectarian tensions coupled with regional separatist movements grip much of South Asia and threaten the peace of the countryside.

The Hindu-Muslim and caste-based tensions in India, which date at least to Partition, are not restricted to a particular ethnic group or territory, but rather are imbedded in the personality and structure of the Indian secular state. A potential for the pan-India tensions to flare into violence exists virtually everywhere in the country. In many places of India, however, and throughout the rest of South Asia, the ethnic struggles have a clearly defined territorial basis. As of this writing, over forty ethnic struggles are in existence in the South Asian region.

To the extent that some of them are successful, they will redraw the political map of the world. Wherever they exist, the possibility for political instability and communal violence is present.

The geographical conflict in South Asia is largely a product of its cultural history and the more recent government policies that intervene there. The prospects for competing territorial claims, both between insurgent groups and the State and among ethnic groups, are enormous throughout the region. Moreover, the aspirations of the various groups are mixed. Some of them may struggle for more recognition and participation in political affairs, while others seek greater autonomy or complete independence. Even within the ethnic movements, competing factions exist and members may have quite different goals. In Kashmir, for example, some insurgent groups seek full independence while others wish to join Pakistan.

In the Punjab, a gradual change is taking place away from the earlier radical call for a separate Sikh homeland to more moderate desires for Sikh engagement with the central government of India. In the hill lands of Uttar Pradesh, the separatists want their own state but not independence from India. The ethnic Nepalese who were forcefully evicted from Bhutan during 1990-1992 now live in United Nations camps in eastern Nepal as frustrated and disenfranchised refugees. The list goes on. In the sections that follow, I highlight some of the important regions where territorial struggles are currently being waged. Collectively, they show South Asia to be a place of enormous potential for territorial conflicts.

A commonly-held perception of the Himalaya Mountains is one of serenity, as if the region's geographic isolation and resident cultures may somehow guarantee the absence of turmoil. Current events, however, show it to be otherwise. The western mountain regions in Pakistan and Kashmir are embroiled in both tribal and international warfare. In the central sector of the range, the Pahari-speaking people of Uttar Pradesh struggle for a separate state called Uttarkhand.

In Nepal, Maoist insurrection has gripped much of the countryside, especially in the west, as communist agitators infiltrate the tribal regions, and in the east where refugee populations from Bhutan swell the ranks of the villages and resettlement camps. In the hills of Sikkim and Darjeeling, meanwhile, ethnic Nepalese call for a separate homeland called Gorkhaland. And in the far eastern Himalaya, north of the Brahmaputra River, various indigenous peoples, including the Assamese and Bodo tribes, seek independent homelands and control over local resources.

The Pathan (Pashtun) tribes have lived in the arid mountains of the western Himalaya for centuries, securing them against the advances of such would-be conquerors as the Mongols, the Moghuls, the British, and most recently the Russians. They have successfully repelled all those invaders. However, as a result of the British annexation of 40,000 square miles of land along the Khyber Pass and Indus river in 1893 (which formalized the Durand Boundary Line), the Pathans now find themselves under the divided control of Afghanistan and Pakistan. In both countries, they constitute a federation of closely-allied tribes and clans with a strong sense of Pathan nationalism. Since 1947 there have been numerous efforts toward a re-united Pathan homeland called Pashtunistan.

The Pathans look back on a history of fierce independence and a shared honor that dates to at least the 8th century. They derive their cultural identity from the bonds of Pashtunwali, a tribal code that stresses autonomy, bravery, and self-respect. During the 1950s and 1960s, the Pathans agitated heavily for an independent territory that would include parts of both Afghanistan and Pakistan. Pathan insurrection again flared up in the late 1970s, following the Soviet invasion of Afghanistan.

Today, the Pathans are a heavily militarized group in Pakistan, with abundant weaponry imported during the Afghan war with Russia. Guns and ammunition are casually sold on the streets in most villages and towns under Pathan tribal authority. Such transactions bring the appearance of lawlessness to the region. Pathan nationalism in the 1990s centered on halting the exploitation of tribal homelands by the Punjabi government. In fact, most of the land in northern Pakistan is under some form of tribal authority, with the State exerting only nominal control in the countryside.

One of the most contentious regions in the Himalaya is the Kashmir valley. When I first visited there in 1975, I found it to be a peaceful place that befitted the tourism descriptions of serene lakes and dramatic mountain beauty. At the time, I had no real understanding of the ethnic tensions that even then simmered just beneath the surface of the place. But at least the countryside was not embroiled in the violence that now occurs there on a daily basis. The separatist struggles of the Kashmiri insurgents and the militaristic actions of the Indian Army combine to create a highly charged atmosphere of disorder, violence, and human rights abuse across the region. In the words of a Kashmiri friend who last wrote to me in the summer, 1998, "Kashmir is hell on earth."

That assessment is a far cry from the acclaim of the Moghul prince Jehangir who once wrote about Kashmir, "If there be a heaven on earth, then this is it." The ethnic conflict in Kashmir centers on the Kashmiri Muslims, who are a majority in the region, and Hindu Pandits, who predominate in the southern section. But the conflict also embroils Pakistan and India in a border dispute that dates from 1947, when India gained Kashmir against the claims of Pakistan. The two countries have fought three wars over the region (in 1947, 1965, and 1971) and the inhabitants of Kashmir are divided in their loyalties.

The conflict that has raged throughout the 1990s is fueled in part by the assistance provided to the separatists by Pakistan, but the insurgency actually splinters into over 100 different groups with various competing aspirations, so that any resolution to the conflict appears far off. Estimates of the number of persons killed in Kashmir since 1990 range as high as 50,000. Today, even the spectre of thermonuclear war haunts the region as Pakistan and India turn to atomic weaponry in their efforts to establish respective control over Kashmir.

In the hills of Darjeeling, southern Sikkim, and southern Bhutan live ten million ethnic Nepalese. Their predominance in the region is a result of large scale migrations from Nepal beginning as early as the middle of the 19th century. In 1891, when the first official census of India was made, the ethnic Nepalese comprised over two-thirds of the hill area population.

In 1940, Nepalese activism led to the formation of the Gorkha League, which was established to represent the interests of the hill residents as well as the 80,000 Nepalese Gorkhas serving in the Indian Army. The Gorkha League in the 1940s first proposed the idea of a separate Gorkha State, to be carved out of areas of Sikkim, North Bengal, Cooch Bihar, and Bhutan. The demand was dropped in 1950, but in 1973 the Nepalese again spearheaded an independence movement. Partly as a result of that movement, Sikkim merged with India in 1975. In 1986-88, the Gorkha Nepalese staged a series of violent uprisings in Sikkim that spilled onto neighboring India and Bhutan in the form of demonstrations, terrorism, and killings.

The Gorkhas have not gained regional autonomy as a result of their efforts, but their movement for independence continues today. The most current proposals for a Gorkhaland include a potentially volatile mix of ethnic Nepalese, including the Gorkhas in the Indian Army, the refugees in the camps in Nepal, the Lhotshampas (ethnic Nepalese) living in Bhutan, and the Nepalese majority populations in Sikkim and Darjeeling. In 1993, Bhutan accused Nepal of allowing the refugee camps in eastern Nepal to become training grounds for Gorkha insurgents. That accusation included the fear that arms and munitions were being collected and stored in the camps, including a supply of AK-47s coming from China.

The northeast region of India, adjacent to the borders of Burma and China, is one of Asia's last outposts. It remains off-limits to most foreigners and is inhabited by a polyglot of tribes and caste groups, numbering around 22 million persons, who remain independent of much of central state control. Recent immigrations from Bangladesh have added to the cultural makeup and have fueled additional ethnic tensions in the region.

The groups that currently are most involved in territorial insurgencies are the ethnic Assamese, the aboriginal Bodo tribes, and the immigrant Chakma tribes who came from the Chittagong Hills in Bangladesh. A campaign of violence by the Assamese against Bengali Muslims began shortly after 1970, when ten million Bangladeshis fled into the region. In the past decade, the

Assamese have been warring with the Bodo people, who fear the expansion of the Assamese population onto their traditional homelands in the forested hills north of the Brahmaputra valley. The intra-ethnic conflicts in the northeast Himalaya are further complicated by the fact that Assam has a longstanding separatist claim against the New Delhi government. The United Liberation Front of Assam (ULFA) emerged in 1979 as a militant Assamese organization whose purpose was to organize armed action and conspicuous violence as an insurgency tactic.

It has never fully united, however, the diverse tribes inhabiting the region. The peak of the Assamese communal violence against the Bengalis occurred in the mid-1980s when several thousand persons were killed in systematic ethnic pogroms. The Bodo insurgency, meanwhile, was first organized in 1967 under the Plains Tribal Council of Assam and became radicalized in 1984 when the Bodo leaders formed the United Tribal Nationalist Liberation Front (UTNLF). The UTNLF coordinated a campaign of insurgent violence throughout the 1990s against both the Assamese and the Indian military forces posted in the region.

THE SOUTH ASIA LOWLANDS

The lowland regions of South Asia currently host numerous zones of ethnic conflict stemming from territorial aspirations. Two of the most important movements in India involve the Sikhs in the Punjab, who have been waging a struggle for an independent homeland called Khalistan, and the tribal people known as *adivasi*, who live in the forests of east-central India. The *adivasi* (a Sanskrit term for "indigenous peoples") are calling for a new tribal state with the name Jharkhand. In both cases, the current level of violence has waned in recent years due to new government initiatives, but the history of both places is marked by ethnic conflict, and the potential for renewed violence in the future is considerable.

The Sikh population in India, which numbers about 16 million, is united around the Sikh religion and their ancestral occupation of the Punjab region. The development of the Sikh culture, which dates to the 15th century, follows the militancy tenets of the Khalsa, the Sikh brotherhood that is symbolized by the sword and knife. Much of Sikh communal life centers on the temples, whose control in 1920 passed to the Akali Dal political organization. Since Independence in 1947, the Akali Dal has struggled with the central government for control of the Punjab. It became radicalized in the 1960s, and despite the threat of factionalism, emerged in 1972 as the majority Sikh party. Since then, the Akali Dal has called for a Sikh Autonomous Region called Khalistan.

The 1980s ushered in a decade of bloodshed in the Punjab as the Sikh insurgents turned to violent tactics in their bid for sovereignty. The separatist movement benefited from the organization of temples, which provided logistical and administrative support to the insurgents. The Khalistan Movement also received support from international sources by way of remittances and arms shipments.

The political and religious goals of the Sikhs deteriorated in the 1980s to a general lawlessness in the countryside, where terrorism and extortion became a way of life. In 1984, the Indian Army stormed the Golden Temple in Armristar, killing 493 insurgents. In partial retaliation for that invasion, which the Sikhs considered to be a desecration of their holiest temple, Sikh bodyguard troops assassinated Prime Minister Indira Gandhi on October 31st, 1984. Since 1981, over 20,000 people have been killed in the political violence in the Punjab, which peaked in 1990 when 4000 persons died. In the early 1990s, the Sikhs were disunited and divided into numerous extremist, militant, and moderate groups, allowing effective military action against the insurgents. A restless quiet descended onto the Punjab, and in the late 1990s a majority of Sikhs turned toward more moderate political strategies.

The forested hills in east-central India, mainly in the states of Madhya Pradesh, Orissa, and Bihar, are inhabited by numerous tribal groups who collectively are known as the *adivasi*. Until the 17th century, the region remained outside of foreign influence. Beginning in the late 18th century, however, the territory and its inhabitants came into increasing contact with outsiders, first with British and then, following Independence, with central government policies.

Since then, the *adivasi* have experienced a great deal of discrimination and encroachment onto their tribal homeland, especially during the 1960s when the forest and mineral resources were exploited. In the 1970s, the *adivasi* began to agitate for a separate homeland called Jharkhand, meaning "forested area," and in the 1980s the Jharkhand Movement turned militant under the organization of the Jharkhand Mukti Morcha. Jharkhand currently contains almost 75% of India's total tribal population (estimated to be 68 million persons in 1991. The two main tribes, the Chota Nagpurs and the Santals, and the less predominant Bhils and Gonds, are the main agitators in the Jharkhand Movement.

Traditionally, the Jharkhand *adivasi* used the forests for hunting and gathering, and for shifting cultivation. Those activities are greatly curtailed, however, under the new government forest rules. Moreover, outside interests have gained control of tribal land for the purposes of commercial timber cutting, mineral exploitation, and agricultural expansion. Jharkhand also is the location for massive industrial buildup, especially in the Bihar districts, and is slated for renewed mineral development.

The continued agitation of the Jharkhand militants against those encroachments led in 1995 to the creation of the Provisional Jharkhand Area Autonomous Council, and in 1998 to a proposal by the central government of India for the creation of a new state in India called Jharkhand. The eventual establishment of such a new state is predicated, however, on the adoption of the territorial boundaries imposed by the government for Jharkhand; they have not yet been fully accepted by the *adivasi* leadership.

A state of civil war exists in the northern part of the island nation of Sri Lanka as a result of the ongoing ethnic conflict between Sinhalese nationalists and Sri Lankan Tamils. The Tamil presence in Sri Lanka dates to the 13th century, and they currently number 2.23 million persons (1991. living mainly in the northern and eastern sectors of the island. A third group in Sri Lanka, the Indian Tamils (called estate Tamils), are a more recent addition to the nation's cultural blend.

They were brought to the island in the late 1800s to work on the British tea plantations. In the early 1900s, the Tamils (both

Sri Lankan and Indian) moved onto Sinhalese land, fueling Sinhalese resentment and initiating a period of ethnic consciousness which eventually led to economic and political discrimination against the Tamils. A rise of Sinhalese nationalism swept across the island in the 1950s and led to the first wave of anti-Tamil demonstrations and rioting.

Communal riots increased in the 1960s and 1970s, instigated by both Sinhalese and Tamil groups against the other. Tamil nationalism arose in the 1970s, pointedly against the discriminatory policies of the Sinhalese government, and coalesced under various Tamil militant groups. In 1972, the Liberation Tigers of Tamil Eelam, known as the Tamil Tigers, emerged as the leaders of the Tamil insurgency in Sri Lanka. Since the late 1970s, numerous organized campaigns of terror have been waged by the Tamil Tigers against Sinhalese citizens, leading to the deaths of over 50,000 persons. Until the 1990s, most of the violence was restricted to the Tamil-held northern and eastern parts of the island, but the conflict expanded to other areas by the mid 1990s, and in 1996 a State of Emergency was imposed for the entire country.

The primary contention of the Tamil extremists is that the island is their rightful home by virtue of their longstanding residency there. But their prospects for economic and social advancement are dim against the discriminatory policies of the Sinhalese government. Parliamentary procedures have failed to resolve the issue, so the Tamils believe the only way out is to wage an armed struggle for independence. Their goal is an independent Tamil homeland in the northern and eastern parts of the island. The Sri Lankan government's strategy, meanwhile, is to use military force to suppress the insurgency. Very little accommodation has been made by either side, so that the prospects for peace in the country in the near future look dim.

The mixture of ethnic groups with different territorial aspirations creates an unstable political landscape in much of South Asia. In places, ethnic groups are in conflict with the central state, elsewhere they fight against one another. Moreover, the localized struggles often are overshadowed by the pan-India secular tensions, mainly between Hindus and Muslims but also among caste groups, so that the local violence may go unnoticed. The regional movements are further complicated by two additional facts.

One, many of the ethnic groups in conflict are transborder groups, so that the regional ethnicity problem immediately becomes an international one; and two, some of the ethnic struggles actually disguise power and territorial movements between countries. The latter is true, for example, for the Kashmiris (India and Pakistan), the Pathans (Afghanistan and Pakistan), the Tamils (Indian and Sri Lanka), the Assamese (Bangladesh and India), and the Gorkhalis (Bhutan, India, and Nepal). In such ways, the ethnic struggles exhibit complex elements of regional, national, and international aspirations. The local insurgencies produce a tense and often violent atmosphere in many places, and altogether they threaten to rearrange the landscape of South Asia by altering the size and shape of existing political territories and by adding new ones with different names.

6

Development of Bangladesh in the 1980s

Bangladesh faces some of the most difficult problems of development in the world. The difficulties arise from the following: a very low level of development as indicated by the low level of per capita income and the prevalence of poverty, malnutrition and illiteracy among large segments of the population; a demographic pattern characterized by one of the highest population densities in the world, which continues to rise with population growth; a poor resource and infrastructural base in a deltaic plain vulnerable to a variety of natural catastrophes; and certain social and economic organizational deficiencies inherited from the country's centuries-long hinterland status within a vast empire.

To these difficulties are added certain external factors, e.g., a threatened loss of markets for the country's few traditional exports that could help sustain incomes and support development by financing capital goods imports; the influence of imported ideas, expectations and aspirations about standards of private and public consumption that generate undue demand on the meagre available resources, that tend to develop dual economic and socio-cultural standards in the country and thus create disharmony and potential social instability. This complex background has given rise to pessimistic prognoses about the future prospects of Bangladesh, though there have been a few optimistic ones as well. To be optimistic is not easy given the country's objective circumstances. To be pessimistic, however, is not helpful and could impede the serious national and international efforts required to find reasonably satisfactory solutions to the country's problems.

PATTERNS OF DEVELOPMENT

Bangladesh became a separate political entity in 1947 as the East Wing of Pakistan. At that time the population numbered nearly 42 million. Population recorded no increase between 1941 and 1951, largely because of the effects of the 1943 Bengal famine and large-scale emigration from the territory that was to become Bangladesh, following the partition of Bengal in 1947. Between 1950 and 1960 the population increased by 2 per cent, or 2 per cent per annum, and at an estimated annual rate of 3 per cent during the 1960s. Against this trend in population growth, the economy remained virtually stagnant during the decade of the 1950s, resulting in a declining per capita income. During the 1960s, the recorded GDP growth rate of 4.4 per cent per annum permitted per capita income to grow at a rate of 1.4 per cent.

Bangladesh started its industrialization virtually from scratch in 1947. In 1949/50, large-scale manufacturing accounted for only 0.6 per cent of GDP, while small-scale manufacturing contributed 3.4 per cent. The contributions of other sectors were: agriculture 65.2 per cent, construction, transport and power 5.6 per cent, and services, 25.3 per cent. By 1969/70, the shares of agriculture and services had declined to 55 per cent and 23 per cent respectively, while the shares of construction and manufacturing had increased to about 9 and 13 per cent respectively. Within the manufacturing sector, the share of small industries declined from 3.3 per cent of GDP in 1949/50 to 2.9 per cent in 1969/70. At the same time the share of large-scale manufacturing rose from 0.6 per cent to 6 per cent of GDP. This structural change resulted mainly from the expansion of jute processing facilities to supply the growing export trade in jute goods. Industrial capacities were created in a few other activities as well but their utilization remained low, resulting in an insignificant contribution to production.

Given the dominance of agriculture in the Bangladesh economy, the differing rates of sectoral growth did not portend well for the future of the economy. The slow growth in agriculture in the presence of rapid population growth and diversification from rice to jute caused the food-population balance to deteriorate. Production of rice, the major cereal crop and calorie source increased at an annual rate of barely 2.5 per cent, against an estimated 3 per cent rate of population growth.

As a result, the country's food imports increased from 0.69 million tons in 1960/61 to 1.55 million tons in 1969/70. By and large, agricultural production pattern remained undiversified. Rice, taking 80 per cent of the cropped area, and jute, taking 8-10 per cent, dominated the crop sub sector. Cultivation of a few minor crops such as potatoes and bananas expanded but were still insignificant in terms of both production and consumption; starchy roots, for instance, provided only 1.5 per cent of the total calories.

With Bangladesh as its Eastern Wing until 1971, Pakistan's development up to the mid-1960s was based on a strategy of rapid industrialization aimed at an early transition to self-sustaining growth. This led to the comparative neglect and lack of development of the agricultural sector. The crisis in agriculture remained submerged under the umbrella of the United States commodity assistance programme until the mid-1960s, when the flow of such assistance started to dry up. The slackening of commodity assistance drove home to the planners the urgency of increasing agricultural production, and programmes were launched to attain food grain self-sufficiency within the shortest possible time.

This increased urgency fortunately coincided with the availability of "green revolution" rice technology and production was pushed as quickly as possible. But the physical, financial and institutional bottle-necks could not be overcome in a short period and, although some successes were achieved, food self-sufficiency was not achieved in East Pakistan. The emphasis on industrialization on an all- Pakistan basis, without special regional focus on the problems of East Pakistan, proved unhelpful for the overwhelmingly agrarian economy of East Pakistan. The industrial strategy was based on the promotion of private enterprise and, to this end government fiscal, commercial and monetary policies were geared to making private investment attractive.

Lacking an entrepreneurial tradition, a rich landlord class with a surplus to invest in trade and industry and the institutional framework needed to provide direct and policy support to private industry, East Pakistan failed to benefit from the industrialization strategy. To the extent that the national industrialization programme was sustained by low-priced imports (by means of an over-valued exchange rate for the domestic currency) financed by exports of agricultural products such as jute, East Pakistan in effect subsidized the industrialization of West Pakistan. This pattern continued up to the last days of united Pakistan.

In the 1960s, East Pakistan promoted industrialization with the pioneering efforts of the East Pakistan Industrial Development Corporation (EPIDC), in circumstances of increasing financial stringency which resulted from Pakistan's growing balance-of-payments deficit and a slow-down in foreign assistance inflows. West Pakistani and expatriate entrepreneurs showed some eagerness to exploit the market opportunities and the favourable conditions created by government policies in East Pakistan; as a result the few processing industries which developed came to be owned by outside interests.

The role of the private sector in industry remained very small, with only marginal participation by East Pakistani entrepreneurs. EPIDC emerged as the largest holder of industrial assets prior to the nationalization of these industries in 1972. Lack of development in agriculture and industry was parallelled by and contributed to low levels of investment and performance in infrastructural development, including transport and communication, flood control and irrigation and power facilities. Equally poor, if not poorer, was the development of social sectors such as health, housing and education.

STRUCTURAL CHARACTERISTICS

In 1970, the Bangladesh economy displayed all the typical characteristics of underdevelopment. The low level of per capita income was accompanied by low rates of saving and investment, low rates of participation in foreign trade with tendencies toward widening trade and payments gaps, low rates of urbanization and literacy, and a high rate of population growth. In terms of both income and employment, agriculture dominated the economy; the share of agriculture in GDP was 62.4 per cent and in total employment, more than 80 per cent. Industrial production accounted for only about 8 per cent of GDP.

Agriculture remained relatively little diversified; the crop sub sector accounted for more than 80 per cent of agricultural value added. Rice production alone accounted for 78 per cent of the total cropped area and 65 per cent of agricultural value added. Cultivation of wheat was insignificant in terms of both acreage and output, although there were indications of gradual expansion. Jute, tobacco, tea and sugarcane were the most important cash crops, providing industrial raw materials and foreign exchange earnings. Agricultural production was characterized by low land and labour productivity. The total land cultivated (at an intensity of 115 per cent for wheat and the three seasonal rice crops) could not produce enough food grains to feed the country's population at a level corresponding to minimum requirements.

In the industrial sector, about two thirds of value added was accounted for by large-scale industries. Forty-three per cent of industrial production consisted of jute and cotton textiles; food, beverages and tobacco accounted for another 30 per cent and other industries contributed 27 per cent.

The country's physical infrastructure remained extremely weak. With a railway network of 1,776 miles and about 2,400 miles of paved roads, the country had railway and road densities of 3.2 and 4.4 miles respectively per 100 square miles of territory. The railway network remained divided into two independent segments in the north-west and south-east halves of the country, interrupted by the mighty Brahmaputra River system. The road network remained fragmented by many unbridged rivers, requiring frequent ferry transfers of traffic, with consequent delay and congestion. With its 3,500 miles of perennial river routes, extending to some 5,000 miles in the monsoon flood season, river transport carried about 60 per cent of the country's freight and 40 per cent of passenger traffic. Conditions of service in all transport modes remained unsatisfactory.

Bangladesh had an electricity-generating capacity of 545 MW in 1970. Per capita consumption of electricity amounted to only about 20 kWh, and peak load use was only 223 MW. Modern industrial units, however, were highly dependent on the electricity supply and frequent power failures resulting from the weaknesses of the generation and distribution system hampered industrial production. The limited importance of electrical power is reflected in the fact that the country met more than three fourths of its energy needs from traditional fuels, including straw and rice husks, cow dung, twigs and leaves, firewood and biogases.

With a per capita income level of $US 84 Bangaladesh remained one of the least developed countries in 1970. The rural areas, which sustained more than 90 per cent of the population with about 60 per cent aggregate income, had a much lower average level of income than the urban areas. Income distribution in the aggregate as well as within the urban and rural sectors was strikingly unequal. According to an estimate for 1963/64, the lowest 20 per cent of households received 7 per cent of total household income while the top 20 per cent received 44.5 per cent; the bottom 40 per cent received only 18 per cent of income. According to this estimate the over-all income-concentration ratio (Gini coefficient) was .368, whereas it was .346 for the rural areas and .491 for the urban areas. In the urban areas the top 20 per cent of households received 57 per cent of total income, showing the comparative affluence of some urban groups.

The high incidence of poverty indicated by Bangladesh's low per capita income and unequal income distribution was also reflected in the failure of the population to satisfy their basic needs for food, clothing, housing and health. Although such needs are not easy to define or quantify, available estimates suggest that food consumption met only about 80 per cent of the average minimum calorie requirement in the 1960s. Cereals, of which rice constituted 94 per cent, dominated the people's diet; cereals contributed 85 and 74 per cent of the calorie intake in the urban and rural areas respectively.

The food-population balance deteriorated over the period. Per capita availability of food grains declined from 1965 through

1969, despite annual imports exceeding a million tons. In 1970 there was a small improvement in availability, because of a sharp increase in imports to 1.55 million tons from the previous year's 1.12 million tons. Consumption of nutrients by large numbers of households was far below acceptable levels. Thus in the rural sector the percentage of households with an intake below an acceptable level of calories was 46; protein, 61; calcium, 86; and vitamin C, 60 per cent. In the urban sector, the corresponding percentages were 76, 77, 94 and 59.

Per capita consumption of cloth in 1969/70 has been estimated at 7.5 yards per annum. This might be regarded as the barest minimum to safeguard human decency with hardly any to spare for protection against exposure to the severity of the weather. Housing conditions were extremely bad. In the rural areas the common thatch, mud-floor dwelling often failed to provide adequate shelter from the rains and the cool weather that the country experiences from December to February. Modern sanitation facilities were conspicuous by their absence. A programme of installing hand-operated tube-wells was in progress, however, in an effort to supply safe drinking water. In the urban areas, according to a sample survey, 70 per cent of the houses were temporary construction, 80 per cent were without water connection and 97 per cent without electricity.

The war of liberation in 1971 caused serious setbacks to the economy and to social welfare in Bangladesh, imposing an almost total hiatus on economic activity. Production declined in all sectors; development rends were reversed; there were massive movements of population; the over-all economic situation was worse than at any time in the recorded history of the country. The 10 months of confusion and disruption between March 1971 and January 1972 brought additional physical, social and political difficulties and added a further dimension of human suffering to the country's long-standing problems of chronic poverty.

The first year following independence was devoted to the immediate tasks of rehabilitating the people displaced and disabled by the war, repairing vital transport and communication links, and restoring institutions and organizations in various fields. To facilitate the task of economic recovery, a 5,020 million taka Annual Reconstruction and Development Plan was launched in July 1972. However, by the end of the year the economic situation had deteriorated further, owing to a severe drought, which caused a decline in food grain production to 9.8 million tons from the 11.8 million tons of 1969/70.

During the year, 2.8 million tons of food grains were imported with international assistance and distributed with the help of the United Nations Relief Operations in Dacca (UNROD), averting a potential catastrophe. Food grain consumption nevertheless declined from 15.4 oz per capita per day in 1969/70 to 12.9 oz in 1972/73. Industrial production revived only partially. For instance, the production of fertilizer was only 15 per cent of that of 1969/70. The vital jute and cotton textile industries reached production levels of 70 (jute goods), 42 (cotton yarn) and 62 per cent (cotton weaving) of the 1969/70 base.

The termination of textile imports from Pakistan, on which consumption in Bangladesh was heavily dependent, caused an acute shortage of textiles in 1972/73. Per capita cloth consumption fell to 5 yards during the year compared with 7.5 in 1969/70. In sum, real GDP in 1972/73 recorded a fall of 14 per cent from 1969/70.

In these extremely difficult circumstances, Bangladesh launched its first five-year plan in July 1973. With a proposed total outlay of taka 44,550 million (at constant 1972/73 prices) the plain aimed at: (a) the rehabilitation and restoration of the economy to the 1969/70 level during the first year; (b) a 5.5 per cent annual growth in GDP and a 2.5 per cent annual increase in per capita income; (c) the transformation of the institutional and technological base in agriculture to attain self-sufficiency in food grains; (d) reduced dependence on foreign aid by domestic resource mobilization, export expansion and import substitution; (e) the reduction of the population growth rate from 3 per cent to 2.8 per cent; and (f) maintenance of price stability.

The foremost objective of the plan was the reduction of poverty, which was to be achieved by the accelerated growth of national income and its more equitable distribution, the expansion of the output of essential consumption items to provide the minimum consumption requirements of the masses, the expansion of employment opportunities (for which a target of 4.1 million new job was set), and a wider diffusion of employment opportunities in traditional and informal sectors in both urban and rural areas.

The launching of the plan coincided with sharp rises in the world prices of food and energy, on both of which Bangladesh was heavily import-dependent. The subsequent international recession adversely affected the country's export trade, which was already suffering from the disruption of established trade links upon its independence from Pakistan. By 1974/75 the terms of trade had declined by almost 50 per cent from 1972/73. These difficulties were accompanied by a reduction in foreign aid.

A severe foreign exchange crisis developed, requiring drastic cutbacks in essential imports, which in turn entailed a huge resource shortfall for plan implementation. This was indicated by an actual outlay of taka 7,130 million during the first two plan years against a plan provision of taka 11,700 million (at 1972/73 prices). The GDP level in 1974/75 was still below that of 1969/70, pressing down on the per capita income level. Adding to these burdens, the country suffered severe flood damage in 1974/75, causing agricultural production to decline by 2 per cent during the year and generating a famine situation.

Following the frustrating experiences of the initial years of the plan, planned programmes and priorities were re-examined. A three-year hard-core programme was drawn up for the remaining three years of the plan period which did not effect any major change in the economic and social objectives of the plan but recast its priorities to permit maximal realization within the limits of available resources. This was to be accomplished by ensuring the efficient use of existing capacity, augmented in the shortest possible time by raising the level of investment and allocating it to potentially productive sectors. Furthermore, the relatively strong emphasis in the first five-year plan on social services and housing was reduced in favour of increased agricultural and industrial productivity.

Evaluation of plan achievements indicates that only 50 per cent of the plan's financial targets were met. The recorded growth rate of 4 per cent in GDP over the plan period was largely the result of a 3.7 per cent growth rate in agriculture. In view of the flood damage of 1974/75 and the drought of 1976/77, the performance of the agriculture sector was encouraging. A precarious balance was maintained between food output and population growth. Nevertheless, the balance was periodically upset by adverse shifts in weather conditions in 1972/73, 1974/75, 1976/77 and 1978/79. Moreover, the performance of the manufacturing sector, with an annual rate of decline of 0.3 per cent, was most unsatisfactory. In keeping with this mixed performance, the major physical targets remained largely unfulfilled, particularly in respect of food and other essential consumer items.

A number of factors prevented Bangladesh from launching a second five-year plan immediately after the termination of the first in June 1978. After the policy changes introduced in 1976/77, the economy passed through a transition which warranted some delay before attempting to determine their effectiveness. In view of the large number of unfinished projects at the end of the first plan period, the outlook for further investment was not clear. To allow time to evaluate policies, to improve utilization of existing capacity and complete projects under execution, and to formulate strategies for the longer-term problems which the second five-year plan should address, it was decided to defer the second five-year plan until July 1980.

For continuity in planning during the interim period, a two-year plan was drawn up with aims and objectives similar to those of the first five-year plan. With an outlay target of taka 38,610 million, the plan aimed at an annual GDP growth of 5.6 per cent, for a growth rate of per capita GDP of 2.8 per cent if the rate of population growth were held to 2.8 per cent. A severe drought in 1978/79 limited the agricultural growth rate to 1.3 per cent against the target rate of 4.1 per cent.

Production of food grains declined from the previous year's 13.9 million tons to 13 million tons, threatening a food shortage of critical proportions. At the current level of production, Bangladesh runs a normal food grain deficit of roughly 1.5 million tons. Continuing high rates of population growth make it difficult to eliminate this deficit by increasing production. Recurrently unfavourable monsoons disrupt food grain supply and upset the precarious food balance, causing severe strain on domestic price and wage levels and the balance of payments. Thus food shortages remain the most critical bottle-neck of the country's development.

Reduction of dependence on foreign aid by greater mobilization of domestic resources was a basic objective of both the First Five-year Plan and the Two-year Plan. The first Five-year Plan postulated a share of external financial resources in the development plan reduced to 27 per cent in 1977/78 from 62.2 per cent in 1973/74. In the public sector, with 89 per cent of total planned expenditure, the shares of domestic and external financial resources were to be 57 and 43 per cent. External financial resources actually accounted for 80 per cent of the total investment during the plan period.

Of the total public sector expenditure, three fourths was provided by external financial resources and the remainder by domestic resources. The heavy dependence on external resources for development financing is evident. Nevertheless domestic resource mobilization efforts were improved during the three-year hard-core programme. During the last three years the larger share of investment in GDP reflects both increased mobilization of external financial resources and a larger proportionate contribution of domestic resources.

Of the taka 5,300 million targets for private investment during the plan period, taka 3,430 million, or about two thirds of the target figure, was realized. As an annual average, the proportion was about three fifths. The plan sought to limit the role of the private sector by allocating only 11 per cent of total expenditure to this sector. Together with nationalization of all large-scale enterprises, the Government put a ceiling of taka 2.5 million on private investment, to be allowed to increase to taka 3.5 million by ploughing back profits. Although the original aim was to permit the private sector to operate only on a small-scale basis, the policy was subsequently revised to provide greater incentives to, and enhance the scope of private investment.

The response of the private sector to these incentives was not especially encouraging. With three fifths realization of the private investment target compared with 50 per cent realized by the public sector, however, the private sector performed less poorly than the public sector. Private investment was largely financed by equity capital supplemented by institutional credit from specialized agencies. The activities of the latter were strengthened during the latter years as part of the policy to support and encourage private enterprise.

The pattern of resource availability in the Two-year Plan was not much different from that realized during the First Five-year Plan. Of the taka 31,030 million spent in the public sector (84 per cent of the total), about three fourths was to be provided from external sources. Of the taka 6,000 million of private investment, 40 per cent was to come from private domestic investment and the remainder from private foreign investment and borrowing from the banking system, mainly in the form of foreign exchange loans.

Estimates of domestic savings during the Two-year Plan do not indicate any improvement over the performance during the First Five-year Plan. Savings during the later plan period averaged about 1.5 per cent of GDP, against the target of 4.2 per cent.

The balance-of-payments deficit on current account ran at above a billion dollars in 1978/79, roughly matching the investment-saving gap. Only some 57 per cent of the export targets for the First Five-year Plan were realized and a 13 per cent shortfall occurred in foreign aid receipts. Resources were thus insufficient to meet the plan's import needs and production targets.

Some 78 per cent of the over-all import-payment targets were realized but payments for food grain imports were more than double the plan target as crop failures and rising import prices meant a need for food imports that was greater than anticipated. While the allocation for import payments for intermediate goods was almost fully utilized, payments for capital goods imports were less than two fifths of the target amount. Rising prices caused severe shortfalls in import volume, which hampered productive activities.

It is clear from the foregoing that past developments in the Bangladesh economy have failed to exert an appreciable impact on the general level of poverty in the country. Between 1969/70 and 1979/80, per capita income increased at an annual rate of 1.1 per cent, rising from $US 84 to $US 94, about the same rate of growth as had been recorded in the 1960s, following a decline in the preceding decade. This rate of increase in per capita income was insufficient to permit any meaningful increase in per capita consumption.

Defining absolute poverty in terms of a monthly per capita income sufficient to provide an intake of 1,935 calories per day (90 per cent of the FAO recommendation for an average Bangladeshi), one study has placed the proportion of the "absolutely poor" in rural Bangladesh at 40 per cent in 1963/64, 76 in 1968/69, 78 in 1973/74 and 62 in early 1975. At an incidence rate of 60 per cent in absolute poverty, 54 million of the estimated 90 million 1979/80 population are impoverished.

With such massive poverty and with such a low average income level, the question of distribution may appear largely irrelevant. Certainly policies for the redistribution of existing income and wealth could achieve little. However, the question of distribution assumes significance from other points of views. The rich of Bangladesh may not be especially affluent in comparison with those in other countries but they are able to enjoy a consumption standard totally incompatible with that of the masses of the poor.

This is detrimental to the development of a cohesive sociopolitical order essential for rapid development. Moreover, the danger exists that development will widen the disparity between the impoverished masses and the rich minority, who are often the major beneficiaries of development in poor societies. Studies suggest that poverty and inequality in Bangladesh have intensified over time. Income distribution data, however, do not suggest any substantial change; such data may be an imperfect guide to the actual changes in household and personal income distribution over time.

Changes in income distribution apart, massive unemployment and underemployment and the landlessness of the rural masses are unmistakable evidence of poverty. Nearly

11 million people, more than a third of the labour force, were unemployed or underemployed at the close of the 1970s. More than two fifths of the agricultural labour force was unemployed or underemployed in 1978/79. This massive underutilization of human resources is undoubtedly a major proximate cause of poverty in Bangladesh but the more fundamental causes lie in the lack of access to productive assets, preeminently land. Underutilization is heavily concentrated in agriculture and is fundamentally the progeny of the pattern of land ownership. Total arable land in Bangladesh amounts to about 23 million acres, or roughly an acre per agricultural worker. However, the land is by no means equally distributed.

The widespread poverty of rural Bangladesh derives most obviously from the grossly unequal distribution of land. Of the total number of rural households, 11 per cent owned no land whatsoever in 1977. Of the total households that owned land, more than half owned one acre or less (0.4 ha) and some 70 per cent owned less than two acres (0.8 ha). Although the availability of irrigation water and variation in fertility render a precise assessment impossible on the basis of these figures alone, the households that owned no land and those owning not more than two acres of land undoubtedly comprise the great bulk of those in poverty.

According to the 1977 figures, this group numbered 8.9 million households and 46.5 million persons. The landowning households of this group (72 per cent of all landowning households) owned less than one fourth of all rural land held by rural households. Thus the remaining three fourths was owned by some 28 per cent of landowning rural households. If landholdings greater than 3 acres (1.2 ha) are taken as economically viable, the rural households owning economically-sized holdings numbered 1.9 million, or 18 per cent of all landowning rural households and 16 per cent of all rural households.

As the available data show a systematic increase in household size associated with the size of holding, it is necessary to note that the total number of persons living in households with more than three acres of land amounted to 15.7 million or nearly 23 per cent of the 69 million rural residents in 1977. By clear implication, the great majority of the remaining 53 million lived in some degree of poverty in rural Bangladesh.

There is legally no tenancy in Bangladesh other than the so-called cultivating tenancies. In such tenancies, the land belongs to the cultivator in respect of all its ownership attributes, namely, possession, use, transfer and inheritability, with the State retaining the right to collect rent. There is no intermediate tenure holder between the State and the cultivator. This is the definition from the tenancy legislation enacted in the 1950s, which abolished all types of intermediary tenures and prohibited non-cultivating ownership of land. Nevertheless, the

7

Towards a Human Rights Regime

Today, in Southeast Asia, redress of human rights violations may be far from being realized. However, following the Asian financial crisis in 1997 there has been modest progress in terms of the proliferation of discourse on human rights and democracy throughout the region. More arguments have also been propounded to tailor human rights language, culture, and its implementation to local contexts and sensitivities. But Southeast Asian governments have continued to regard human rights as an ambivalent subject in national development.

At the same time, they have been forced to engage with the issue, for a variety of reasons-from paying lip-service to an increasingly assertive public demand for accountability to using it as a means for shoring-up political credibility in a climate of regional economic uncertainty, to building up an image more acceptable to prevailing international norms.

While the debate on whether human rights is a universal or relativistic norm rages on, different elements are shaping a new climate for human rights understanding and advocacy. For example, the imminent manifestation of an International Security Order in the wake of the terrorist attacks in the United States on 11. September 2001 will leave both critics and defenders of universal human rights groping for renewed answers to an old issue. The pervasiveness of the discourse on security over respect for human freedom has now become one of the stumbling blocks against progress in human rights, replacing the previous divisiveness stemming from the "universalist versus relativist" debates, with authoritarian states promoting the position of the latter. Post-September 11 has turned out to be an opportunity for the nation-state to exert its sovereignty even more forcefully and to sideline the agendas of the global normative movement, one of which being human rights, to a token concern.

The purpose of this chapter is to look at the dynamics of the human rights question by examining the role played by the state in furthering the human rights agenda within Southeast Asia. The chapter is divided into two areas of discussion. The first is on the prospect of a regional body such as ASEAN playing a more committed role in establishing a human rights regime. The assessment of this issue revolves round whether the regional organization, with its avowed stance on noninterference, has responded favourably and accordingly to the human rights challenge.

The second area of discussion is on the four government-established national human rights institutions currently existing in ASEAN. Are these nationally established human rights commissions significantly different from one another, and what have been their successes and failures? It is the contention of this chapter that a human rights regime is difficult to foster in the region because its very existence will be seen to undermine the concept of the strong, autonomous, and economically-sound nation-state that Southeast Asian governments have traditionally promoted.

By assessing the functions and performance of Southeast Asian national human rights commissions, the chapter provides evidence of a strong state-centric resistance against the setting up of an effective human rights regime. In fact, the contestation for a human rights regime has always involved nation-states battling against their domestic civil society and an international movement pushing for a normative global order. The discussion will attempt to draw out this particular dynamic and concludes with some reflections on the future of human rights advocacy in Southeast Asia.

THE PROSPECT FOR HUMAN RIGHTS WITHIN THE ASEAN RUBRIC

ASEAN's early successes were largely related to its role as a regional mechanism operating within the context of Cold War politics. Despite the potentially destabilizing impact of the war in Vietnam, the founding member-countries of ASEAN successfully remained as peaceful and independent entities. The original ASEAN countries were models of a functioning free market economy. Impressive economic development in Singapore, Thailand, Malaysia, and Indonesia for much of the 1980s and 1990s was a successful version of industrialization for developing countries.

Obviously, an issue that is certain to jolt if not undermine the ASEAN principle of "non-intervention" and protection of national sovereignty is human rights itself. By virtue of the fact that human rights violations come within international law (through the International Bill of Human Rights and accompanying instruments), their redress would inevitably involve the questioning, if not the transgression, of national jurisdictions. Another aspect of human rights compliance is the pressure for national governments who are signatories of the United Nations' Human Rights Conventions to enact or amend enabling domestic laws to reflect and promote tenets of the international instruments.

No ASEAN country has ratified all twenty-six international instruments of human rights, while only two ASEAN countries (Cambodia and the Philippines) have ratified all six major human rights conventions. Only the Convention on the Rights of the Child (CRC) has been ratified by all ten ASEAN countries. The most "avoided" international bill of human rights is the Convention Against Torture (CAT) to which only three ASEAN countries are signatories.

It was at the end of the Cold War that the ineffectualness of ASEAN began to be highlighted. Post-1990 economic globalization made way for the deregulation of financial regimes and provided for more liberal capital movements. Given the rapid rate of economic development, there was extensive labour migration within ASEAN itself.

Yet, labour rights policies for a cross-migrating work-force were either avoided or left undeveloped. Another issue which had become perilous to handle because of the ASEAN tenet of non-intervention was the issue of insurgency or secessionism wrought by ethno-nationalists. Some ASEAN countries have been known to have tacitly harboured or supported insurgent or secessionist movements of neighbouring countries, although this has not been brought up openly on an official agenda within the regional body. Terrorism, which is allegedly waged by a cross-network of Islamic militant groups in Malaysia, Indonesia, and the Philippines, is a particularly sensitive issue in which solutions will not be sought easily through multilateral arrangements within ASEAN.

The picture sketched above reflects continuing ASEAN reservations about accepting intervention to uphold the notion of "universality" in the recognition and definition of human rights norms and principles as formally adopted by the United Nations General Assembly in 1948. The 1948 Universal Declaration of Human Rights (UDHR) has now been treated as a document open to reassessment and revision. Questions, doubts, and contentions about the universality of human rights were first raised during the 1993 United Nations World Conference on Human Rights in Vienna.

The purpose of this meeting was to call for a re-strengthened endorsement of the 1948 Declaration. While the ASEAN countries did not withhold their reaffirmation of support for the 1948 Declaration, extensive debate and discourse about the hitherto assumed universalization of the human rights regime was sparked off. Countries expressing their new-found reservations on the 1948 Declaration were largely East Asian, Islamic, and Third World countries.

ASEAN heads of state met in Bangkok prior to the Vienna meeting to draw up the basis of their reservations and doubts on the universality of human rights norms and standards. While the group reiterated its endorsement of the 1948 Charter, many members were not prepared to ratify the various international human rights treaties and conventions. In the Bangkok meeting,

ASEAN adopted instead the Asia-Pacific Declaration on Human Rights (or The Bangkok Governmental Human Rights Declaration, 1993).

The ASEAN governments were specifically uncomfortable with the Universalists' over-emphasis on civil and political rights at the expense of rights to development and basic needs. The meeting tried to offer a concept of a "Universal Declaration of Human Responsibilities" as an alternative to the Universal Declaration of Human Rights. Amidst these criticisms, there was an unavoidable realization that Southeast Asia was one of the few regions in the world that did not have its own regional human rights mechanism.

Why were the ASEAN governments more forceful with their dissent against human rights in the 1990s, even though many had been the original endorsers of the UDHR in 1948? The ASEAN governments' assertiveness was said to be directly linked to East Asia's newfound prosperity as an emerging economic entity. At this time, the notion of an "Asian values" school was being propounded to distance Asian cultural and political systems from those of the West. Many saw this posturing as a justification by the Asian ruling elites to retain their antidemocratic and authoritarian styles of governance.

This was not unrelated to the imperative of the Asian developmental state, which seeks to sustain its market-competitive edge in the global economy by restricting, for example, civil liberties in the form of labour rights. Another emerging idea was the suggestion that a Japan-led Asia was poised to become an influential economic power, enabling it to establish an alternative international order. The coming of the "Pacific Century" to replace the "Atlantic Century" became a much-touted belief.

The ensuing philosophical, political, and polemical debates centering around the notion of "Asian values" has been made possible by an emergent unipolar world at the end of the Cold War. In the early 1990s, vocal East Asian leaders expressed their disquiet about an emerging neo-imperialism wrought by former colonialists. However, the end of the Cold War spelled none of the historical necessity to align with one dominant superpower over the other. The notion of the coming Pacific Century as a challenge to Fax Americana was an attractive idea which Asian leaders were keen to promote in order to bolster their political legitimacy at the domestic level.

One other feature marking this period was the demise of credible political opposition throughout many Southeast Asian states, especially in places where the leadership was most vociferous in asserting the "Asian values" position. Singapore and Malaysia were not only riding high on an economic upturn, but their governments' political legitimacy was also at its most assured. It was this experience of simultaneous economic growth with unassailable political strength which lent a "historic circumstance" to justify an Asian route to development.

The Bangkok "Governmental" Human Rights Declaration of 1993 explicitly stated the concerns of ASEAN in viewing human rights as a tool of Western neo-imperialist agenda. Hence, the ASEAN states were keen to promote the idea that only a regional rather than a global arrangement should best promote and protect human rights in specific regions.

CIVIL SOCIETY PUSH FOR AN ASEAN MECHANISM ON HUMAN RIGHTS

As a result of the expanding discourse on human rights emanating from both governmental and non-governmental quarters, some tangible advancement in the establishment of a human rights mechanism was achieved. Having put forward a challenge to the need for a more particularistic set-up, ASEAN foreign ministers in their joint communiqué at the twenty-sixth ASEAN Ministerial Meeting held in Singapore in 1993, as well as ASEAN parliamentarians in the Kuala Lumpur AIPO Declaration on Human Rights, declared the organization's willingness to establish a regional human rights mechanism.

In 1995, the Human Rights Committee of the Law Association of Asia (LAWASIA) initiated the process by organizing a series of meetings involving representatives from existing national human rights institutions, parliamentary human rights committees, and human rights non-governmental organizations (NGOs) in the region to discuss the possibility of setting up an institutional arrangement to fulfill ASEAN's human rights promise. Arising from these meetings, the Working Group for an ASEAN Human Rights Mechanism was formed in 1996, with its secretariat based in the Human Rights Centre of the Ateneo de Manila University in the Philippines. The ultimate purpose of this Working Group is to push ASEAN towards the setting up of the ASEAN Human Rights Commission.

Many advocates of the above view the ASEAN policy of noninterference and non-intervention as having been upheld "for too long", with governments still harbouring fear of foreign intervention in their internal affairs. Hence, the challenge for the Working Group was to define what exactly a regional mechanism would entail. The options proposed ranged from having an ASEAN human rights charter and a regional human rights court to simple co-operation between national human rights organizations.

Unlike the position taken by the ASEAN governments, the Working Group stressed that the agreement would be in consonance with the principles of the universality of human rights, and that regional and national laws be consistent with international human rights law. However, the reach of the commission would be limited as only countries ratifying the agreement would be subjected to the mandate of the commission. If nothing else, this Working Group would remain as the human rights "conscience" of ASEAN.

NATIONAL HUMAN RIGHTS COMMISSIONS IN ASEAN

In addition to a regional mechanism, the formation of national human rights institutions is considered even more urgent in the overall effort of building a Southeast Asian human rights regime. Currently, in ASEAN, four of its member countries have established their own National Human Rights Commission (NHRC). The NHRC is an institution established by the national government, and its formation is largely induced by an international human rights regime which maintains that the enforcement of human rights standards must effectively and ultimately be the responsibility of national states. National human rights commissions are crucial in the present climate of doubt and debate over human rights, as it is believed that "the lofty ideals contained in the international human rights instruments will remain irrelevant to individuals unless they are actualised in the national context".

The comprehensive principles used to guide and establish the criteria for the formation and functioning of national human rights institutions are known as the "Paris Principles". Elements of the Paris Principles include having a comprehensive mandate to deal with any violation of human rights (including those specified in international conventions not ratified by national governments), having a membership composition that is independent and drawn from a wide spectrum of civil society, and ensuring that national commissions function independently of the government.

In many situations, the existence of the National Human Rights Commission has led to an "unhappy marriage" between the institution and its national government. The national human rights commissions in the Philippines, Indonesia, Malaysia, and Thailand were each established at different times, and under different sets of institutional, political, historical, and cultural circumstances. In institutional terms, the national commissions have very similar goals and functions. However, there are some key differences worth noting, namely: 1. the legal locus of founding instruments, 2. social and political conditions affecting their establishment, 3. their mediation role, and 4. the provision for selection of commission members.

The first difference is in the legal instruments governing the establishment and empowerment of these national commissions. In the Philippines and Thailand, governments were required by popular will enshrined in the constitution to set them up and pass all the necessary enabling legislation. In Thailand, Sections 199 and 200 in the 1997 Constitution enshrine and detail the duties of a national human rights commission. In the Philippines, Article

XII, Sections 17-19 of the 1987 Constitution delineate the composition, functions, and duties of the Filipino Commission on Human Rights (CHR). In comparison, Indonesia's and Malaysia's national commissions stem from presidential decrees, parliamentary decrees, or organic laws, initially promulgated in 1993 and 1999 respectively.

As for the second difference, the four national commissions were each set up under different conditions. The first commission to be established was in the Philippines, which came with the downfall of Ferdinand Marcos and his rule by martial law in 1986. Following Marcos' ouster, a Presidential Committee on Human Rights (PCHR) was set up to investigate and recommend remedies to address human rights violations under the Marcos regime. In 1987, a new "people's constitution" was promulgated, in which a Commission on Human Rights was entrenched. Thus, the commission was established in the midst of a massive wave of political liberalization, where the goals of government were being redefined, and the emphasis was on people's rights, democracy, openness, the rule of law, and transparency.

After the Philippines, Indonesia was the second ASEAN country to set up a national human rights commission, although in radically different circumstances. When the commission was established in 1993 by presidential decree, Indonesia was then still in the grip of Soeharto's rule, with no concomitant flowering of political and civil liberties. Rather, the commission was the result of increased responsiveness to human rights concerns during Soeharto's "New Order" government of the early 1990s.

Indeed, Indonesia's foreign minister played a prominent role in convincing Soeharto to set up a commission. According to one Komnas HAM Commissioner, the years of authoritarian centralized rule were actually "golden years" for the effectiveness of the commission, as it benefited from extensive co-operation of state agencies-including the military and police-which were all directly answerable to the President. However, the good times ended abruptly in 1996 when the commission's activities in investigating an attack o n the offices of the PDI-P opposition party directly threatened Soeharto's political interests. State cooperation ceased, showing the limitations of dependence on powerful political patrons as opposed to rules-based institutional guarantees for human rights.

Thailand was next in establishing the foundations for its own national commission, when the Asian financial crisis in 1997 accelerated a pre-existing movement for political reform, leading to the passing of the long-debated "people's constitution" in October that year. Part of this new emphasis was the entrenchment of broad, liberal panoply of human rights in the constitution, as well as a mandate to establish a national commission to protect and promote those rights. However, from that date, it took nearly four years for the commission to be finally operational, as a result of the slow nomination procedure, and political squabbling over candidates' qualifications.

Malaysia followed closely behind Thailand in establishing its National Human Rights Commission in 1999, also partly in response to a changed political climate in the country. At the time of SUHAKAM's formation, international pressure was being exerted on Malaysia over the highly-publicized case of the ouster of Anwar Ibrahim from the government, and his subsequent imprisonment. Musa Hitam, a former Chairperson of the 52nd United Nations Commission on Human Rights in 1995 and 1998 may have also used his personal clout to persuade the Prime Minister to agree to the establishment of SUHAKAM, of which he was to become its first chairman.

Growing international awareness and condemnation of the sacking as Deputy Prime Minister of Anwar and his subsequent trial bore its weight on the government to salvage its reputation by relenting to a human rights instrument. The third area of difference is in the role of mediation in which the national commissions actively participate. The national commissions in Indonesia, Thailand, and the Philippines all have explicit provisions calling for a role in mediation between parties. However, the Malaysian commission has no such role, only an exclusively advisory one.

Malaysia's commission is highly government-centered and formalistic in its inception. Its annual report does not explicitly mention a role for civil society organizations in ameliorating the human rights situation in Malaysia. In comparison, the formal functions of the Indonesian, Thai, and Philippine commissions actually require them to forge or promote co-operation with civil society nationally, and even internationally. In Indonesia's case, the country's reliance on the international community in its reform efforts is even recognized. The Philippine Commission on Human Rights goes the farthest towards addressing the imbalance between state power and resources an d the capacity of individuals to achieve those rights. The commission even provides in "Assisting victims of human rights violation and/or their families with other forms of services, including legal aid and financial assistance."

The fourth difference to be emphasized is in the provision for the selection of members of the commissions. In Indonesia, the national commission has been mandated to have up to thirty-five members. The commission itself nominates two individuals for every position available; they are then elected by the Legislative Assembly and appointed by the President. Nominees must have experience in human rights work, and have either professional legal experience, government experience, or be prominent figures in civil society. Two five-year terms may be served.

In practice, this process has received many complaints relating to its transparency and the qualifications and credibility of those nominated. In addition, the secretary-general must be a civil servant, which would somewhat compromise the commission's independence by having its top officer holding a rank in a hierarchical, government-controlled bureaucratic organization. Thailand's nomination system, on the other hand, has been praised for being "highly democratic" and it has been noted that it "should produce well-qualified, independent-minded commissioners".

A selection committee, comprising the Chief Justices of the Supreme Court and Supreme Administrative Court, the Attorney-General, the Chairperson of the Law Society, five academics, ten NGO representatives, five political party representatives, three people from the media, in addition to the

Secretary-General of the Commission, must submit a list of candidates to the Senate for selection by vote, with final formal appointment being made by the King.

In effect, this is very similar to the Indonesian system, and in practice has proven to be an agonizingly slow process, given the length of time needed to set up the commission. Furthermore, the nominees must have experience in the field of human rights protection, and cannot concurrently hold any political (party) or government positions or affiliations (they must be full-time commissioners, in comparison to those of Indonesia who are basically unpaid volunteers, which compromises somewhat on their ability to perform their duties efficiently and fairly). They also cannot have any criminal convictions and can serve for only one six-year term. However, the independence of the commission is somewhat compromised in that its secretariat is classified as a ranking office in the bureaucracy, making its officials subject to possible political interference through the hiring process. Indeed, the political system can hold up appointments and manipulate their funding.

The nomination system in Malaysia is the most questionable, as commissioners are appointed on the recommendation of the Prime Minister for short, but renewable, two-year terms. This highly centralized, top-down nomination process curtails the independence of the commissioners, as they are under constant threat of removal if their performance is unsatisfactory to the powers who appoint them. The fact that the head of government should appoint the members of any watchdog commission is a clear case of conflict of interest, open to political pressure and compulsion.

This undermines the credibility of the institution when it comes to reporting on the government's performance, especially when it involves imputing their agents as the perpetrators of human rights violations. While the commission is officially responsible to Parliament, and legally bound to submit its report to the Speaker, the Commission nonetheless gives the Prime Minister an advance preview of the report "out of respect" for his position before rel easing it to the Speaker and the public. This tends to exemplify the strong pull on the commission's activities by the executive power. The latest appointment of new commissioners has been heavily condemned by non-governmental human rights bodies.

In the Philippines, members of the commission are appointed by the President, and their budgets come from public coffers controlled by politicians. No criteria are given in the constitution on how commissioners are to be selected, although it is determined elsewhere that a majority (from a total of five commissioners) must be members of the bar, all must be thirty-five years or older, and should have ten years of experience in human rights work. The low number of commissioners in the Philippines is indicative of the general lack of resources available in that country, and symbolizes a chronic problem the CHR has in its operational capacity.

NATIONAL COMMISSIONS IN PRACTICE

The actual practices of the various national commissions can give further insights into the state of human rights in the various countries. The performance of national human rights institutions is a key indicator in this regard.

THE PHILIPPINE COMMISSION ON HUMAN RIGHTS (CHR)

In the Philippines, as is to be expected from its longer history, the Commission on Human Rights has become deeply embedded in both the operation of government and society, having developed far-reaching networks through years of active co-ordination and co-operation on different projects. In addition to extensive co-operation and co-ordination with civil society and the government, the CHR has also established a wide-ranging regional network of subsidiary organizations, including regional offices, and a system of local baran gay Human Rights Action Centres to extend its presence down to every village.

However, this ambitious plan is plagued by a lack of resources, as there is no budget to support the centers, and the CHR is either unable or unwilling to supervise these bodies effectively. Out of 40,000 villages, only 14,000 have so far established these Human Rights Action Centres. Despite the

Philippines' lead on the holistic approach to human rights, serious obstacles remain above and beyond the lack of resources.

As a function of a highly diversified and liberalized society, Philippine civil society is also highly heterogenized, which entails significant difficulties in co-coordinating action and seeking co-operation from NGOs. Indeed, there is a major ideological split in civil society between the so-called "rejectionists" and the "re-affirmationists", who disagree on whether to work with the government, or to support insurgency to unseat the government. This can be seen most explicitly in the Mindanao conflict, and the waffling of various factions of the Moro National Liberation Front (MNLF) and the Moro Islamic Liberation Front (MILF) between co-operation and rebellion. The same also applies to the remaining supporters of the Communist New People's Army (NPA).

INDONESIA'S KOMNAS HAM

One of the biggest reasons for the early successes of Indonesia's Komnas HAM was, ironically, Soeharto's strong centralized control and his endorsement of the institution. This had allowed for the smooth coordination among government agencies to the advantage of Komnas HAM. However, the range of investigations which the commission could undertake was circumscribed by that same power. Now the situation is completely reversed, as political liberalization has greatly expanded the range of options open, while the fragmentation of power, lack of co-ordination, and institutional decay (corruption) has constrained the effectiveness of all government institutions, including Komnas HAM.

While some civil and political rights have improved for many, some of the most basic rights-to life, freedom from fear, to a home-are more tenuous than ever before for countless others. Indeed, calls have been made by a coalition of prominent NGOs for the entire Komnas HAM commission to resign en masse for their failure to deal with some of the worst excesses of the Soeharto era and the transitional period after he stepped down. Charging that "it's the Commission itself which has become its [own] obstacles [sic]", members of the coalition accused it of shielding prominent personalities suspected of human rights violations.

The problem of political will is particularly serious when it comes to investigating human rights abuses committed by the military in Indonesia, characterized as "anarchy corruption" by NGOs. The major shift in power from the President to the Legislative Assembly leaves Indonesia without a political centre, and a unifying direction. The practical results are devastating for victims of past human rights violations, as the lack of political direction leads to a breakdown of the entire system, as surviving elites from the New Order regime use their significant influence to block any initiatives to incriminate them.

The limited prosecution of past human rights violations remains one of the biggest failures of the post-Soeharto era. President Megawati's own commitment to human rights remains uncertain. Although Megawati has endorsed the need to settle gross violations of human rights in regions of armed conflict and has allowed the prosecution of offences in East Timor, she is personally close to a number of prominent military figures. Thus far, only nineteen of thirty-three East Timor rights violators identified by Komnas HAM have been accepted by the Attorney-General's office as "candidate suspects".

Furthermore, despite the setting up of the Human Rights Court in January 2002 to try at least eighteen senior army officers and militiamen, there has been criticism of the decision by the Attorney-General's office not to prosecute the then defence minister and armed forces chief General Wiranto, alleged by human rights groups to be morally responsible for the violence in East Timor.

MALAYSIA'S SUHAKAM

Malaysia's situation is again different from that of the Philippines or Indonesia. One might expect that the National Human Rights Commission, SUHAKAM, could also benefit from the efficiencies of authoritarian rule as Komnas HAM had done in Indonesia in the mid-1990s. However, SUHAKAM was created at a time of political ferment in Malaysia, when the government was actively repressing the political opposition while putting Anwar Ibrahim on trial. In this context, it was difficult for the commission to ignore all the government's controversial actions, and thus found itself quite vocally criticizing the government.

Despite initial fears that SUHAKAM would be nothing more than window dressing to restore the credibility of the government while it dealt with Anwar, some NGO activists have acknowledged that the Commission has done a commendable job, given the difficult circumstances. However, the very issue of Anwar's trial, and the detention of other dissidents, highlights an important point in the Commission's powers-it cannot address or investigate any issue which is, or has been before the courts. Thus, Anwar's case, and the government's alleged abuse of his rights and those of many of his supporters could not then be taken up by the Commission as a case of human rights violation.

In that respect, it should be noted that the Commission is established on the basis and authority of a parliamentary law, which cannot override other laws as specified in the Malaysian Constitution. In short, the powers of the Commission are circumscribed as it is prevented from going against the tenets of previously enacted laws, such a s the Internal Security Act (ISA), which provides for detention without trial. Despite these limitations, the Commission has had some modest success in putting out frank reports critical of the government's use of the ISA, limitations on freedom of speech, and most recently, freedom of assembly.

SUHAKAM's recommendations, following its first open inquiry into allegations of police brutality in a massive protest rally, on 5 November 2001, along the Kesas highway, have been welcomed by the public. However, this was met with government condemnation of the report as being influenced by "Western thinking" and not in the interest of the nation. However, one of the commissioners reported that such an action had helped to change the attitudes of law enforcers, as some policemen are now conscious of SUHAKAM's possible rebuke, if complaints from the public, no matter how trivial, are not recorded down. However, the fallout of the 11 September 2001 terrorist attacks in the United States has seen the Commission retreating from its own purpose. Soon after 11 September, the chairman of the Commission, Musa Hitam, said that in the light of the fight against terrorism, "human rights must take a backseat".

THAILAND'S NATIONAL HUMAN RIGHTS COMMISSION

Thailand's National Commission was slow in getting started, taking nearly four years from the 1997 constitutional mandate to the opening of its offices in 2001. This was due to the debate over the enabling laws necessary to establish the Commission. Academics, business people, and civil society activists aligned against conservative politicians and bureaucrats over the exact character of the body.

The independence of the Commission became a central issue, as conservatives sought to make it an easily controlled, minor bureaucratic office, in contrast to the activists' vision of an independent, vocal, and effective body. Using the media as their platform and threatening to blacklist politicians supporting conservative proposals in an upcoming election, the activists were successful in forcing a compromise. An acceptable enabling bill was finally passed, with the Commission coming under the Senate for its first five years, and then having the option to become independent.

The complex procedure used for selecting National Commissioners, who seek to build a broad-based social consensus involving all sectors of society directly concerned with the promotion and protection of human rights, has also slowed the starting date of the Commission. Since it only recently opened its doors, just a few comments are appropriate. One issue likely to emerge is the definition of human rights which the Commission will use as its standard. Commissioner Saneh Chamarik has advocated a local definition of rights, with a strong emphasis on the protection of the traditional "way of life" as communities seek to regain some degree of autonomy after decades of rigid centralization. Others have argued for the use of international standards, which, in turn, have been criticized by nationalists resentful of foreign domination.

In Thailand, the Office of the National Commission and its staff are considered "an agency of the National Assembly", leaving control over hiring and funding in the hands of professional politicians, many of whom still operate according to more traditional client list patterns. Within the context of Thailand's rapidly changing political landscape, it remains to be seen what impact such constraints will have. As political parties merge and the power of party leaders grows, there have been many concerns about how such a powerful political force can dominate the system and society. This is seen in recurring concerns over the current government's stifling of the media and other critical voices in society, as well as corrupting such institutions as the Supreme Court through the inappropriate exercise of political power.

This survey has shown that the various reasons behind national governments' wariness of the human rights agenda have not been successfully allayed despite efforts to pave the way for a human rights regime. Mistrust of the human rights agenda has continued to be firmly entrenched within official mindsets on the basis of the contention that international laws and norms on human rights are still viewed as threatening to national sovereignty and jurisdictions.

There is a pervasive ideology, either "manufactured" or entrenched that only a strong, benevolent, and authoritarian national state can act as the nexus of stability, order, and cohesion. In some ASEAN countries, citizenship rights are not of equal worth. Inequality in terms of gender, ethnicity, and religion is still an uncontested legal provision, making human rights advocacy impossible without prior societal restructuring at its most basic but politically taxing level, so as to elicit a minimal premise for human rights acceptance.

In terms of periodic trends, one can observe four watershed periods in discerning the vicissitudes of a Southeast Asian engagement with the human rights question:

- 1999-93: The beginning of Difference. In the post-Cold War era, "Asian values" were first asserted to promote Asian capitalism and the efficacy of the developmental state. In terms of major markers, there existed an official position to distance the ASEAN stance from that found in the Universal Declaration of Human Rights through the 1993 Bangkok Governmental Declaration on Human Rights.

- 1993-97: A period of great contestation and reassessment. At this time, an active debate was waged between the relativist and the universalist schools of human rights. There was an assertion of Asian and Islamic paradigms as credible counterweights to Western and liberal systems.
- 1997-2001: The outbreak of the 1997 Asian financial crisis exposed the vulnerability of the "Asian values" school, providing a boost for the proponents of human rights universalism, witnessed by the outbreak of democratization movements in Indonesia and Thailand. In Malaysia, the formation of its national human rights commission was largely prodded by this public sentiment.
- 2001: The beginning of Doubts. A discourse on "safety and security" following the 11 September 2001 fallout overtook that of "freedom and rights", causing many ASEAN governments to retreat from the hitherto "thawing" receptivity to a human rights commitment.

Throughout the post-Cold War period of East Asian economic take-off, ASEAN and the national governments were compelled to respond to some of the human rights challenges posed to them. They have gone reasonably far as to provide organizational support for a Working Group towards the formation of the ASEAN Human Rights Commission. Another limited, though significant, success of national governments has been the formation of at least four national commissions on human rights in the region. Although all the commissions have had their share of successes and setbacks in the discharge of their functions and independence, an "official channel with clout" has minimally been provided for human rights complainants.

Undoubtedly, there have been setbacks to the progress on human rights in the region due to the fallout of 11 September. The playing up of security issues has provided a convenient opportunity for a few ASEAN governments to deflect the population's attention away from the state's eroding "performance legitimacy" as they struggle with the continuing prospect of an uncertain economic rebound and renewal.

Clearly, a human rights culture is not inimical to the realities of local conditions. The biggest stumbling block remains the nature of the modern nation-state itself. Human rights mechanisms, enhanced by international instruments, are persistently seen as a threat to national sovereignty. Furthermore, the identity of Southeast Asian nation-states is crafted upon its ability to deliver economic welfare, which is, in turn, pedalled by the state as predicated upon the preponderance of public security and order. Thus, while the battle for the promotion of human rights may win the approval of the public, the war against the tyranny of the nation-state has yet to be won by the proponents of a universal normative cause such as that of human rights.

INDIA: A SOCIETY IN TRANSITION

Sample this: Dinesh Chand Jaiswal, a young constable with the Central Reserve Police Force, is proud holding a small trophy won on a debate on human rights. "I feel really good since I've been participating in this debate in 2002, and this year I have won it", he says with a grin while his battalion mates crowd around listening to him. "Yes, I've learned that our operations, conducted while pursuing terrorists and anti-social elements, can be carried out by ensuring that human rights are not abused." Like what? "I know that innocent people, who may happen to be there, have to be protected at any cost, and its compulsory to involve elders from the community when carrying out search operations ... and always take along a woman constable to deal with women in such operations", he adds.

An eight-year-old girl has just found her way to the bustling community of "Prayas" (meaning the effort). Her mother earns 1,300 rupees (some $28. per month and has three other daughters to look after in her little slum house on the outskirts of New Delhi. At the Prayas-run shelter for destitute children, she will get an education, regular meals and a hope to make something of her life-her amputated arm notwithstanding. In another part of India's capital, in a small ordinary office sits a small group of researchers pouring over media reports and meeting "sources" to collect data on torture and extrajudicial killings. While local media reports are agog with stark pictures of a baby born and dying outside one of India's top hospitals, photographers persuade the distraught mother to uncover the tiny bundle on her lap for their shoot for the "audience".

At the same time, the citizens are divided over an army of bulldozers that have descended in some middle-class colonies on direction from the highest court to remove "unauthorized" portions of residential and commercial buildings. Some bay for blood of municipal officials who "allowed" these buildings to come up. "It is my home and I won't allow you to demolish it", says a young girl as she shakes her fists at two police officers sitting atop a crane, who are trying to persuade her to leave her balcony and allow officials to carry on their work. "It is our right", says everyone in a society filled with a new found awareness fueled by media focus on abuse and violation, moving of the wheels of human rights institutions-an exceptionally devoted community of non-governmental organizations and a high-pitched, philanthropy-driven endorsement of social causes by celebrities.

Public debates focus on fairness, be it for the alleged "moll" of an international terrorist who had just been extradited to India by Spain, or the dropping out of a former captain of the country's cricket team, on which a debate was scheduled even in Parliament. Vigilant Indians are waking up to their rights and coming forward to fight for them. "Everyone is talking about rights, but the only drawback is that people do not know the process. The awareness is therefore incomplete", says Archana Chaturvedi of the Indian Social Institute, which publishes several magazines on the issues of human rights, women and civil society. "And the most vulnerable section is women and they have to be made aware of the processes", she adds.

"Laws are present, but awareness is not there", echoes Sadhana Ramachandran, a lawyer practicing human rights law for the past ten years. "Laws relating to women's inheritance of property, domestic violence and dowry deaths have been made, but people still need to be adequately educated about them", she adds. Children, along with women, bear the brunt of societal and economic torment, even though all rights are guaranteed by the country's Constitution.

"The right to move the Supreme Court for violation of a fundamental right is now almost a fundamental right", she says, so institutional support emanates from the top. "Political will is perhaps lacking in this support. There is so much child labour in India, which is equal to the number of unemployed adults, so why can't we just have policies to switch the two and send these children to be educated. The police, armed forces and the lower judiciary need to be sensitized the most to make human rights implementable in our country," Ms. Ramachandran says.

"Torture in custody and extrajudicial executions are a major problem across South Asia", says Rineeta Naik of the South Asia Human Rights Documentation Centre. "This is evident from the number of complaints sent to the National Human Rights Commission of India (NHRC)." One of the main causes of the persistence of such violations is the lack of accountability. Certain laws grant immunity from prosecution to all public officials, she says, and under the Armed Forces (Special Powers) Act of 1958, all security forces are given unrestricted and unaccounted power to carry out their operations once an area is declared disturbed.

Even a non-commissioned officer is granted the right to shoot to kill based on mere suspicion that it is necessary to do so in order to 'maintain the public order'." Further, she adds, the NHRC is not allowed to independently probe violations by the army, which is a serious lacuna in the process of ensuring justice to victims. The Commission has been seeking more power to increase its effectiveness in upholding the citizen's rights for the last few years. Justice (retired) A. S. Anand, the NHRC Chairperson, is a proponent of putting the Commission at the forefront of the battle to prevent violations of human rights in the country; and with 75,000 cases registered with it in 2004; it's a Herculean task to increase efficiency and effectiveness.

According to Mondeep Tiwana, co-author of a "citizen's handbook" on human rights commissions, the reform areas that are widely endorsed are powers of the commission and appointments. "Though the NHRC was set up under the Protection of Human Rights Act 1993, it is not fully in accordance with the Paris Principles. While commissions should be given as broad a mandate as possible, the NHRC only has powers to recommend to the Government", he says, adding that "these should be made binding to increase effectiveness and provide quick relief to victims of abuse and their families.

The follow up by authorities is very poor both at the centre and the different states of India". Currently, 16 states have constituted commissions under the 1993 Act. "Also, they can get bogged down because of inadequate staff; and out of the 75,000 cases, many would be frivolous complaints by citizens", Mr. Tiwana says. He cites custodial deaths, torture by the armed forces and the police, trafficking of women and children, and child abuse as "serious" human rights issues that India is grappling with.

But that's not all, feels Lola Nayyar, a writer on development issues for the past 20 years. "Violence against individuals is not the only human rights abuse-it starts from day one. When a child is born and is not given proper medical care that is promised free of cost by the Government, and this child grows, the violations continue, be it pertaining to education, the right to clean drinking water, unpolluted environment or a safe society to live in", she says, adding that even a dangerous road to walk or drive on is a violation of a citizens right, and the violators are the States who fail to provide these basic living facilities to their citizens.

8

Development in South Asia

According to the recently released 1996 revision of the official United Nations population estimates and projections, at mid-1996, world population stood at 5.77 billion persons. Between 1990 and 1995, the world population grew at 1.48 percent per annum, with an average of 81 million persons added each year. This is considerably slower than the 1.72 percent per annum growth rate of the 1975 to 1990 period. Additionally, the annual increment is notably less than the 87 million persons added each year between 1985 and 1990. In South Asia-Afghanistan, Bangladesh, Bhutan, India, Maldives, Nepal, Pakistan and Sri Lanka-the population exceeded 1.2 billion people in 1996, which is more than one-fifth of humankind.

The sharp decline in South Asia's death rates in the post-Second World War era has been accompanied by a much slower reduction in birth rates. As a consequence, the region's population has grown rapidly, adding significantly to its large population base. This rate of growth continues to challenge and constrain the ability of governments to improve the quality of life, with the result that South Asia has the bulk of the world's poor in its midst as well as the highest concentration of need for reproductive health (RH) and family planning (FP) information and services. Therefore, the provision of comprehensive reproductive health services, the empowerment of women, improved education for girls and a commitment to gender equality and equity will be critical to achieving sustainable development.

Adult Illiteracy Rate (UNESCO) and GNP Per Capita (World Bank database) - in UNESCO, World Education Report 1995 defined a person as illiterate who is unable both to read and write a short simple statement on everyday life with understanding.)

It is clear that on the eve of the 21st century the countries of South Asia face several challenges in the area of population and sustainable development. According to the Programme of Action, which emerged from the 1994 International Conference on Population and Development (ICPD), sustainable development is defined as, inter alia, long-term sustainability in production and consumption relating to all economic activities including industry, energy, agriculture, forestry, fisheries, transport, tourism and infrastructure in order to optimize ecologically sound resource use and minimize waste. Macroeconomic and sectoral policies have, however, rarely given due attention to population considerations. Explicitly integrating population into economic and development strategies will both speed up the pace of sustainable development and poverty alleviation and contribute to the achievement of population objectives and an improved quality of life of the population.

At the 1994 ICPD, representatives from 179 countries, including those of South Asia, agreed on and endorsed a Programme of Action delineating population and sustainable development objectives and goals for the next 20 years. These include: sustained economic growth in the context of sustainable development; improvement of education, especially for girls; gender equality; reduction in infant, child and maternal mortality; and the provision of universal access to RH services, which include FP and sexual health. The Programme of Action, firmly anchored in a human rights framework, underscores the centrality of the human person as the subject of development, emphasizing that, "people are the most important and valuable resource of any nation "and," the right to development is a universal and inalienable right and an integral part of fundamental human rights."

Key to this approach is the empowerment of women, gender equality and equity, reproductive rights and reproductive health.

The new paradigm that emerged at the ICPD marks a distinct shift from a focus on demographic targets to a focus on people-centered development.

This chapter focuses on the following key issues that countries in South Asia must address to achieve sustainable development: population growth; migration and urbanization; poverty eradication and the provision of basic social services for all; empowerment of women; gender equality and equity, including special attention to the girl child; and reproductive health, family planning and sexual health, including HIV/AIDS prevention. Undoubtedly, in each country the policies and programs to meet these challenges will be shaped by national priorities and particularities. However, any effective strategy will require development partnerships between governments, non-government organizations (NGOs), multilateral and bilateral agencies, the private sector and civil society Increased resource mobilization and strong advocacy at all levels will also be required for population and sustainable development.

FERTILITY IN SOUTH ASIA

While fertility reductions in South Asia have been slower than in certain other regions, there have been some impressive recent changes. Sri Lanka is the only South Asian country that has completed the transition to replacement level fertility-that is to approximately two children per woman. Its fertility decline began in the 1950s, largely as a result of the rise in the marriage age, and subsequently through a fall in marital fertility as a result of increased contraceptive use, particularly female sterilization. Sri Lanka's fertility transition, like that in the Indian state of Kerala, appears to have been facilitated by a relatively equitable distribution of wealth and welfare benefits, the high status of women and high levels of female literacy.

In the mid-1990s, women in Bangladesh and India were having between three to four children on average. The remarkable relatively recent fertility decline in Bangladesh since the early 1980s contrasts sharply with the much steadier change that has occurred in India. In India, however, national trends in aggregate fertility levels conceal state variations. Thus, for example, whereas fertility in the southern states of Kerala and Tamil Nadu is near replacement level, women in poorer states, such as Bihar and Uttar Pradesh, are still bearing approximately five or more children.

The areas where fertility has declined most are those where social progress has been greatest. Relatively high adult female literacy, later age at first marriage, low child mortality together with active family planning programs are characteristics of states where fertility is lowest. In Pakistan and Nepal during the mid-1990s, women were having between five and six children on average. Although fertility levels are higher than those prevailing in the other South Asian countries, there is evidence of some recent decline, which is consistent with a small rise in the age of women at first marriage.

Key factors in the persistence of high fertility in both countries appear to be a large need for reproductive health and family planning (RH/ FP) information and services, the low status of women, and low levels of female education. To remedy the situation and meet the need for quality RH/FP, governments of countries in South Asia are beginning to implement integrated RH/FP programs. For example, Pakistan has already trained and deployed 30,000 (of an anticipated 100,000) Lady Health Workers to increase coverage and enable a larger number of rural people to have access to RH/FP services.

These workers are in addition to 12,000 village-based workers already in place. Nepal, too, has developed a national primary health care outreach strategy to ensure universal access to quality RH/FP services. Although survey data indicate that by the mid-1990s knowledge of contraception was very widespread among women in Bangladesh, India and Sri Lanka, contraception is less well known among the populations of Nepal and Pakistan where the programs have had less impact. As might be expected from trends in levels of fertility the use of contraception has been uneven. Sri Lanka has long been, and remains, significantly ahead of the other countries in the level of contraceptive use.

Indeed, Sri Lanka, with its strong family planning program and history of investing in health and education, represents a population success story. It has low infant and maternal mortality rates, high contraceptive prevalence rate (66.1 percent), a high female literacy rate (83.1 percent) and low population growth rate (1.3 percent). In the light of the ICPD Programme of Action, Sri Lanka is broadening its program perspective to a comprehensive reproductive health approach and increasing its emphasis on such issues as improved quality of care and increased access to RH/FP services.

A particular attempt is being made to reach neglected and/or under-served groups such as youth and adolescents and women workers in the industrial free-trade zones and the tea-plantations. Advocacy, training and the increased involvement of other actors such as the private sector and civil society are also being encouraged. Over the past decade, Bhutan has achieved similar striking achievements in improving the health of its people as shown by the declines in infant mortality and maternal mortality between 1984 and 1994. At the same time, population grew rapidly at a rate of 3.1 percent in 1994. To meet this challenge, the Kingdom of Bhutan is encouraging its people to adopt family planning and is introducing RH/FP services as a major component of the health sector program.

India, in reorienting its national family welfare program, has moved away from a target-driven approach focused primarily on increasing the number of contraceptive users to a service-oriented approach, emphasizing improved quality of care and the delivery of a constellation of services to clients. Reflecting the ICPD Programme of Action, this new approach focuses on expanding services and meeting the need for quality RH/FP information and services. The government of India is also focusing on increased training for service providers and collaboration with NGOs and international agencies. Additionally; to enhance the empowerment of women within the framework of decentralized planning and decision making, women have been guaranteed one-third of the seats in local councils.

URBANIZATION AND MIGRATION

By the year 2015, nearly 56 percent of the global population is expected to live in urban areas, compared to less than 45 percent in 1994. The most rapid rates of urbanization will occur in developing countries. The urban population of the developing regions was just 26 percent in 1975, but is projected to rise to 50 percent by 2015. This change will place enormous strain on existing social services and infrastructure, much of which will not be able to expand at the same rate as that of urbanization. The two decades ahead are likely to produce a further shift of rural populations to urban areas as well as continued high levels of migration between countries.

While these migrations are an important part of the economic transformations occurring around the world, they present serious new challenges which must be addressed with greater emphasis on population and development policies. In South Asia, the mega-cities Mumbai (Bombay; India), Karachi (Pakistan) and Dhaka (Bangladesh) grew by 3.7, 4.7, and 7.6 percent, respectively, between 1970 and 1990. These growth rates will moderate before 2015. However, Dhaka, Hyderabad (India), Karachi and Lahore (Pakistan) are projected to grow faster than 3 percent annually from 2000 to 2015.

Cities appear to draw migrants with the promise of higher living standards, but the wealth produced in cities does not necessarily translate into prosperity for all. Increasing urbanization has the potential for either improving human life or increasing misery The cities can provide opportunities or frustrate their attainment; promote health or cause disease; empower people to realize their needs and desires or impose on them a simple struggle for basic survival.

A successful urban future depends as much as anything else on engaging all members of the community; especially women and the poor, in a constructive political process. Partnerships between governments and members of civil society, including women's groups, are one of the keys to achieving social cohesion and economic progress. A good example of this is found in Mumbai, where the Society for Promotion of Area Resource

Centres, in collaboration with other NGOs, has shown that pavement/sidewalk dwellers, mostly women and children, can save for better housing and can avert or cope with the demolition of their squatter homes. Working with the government, area committees headed by women conducted surveys and planned for alternate settlements.

Women collaborated with architects and engineers in the design of new dwellings. Such collaborative development partnerships are necessary to meet the growing demand for education, health services, housing and other basic social services that results from increased urbanization. The provision of RH/FP information and services is indispensable for human well-being, and it is also an essential component of population and development strategies seeking to balance population growth and resources.

Migrants are not only a rapidly growing urban population but also a group with special reproductive health needs. Research findings indicate that migrants and their families face greater health problems than long-term residents. Providing basic social services to migrants, including the provision of reproductive health care, requires more focused communication and service delivery

POVERTY ERADICATION AND THE PROVISION OF BASIC SOCIAL SERVICES

One of the greatest challenges facing countries in South Asia is the eradication of poverty and the provision of basic social services, with particular emphasis on safety nets for the marginalized and vulnerable population groups. Eradicating poverty is an indispensable requirement for sustainable development in order to decrease the disparities in standards of living and better meet the needs of the majority of the people. While the achievement of sustainable development, in large measure, depends on economic growth, it is critical to recognize that economic growth is not a panacea for all development problems, nor does it automatically translate into sustainable development with a better and more equitable life for all.

This key lesson, learned from decades of development experience, must inform and shape population and development planning in South Asia. Indeed, countries and larger states of federal unions frequently accord lower priority to investments in social services and infrastructure than to industrial development. Those that have invested in education, particularly women's education, and basic health services, including reproductive health and family planning, have had striking results. For example, Sri Lanka, Bangladesh and Kerala state in India have attained higher levels of education and health than other societies with similar economic status and urban burdens.

Following the ICPD, countries in South Asia are investing more in education, and focusing greater attention on education for the girl child. The Education for All (EFA) initiative of the Nine-High (E-9) which includes population countries, Bangladesh, India and Pakistan has succeeded in mobilizing an unprecedented level of political support for the goals of EFA, including: full access to basic education for all members of society, particularly, equity of access for girls and women.

The three South Asian E-9 countries-Bangladesh, India and Pakistan-reported increased allocation of national resources to education. In Pakistan, the overall allocation of the GNP for educational development and recruitment has risen from 2.1 to 2.5 percent since the 1993 EFA Delhi Summit, and is expected to increase beyond 3 percent before the close of this century The Government of Pakistan has undertaken an integrated $4 billion education policy that focuses on improving quality as part of a broader strategy for human development. Bangladesh has increased the share of gross domestic product (GDP) spent on education by nearly 3 percent from 1994 to 1995.

Education expenditure as a share of total government expenditure also rose from 9.4 percent during the First Five-Year Plan (1973 to 1978. to 13.6 percent during the Fourth Five-Year Plan (1990 to 1995.. In India, allocations for education have doubled from 9,770 million Rupees in 1991/92 to 18,250 million Rupees in 1995/96; and 46 percent of the education budget is allocated for primary education. Meanwhile India also reaffirmed its commitment to increase allocations for education from the present level of 3.7 percent of GDP to 6 percent by the end of this century.

WOMEN'S EMPOWERMENT AND GENDER EQUALITY AND EQUITY

South Asia gave the world the first female prime minister of a nation (Sri Lanka), and subsequently there have been four other women prime ministers in South Asia (in India, Pakistan and Bangladesh). It is, therefore, ironic that in a region where many women have attained high rank in such elite areas as the government, diplomacy, education, medicine and even the armed forces, the vast majority of South Asian women suffer a low socioeconomic status with even their basic needs and fundamental human rights denied. Since discrimination on the basis of sex often starts at the earliest stages of life, greater equality for the girl child is a necessary first step in ensuring that women realize their full potential and become equal partners in development.

The empowerment of women and the achievement of gender equality and equity is pivotal to poverty eradication and sustainable development. Governments in South Asia need to actively promote women's full involvement in all policy- and decision-making processes at the international, national and local levels. By providing education, employment and health services, the autonomy and empowerment of women can be enhanced and their socio-economic life and health status improved. In designing programs and policies to meet the basic needs of women, it should be ensured that women themselves are active participants-indeed, are the architects in the processes of project design, implementation, monitoring and evaluation.

The value of girl children to both their family and society must be expanded beyond their definition as potential child-bearers and care-takers, and reinforced through the adoption and implementation of educational and social policies that encourage their full participation in the development process. Leaders at all levels must speak and act forcefully against patterns of gender discrimination within the family based on preference for sons. Special education and public information efforts are needed to promote equal treatment of girls and boys with respect to nutrition, health care and education, as well as social, economic and political activity. Specific governmental measures are needed to prevent female infanticide, prenatal sex selection and trafficking of girl children and use of girls in prostitution and pornography.

At the same time, governmental, non-governmental and community efforts must be undertaken to eliminate all forms of discrimination against the girl child and the root causes of son preference. The media in South Asia can play a key role in increasing public awareness of the value of the girl child while promoting the elimination of gender stereotypes. Countries must recognize that, in addition to expanding education for girls, teachers' attitudes and practices, school curricula and facilities must also change to reflect a commitment to eliminate all gender bias and recognize the specific needs of the girl child.

Education is one of the most important means of empowering women with the knowledge, skills and self-confidence necessary to participate fully in the development process. Experience shows that population and development programs are most effective when steps have simultaneously been taken to improve the status of women. Changes in men's and women's knowledge, attitude and behavior are necessary conditions for achieving a harmonious partnership.

In South Asia, as indeed in most societies, men play a key role in bringing about gender equality since they exercise preponderant power in nearly every sphere of life. For men and women to become equal partners in public and private life, it is essential to improve communication and understanding between them on issues of sexuality and reproductive health. Men and women should also share responsibilities in the care and nurturing of children and the maintenance of the household. Career options for women should be increased and marriage should not be automatically assumed to be the final destiny of all women in South Asia, or anywhere else in the world. Creating choices for women and an enabling socio-economic and cultural environment that supports those choices is a major challenge facing countries in South Asia as they seek to empower women.

In Pakistan, one significant step has been the introduction of a Compulsory Primary Education Act by the Government of Punjab. In order to eliminate both gender disparities and those between rural and urban areas, all new schools will be mixed and more than 60 percent of the teachers will be female. The recruitment age has been lowered to increase the supply of available teachers. Girls, particularly in rural areas, are being encouraged to stay in school through the implementation of food programs and provision of free textbooks and stipends. Female enrollment rates have already increased and drop-out rates have decreased.

In an innovative project in the north Indian state of Haryana, the United Nations Population Fund (UNFPA) is assisting the Indian government to implement a project that addresses the issues of women's status, health and development in a comprehensive manner. Haryana is seen as an important test field because the state has experienced impressive economic progress, but human development achievements are among the lowest in the country A women's collective is the fulcrum of the project and is mobilizing women as an empowered group through an intensive awareness campaign, supported by the media, for all-round development of women with a focus on education, health care, nutrition, sanitation, delayed marriage, small family norm and methods of child spacing. Women's marketing groups are supporting income-generating activities.

To increase access to education and school attendance, various schemes have been implemented, including the provision of escorts for girls and an allowance for uniforms, stationery and books. Sensitization of men to gender issues and raising their awareness has been undertaken to highlight women's socio-economic contributions and to counteract the "invisibility" of women's work and worth. The overall emphasis is on training, enhancing the capacity of rural women to make informed choices and creating a cadre of confident and aware women who will play the role of catalysts to bring about an appreciable change in the status of women.

In predominantly Muslim Pakistan, a major innovation in expanding access to education has been the use of mosques as schools in addition to being places of prayer. The mosques now account for the majority of non-formal schools in Pakistan. They have also been a major factor in increasing the enrollment of girls.

Although many Muslim parents may not favor co-education, they tend to accept it in a mosque setting. Also in Pakistan, where child labor is a major obstacle to education, a bold scheme has been launched to give cash compensation to parents of working children who attend class regularly.

Reproductive rights and reproductive health, including family planning and sexual health, are critical to human wellbeing and human development. The empowerment of women is a fundamental prerequisite for their reproductive health. In implementing the Programme of Action of the ICPD, governments in South Asia (and other regions) are emphasizing a reproductive health care approach within primary health care. However, many factors influence reproductive health, and its attainment is not determined by interventions in the health sector alone. Socio-economic factors including education, employment, living conditions, family environment, social relations, gender relations and legislation, as well as cultural and traditional practices, all affect reproductive health.

Thus, it is critical that reproductive health programs adopt an inter-sectoral as well as a multi sectoral and multidisciplinary approach, i.e., reproductive health programs will need to be designed in ways that include and cross-cut various sectors, such as health, education and employment. At the same time, the programmatic approach will need to be informed by various disciplines so as to better focus on meeting the needs of individuals and improving human well-being.

At the ICPD, the countries present, including those of South Asia, agreed that all countries should strive to make reproductive health accessible to all individuals of appropriate ages through the primary health care system as soon as possible and no later than 2015. The ICPD Programme of Action defines reproductive health care as the, constellation of methods, techniques and services that contribute to reproductive health and wellbeing by preventing and solving reproductive health problems. It also includes sexual health, the purpose of which is the enhancement of life and personal relations and not merely counseling and care related to reproduction and sexually transmitted diseases.

The Programme of Action goes on to state that reproductive health care in the context of primary health care should, inter alia, include: family-planning counseling, information, education, communication and services; education and services for prenatal care, safe delivery ,and post-natal care, especially breast-feeding, infant and women's health care; prevention and appropriate treatment of infertility; abortion as specified in paragraph 8.25 (of the Programme of Action)including prevention of abortion and the management of the consequences of abortion; treatment of reproductive tract infections (RTIs); sexually transmitted diseases (STDs) and other reproductive health conditions; and information, education and counseling, as appropriate, on human sexuality, reproductive health and responsible parenthood.

Reproductive health is a lifetime concern for both women and men. For women, reproductive health concerns begin even before birth, with the possibility of sex-selective abortion; they continue in infancy as a result of son preference; through childhood and adolescence, when issues of education, nutrition and appropriate health care are most prominent; and continue into the reproductive years with concerns for family planning, STDs and RTIs, adequate nutrition and care in pregnancy; and the social status of women; and continue to old age, with concern for heart disease, osteoporosis as a result of estrogen deficiency and the social role of older women in passing on information and setting rules for behavior. Men need early socialization in concepts of sexual responsibility to promote healthy sexual and family formation behavior. Thus, gender sensitive training should be imparted in early boyhood.

Usually women's routine health care has been available only through maternal and child health services. These services have generally put the emphasis on child health and addressed only a restricted set of women's health needs. They ignored young unmarried women, women suffering from reproductive tract infections and infertility, and women past child-bearing age. Women's long-term reproductive health problems often stem from lack of care in infancy, childhood and adolescence.

For example, boys are more likely to be hospitalized for treatment of protein-energy malnutrition, though it is more prevalent among girls, who may have less access to whatever nutritious food is available. A comprehensive reproductive health care approach focuses on addressing women's health care needs over the entire life-cycle and not just during the child-bearing years. Reproductive health offers women the freedom from which other freedoms flow. These include the freedom to seek education, employment and a better life for themselves and their families. Children born by choice and not by chance are more likely to have a healthier and happier future with better opportunities for education and employment. The role and involvement of men is central to the reproductive health of both sexes.

Adolescents have special needs related to reproductive health but these have largely been ignored in existing reproductive health services. The response of societies to the reproductive health needs of adolescents should be based on information that helps them attain a level of maturity required to make responsible decisions.

In particular, information and services should be made available to adolescents to help them understand their sexuality and protect them from unwanted pregnancies, sexually transmitted diseases and subsequent risk of infertility This should be combined with the education of young men to respect women's self-determination and to share responsibility with women in matters of sexuality and reproduction. For young women, early marriage and early motherhood can severely curtail educational and employment opportunities and are likely to have a long-term, adverse impact on their quality of life and that of their children. It should also be underscored that motherhood at a very young age entails a risk of maternal death that is much greater than average, and the children of young mothers have higher levels of morbidity and mortality.

Throughout South Asia, there is considerable evidence of unmet need for reproductive health and family planning services. The challenge is to increase access to quality RH/FP information and services, particularly to underserved, marginalized and vulnerable population groups. Programs should promote the following basic concepts: involvement of women and women's organizations in the planning, implementation and monitoring of RH/ FP services and programs; men's participation in RH/

FP programs and responsibility for their sexual and reproductive behavior; assurance of the highest level of quality of care in the provision of information and services, with specific regard to client needs for confidentiality and privacy, and positive client-provider interrelations; provision of a constellation of linked or integrated services; availability of a wide range of safe, effective and affordable methods of family planning approved by the World Health Organization; creation of a better understanding of the social, cultural and behavioral context within which reproductive ill-health occurs; and coordination of national RH/FP programs among governments, multilateral and bilateral agencies, NGOs and the private sector.

HIV/AIDS prevention measures should form an integral part of the spectrum of reproductive health services, with special attention focused on the health and information needs of youths and adolescents. The HIV/AIDS pandemic is not just a serious health challenge but a critical human development challenge with complex socio-economic impacts and costs. The Joint United Nations Programme on HIV/AIDS (UNAIDS) estimates that as of December 1996, 22.6 million people are living with HIV infections or AIDS and of these, 21.8 million are adults and 830,000 are children.

An estimated 5.2 million persons are living with HIV/AIDS in South and Southeast Asia with the epidemic spreading explosively in some parts of South Asia. For example, in Mumbai, over a very short period of time, HIV prevalence has reached 50 percent in sex workers, 36 percent in STD patients and 2.5 percent in pregnant women attending clinics for antenatal care. In addition, HIV may be spreading rapidly to India s rural areas through migrant workers and truck drivers, as has happened in many other countries. For the countries of South Asia, which already face demanding development challenges, the HIV/AIDS pandemic poses an additional major challenge requiring inspired leadership and effective preventative strategies and programs.

Information, education and communication strategies as well as the provision of condoms, counseling, the promotion of safe and responsible sexual behavior and ensuring universal precautions in health settings are critical components of HIV/

AIDS prevention and control strategies. In particular, special attention should be focused on reaching those at high risk of acquiring HIV infection, including adolescents and women whose vulnerability is often greatest. Through its reproductive health and family planning programs, UNFPA is assisting governments in over 100 developing countries-including those of South Asia-in HIV/AIDS prevention.

In Bangladesh, UNFPA is supporting a project that provides reproductive health care services for commercial sex workers, including the provision through a local NGO of counseling and condom promotion, distribution and diagnosis and treatment of RTIs/STDs. Under a UNFPA-supported population education project, HIV/AIDS prevention information has been incorporated in school textbooks. In Bhutan, HIV/AIDS prevention has been integrated in the UNFPA-supported maternal and child health (MCH) and family planning project and includes the free distribution of condoms through MCH clinics and public toilets.

In India, through a UNFPA-supported project on population education, a mandatory course which includes AIDS prevention information has been introduced in all universities and colleges in 1996. This course is supplemented by awareness-raising student activities, such as debates, essay writing/painting contests, street plays and TV spots through class-room telecasts. Additionally, a telephone counseling service called "Help Line" has been established at the University of Delhi. HIV/AIDS prevention education activities have also been undertaken to reach in-school and out-of-school youth and adolescents. UNFPA is supporting similar activities in other countries in South Asia.

ESTABLISHING DEVELOPMENT PARTNERSHIPS

In each country of South Asia, a key point that should be underscored in all population and development planning is that the provision of and access to basic social services including health services, education, shelter, drinking water, and sanitation, as well as access to employment and credit requires synergistic partnerships among governments, bilateral and multilateral agencies, NGOs, the private sector and civil society. Since no one organization can single-handedly address the task of meeting basic human needs and providing basic social services for all, the forging of development partnerships at all levels is imperative. Such partnerships pay higher dividends on investments in the social sector.

Facing the challenge of increasing demands and limited resources, governments in South Asia need to capitalize on the areas of comparative advantage of NGOs, the private sector and civil society Many United Nations organizations, including UNFPA, have a long history of collaborating with NGOs. Following the recent global conferences, new efforts are underway to increase interaction with NGOs, both foı program implementation and for monitoring and evaluation.

A well-established family welfare and credit program in the slums of the city of Madras and four rural districts in Tamil Nadu, India, present a good example of effective collaboration between an international organization, UNFPA, and a local NGO, the Working Women's Forum (WWF). The WWF is a non-governmental grass-roots trade union for poor women workers. Funded by UNFPA since 1989, the project provides support for community-based family planning motivation, education, and referral and credit for income-generating activities. Project achievements include: an increase in contraceptive use from 36 percent of 119,000 eligible couples in 1990 to 68 percent by August 1992; provision of 4,549 loans to women, totaling more than $167,000; increased immunization of children under the age of five years, from 43 percent to 71 percent; and provision of training to credit groups, households and child labor rehabilitation centers. The project demonstrates the success of the promotion of income-generation activities as a catalyst for creating demand for family planning and reproductive health services.

The Self-Employed Women's Association (SEWA) of India and the Grameen Bank of Bangladesh offer two rich examples of micro credit enterprises serving the needs of poor women. Formed in 1972, SEWA is a trade union that reaches out to poor, illiterate, self-employed women who are economically active. SEWA develops women's economic potential through the formation of co-operatives. There are more than 60 urban and rural co-operatives whose women members include vendors and traders, home-based skilled and semi-skilled workers and service providers in rural and urban sectors.

SEWA's first cooperative, a credit society formed in 1974 through the collective effort of 4,000 women, had bloomed into a full-fledged cooperative bank with 43,000 members by 1994. Mahila SEWA Bank, the first women's bank of its kind in India, works with and for poor, illiterate and self-employed women. For example, women operate their own savings accounts, obtain loans for domestic, social or vocational uses, buy tools, equipment and raw materials through credit facilities and borrow capital to initiate and enhance their trade.

In addition to providing enhanced economic opportunities, SEWA has had a positive impact on many other aspects of its members' lives: it has helped women to enhance their self-esteem and confidence and enabled them to improve their economic and social well-being. It has also positively impacted families through, for example, better nutrition, education and health care.

The Grameen Bank of Bangladesh advocates credit as a human right for the poorest and focuses on lending money to the landless poor, particularly to poor rural women, to assist them in their self-employment activities such as paddy processing, poultry and livestock purchase, traditional crafts, and small trade. Members attend regular meetings and make timely deposits into a group savings account from which the loans are drawn. Grameen Bank members are also asked to learn the "Sixteen Decisions," which include rules for good nutrition and health, and emphasize the benefits of education and small families.

While credit programs in Bangladesh do not offer health care services directly; they do encourage women to have small families and to make use of family planning. In villages where the Grameen Bank program has been established, contraceptive use increased among both members and non-members. This is because contraceptive use and small families became more acceptable in the villages than they had been before the credit programs were established.

South to south cooperation, i.e., technical cooperation among developing countries is yet another mechanism to expand development partnerships among the countries of South Asia. At the ICPD, 10 developing countries, including Bangladesh launched the "Partners in Population and Development with the objective of strengthening the capacity of developing countries for south-south cooperation. UNFPA and the Rockefeller Foundation have provided assistance in the development of this initiative and a small secretariat has been established in Dhaka, Bangladesh. The reach of the program is likely to expand further, given other South Asian countries interest in joining the Partners in Population and Development.

The high levels of need in various sectors in South Asia make the challenge of mobilizing resources even greater. Countries in South Asia need to specifically tap non-traditional sources of funding, including the private sector, partnerships with NGOs, cost-sharing with clients and other forms of community participation. At the same time, it is imperative that available resources are deployed in the most cost-effective and cost-efficient manner, balanced by the highest commitment to people-centered development.

To sustain governmental and public interest in population and development issues and to mobilize resources, domestically and internationally, vigorous advocacy for these issues is essential. Advocacy; for example, can play a key role in catalyzing and sustaining political commitment to reproductive health and the empowerment of women, including through the promotion of legislation and an enabling socio-economic and cultural environment. Continual advocacy, using dynamic and attention-getting messages, is needed to capture the interest of audiences and motivate them to action. A shared understanding of reproductive health and women's empowerment can be developed and promoted through national and local consensus-building in the countries of South Asia.

While rapid population growth is a major global concern, our first concern should be the lives of millions of people, most of them women, who are impoverished both materially and spiritually because they cannot exercise their reproductive rights. If we respond to individual reproductive health needs, the global need for slower and more balanced population growth will largely take care of itself. That is the true message of the International Conference on Population and Development.

STATEHOOD IN SOUTH ASIA

In the vast region now known as South Asia at the beginning of 1997, most of the major states-including India, Pakistan, Bangladesh and Sri Lanka-have some form of democratic government for the first time since the formal British withdrawal in 1947. All of these nations are engaged in measures of economic liberalization, moving away from government control of resources toward a market economy. All are also seeking, however tentatively, to increase and strengthen interregional relationships. Although democracy, economics and foreign policy have been important, the overarching concern in all the states and the one that shapes all the other issues is the quest for national unity. The process of decolonization that led to the formation of the separate states of South Asia meant that the externally imposed unity of the colonial state had to be replaced by policies that required the assent of the governed.

It is this theme of the search for national unity that will be analyzed in this chapter through brief examinations of three of the states, with a fourth, Bangladesh, being noted in relation to India and Pakistan. More attention will be given to India, since the same factors that give India a special prominence within the region make it an excellent starting place for considering the South Asia region in general. The first factor that explains India's prominence in the region is its overwhelming dominance in population, industrial development and military power. Equally important is the geographical factor. Since the state of India comprises almost three-quarters of the subcontinent, which is bound by mountains and seas, it is an "intelligible isolate."

A third factor is that the civilizations and cultures of India have made an impression on all the states of the region, despite the other states' own strong indigenous cultural and religious characteristics, such as Islam and Buddhism. A fourth factor giving India a special importance is that all the states in the region, especially the four largest ones, have experienced political trends rooted in what is now the state of India. Beginning with the Mauryan Empire in the fourth century B.C. and continuing into the modern era, political forces have emanated from India throughout the region. India had a special importance for the

British Empire and had a legal and political status different from any of the other colonies. It was regarded as the dominating power in the region. Lord Curzon, as governor general, expressed a grandiose but widely held vision of India's hegemony in 1909 when he wrote:

On the west, India must exercise a predominant influence over the destinies of Persia and Afghanistan; on the north, it can veto any rival in Tibet; on the north-east it can exert great pressure upon China, and it is one of the guardians of the autonomous existence of Siam.

This was a dangerous legacy for the Government of India to leave to its successor state, the Republic of India, as the world discovered when India and China quarreled over the borders that had been left by the British. Upon British departure in 1947, India's influence in the area continued when it began to interact with the new border states of Pakistan, Nepal, Bangladesh, Sri Lanka, Bhutan and Sikhim. The word "empire" is defined by the Oxford English Dictionary as "the aggregate of many states under one common head." The British viewed their empire in these terms. Britain had conquered and brought under one rule what was a hackneyed congeries of states and kingdoms in the geographical area that Europeans had called "India" since ancient times. That the official and legal documents usually referred to the "Government of India" and not "India" reflects that the British perceived India as a government, but not a state and certainly not a nation.

Looking back over 50 years of independent statehood in South Asia, one can identify dominant issues and concerns in each of the states. First, a variety of economic strategies emerged, all of which required an active role for the national government. These strategies were devised to address age-old problems of poverty while providing for the infrastructure of a modern state, including defense, communications, education and health services. These strategies were a post-colonial rejection of the laissez-faire economic policies that had characterized British rule.

Second, dominant trends have emerged from the function of religion in national life in all the countries of South Asia. Religion has been closely related to the question of national language. Third, democratic forms of government according to the Western model were established in all the states, although with many modifications. Fourth, foreign relations have been a constant preoccupation. Only recently has cooperation been embraced with the creation of the functionally-limited South Asian Association for Regional Cooperation in 1983. Despite South Asia's limited independent history, post-independence regional animosities and the fear of Indian hegemony have prevented the growth of normal economic and cultural contacts. Relations with the wider international community during the Cold War era were focused on the United States, the Soviet Union and China. As noted above, however, all of these concerns of the different South Asian states were deeply affected by the necessity of maintaining territorial integrity while fostering a sense of national consciousness.

During India's half-century of independence, the concern for national unity has had two broad aspects. One is the preservation of territorial integrity; which has been tested by wars with China and Pakistan and by internal insurgencies. The other aspect is the creation of a unifying national consciousness and this, in India as elsewhere, has been far more difficult than defending territorial integrity.

Indian territorial integrity was challenged first in 1962 when China and India went to war over territories in the Himalayan borderlands. In 1959, Chinese Prime Minister Zhou Enlai suggested that the borders of India were not legitimate because they were drawn by foreign imperialists. He told Indian Prime Minister Jawaharlal Nehru in an accurate and elegant phrase that the border issue was a complicated question left over by history." This was unacceptable to Nehru, who believed the borders were integral to India's sovereignty and to its sense of nationhood.

In an official note, the Government of India declared its northern frontier "has lain approximately where it now runs for nearly three thousand years," and that the people within the area it enclosed have always regarded themselves "as Indians and remained within the Indian fold." After the war started, Nehru told a New Delhi audience that it would begin "pushing us into the modern world and make us realize the hard realities." One of the hard realities for India was that it would be forced to reconsider its non-aligned status in foreign affairs, in order to obtain outside pressure to deflect the Chinese advance. Nehru wrote to U.S. President John F. Kennedy that India's situation was desperate, and asked for large-scale military assistance, including squadrons of supersonic fighters and B-47 bombers.

The Chinese ceased their advance, either because of the threat of American involvement, or because they believed they had humiliated India and proved that China, as they put it, "was one head taller than India imagined herself to be." The 1962 war with China was a turning point in defining India as a nation. Nehru spoke of it as a blessing in disguise because internal disunity had been swept aside by the Chinese threat and the new mood could be used to achieve industrial advances as well as military preparedness. A variety of militant insurgent movements within India also placed severe strains on the government during the past 50 years. By threatening to secede or demanding a degree of autonomy that the government felt would destroy the nation's unity, insurgencies challenged the government's legitimacy.

Countering rebellions was expensive in material and human resources and left bitter memories of alleged brutalities and grave human rights abuses. All Indian administrations since 1947 have believed, however, that violent and secessionist movements should be crushed quickly. Although the numerous insurgencies had different local origins and agendas and affected widely separated areas, the common threads among them were a sense of grievance, often rooted in perceived economic discrimination. Bonds of language and religion became important characteristics among insurgents because of their belief that the government, in seeking national unity; was trying to replace local traditions with a Hinduized culture.

The longest-lasting example of rebellion began soon after independence in the hilly area in the northeast against the tribal people known as Nagas and was occasioned by what the Nagas saw as an attempt to erode their customs, language and religion by the Government of India. Eventually, the government succeeded in forcing a peace settlement, including the creation of a new federal state, Nagaland, in 1963. However, groups of rebels continued to fight until 1978 when they realized defeat was inevitable and consequently agreed to make peace.

The current insurgencies in Kashmir and Punjab are on a much larger scale. The insurgents are far better armed, have more support from a wider constituency, and are given more ideological coherence by potent appeals to loyalties based on religion, language and history. Furthermore, the insurgents in Kashmir and Punjab have allegedly received support from Pakistan, which has fought India three times since 1947. According to conservative estimates, India had committed a quarter million of its armed forces to quelling armed insurrections in the former princely state of Jammu and Kashmir.

The insurgencies are carried on by many separate groups with different aims and without a unified command. Some want a union with Pakistan, some want independence, and others might settle for a high degree of autonomy within India. This is not an open war between India and Pakistan, but two previous wars between the two countries involved in Kashmir. There is always a danger that a new war may ensue, now with the added peril that both nations could develop and use nuclear weapons.

India's insistence that the accession of the state of Jammu and Kashmir is a closed issue and that its partition or secession cannot be discussed as part of any solution to the problem has angered Pakistan. However, this stance reflects India's fundamental view of its statehood. Indian leaders argue that permitting self-determination to the Kashmiris would lead to a demand from ethnic groups within India to secede, destroying the fabric of the nation's unity. Indian leaders, including Nehru, have argued repeatedly that a concession to a Muslim majority in Kashmir would lead to a new outburst of communal violence against Muslims in India, especially now that Hindu nationalism is ascending.

One thing is reasonably certain: In the foreseeable future, India will violently resist any secessionist attempts or movements for greater autonomy that threaten the state's territorial integrity and stability. While the Kashmir situation attracted more international attention because of the threat of war from

Pakistan's involvement, armed insurgency in Punjab in the 1980s probably affected the people of India more directly Punjab has historically been part of the Indian heartland. It is also one of the most prosperous and progressive Indian states. The conventional explanation of the insurgency was that it originated in a power struggle between political leaders in the Akali Dal party and the ruling party, the Indian National Congress. The Akali Dal represents Sikhs.

However, the element that gave the insurgency its violence and passion was the dynamic leadership of a militant young religious leader, Jarnail Singh Bhindranwale, and his followers who began a crusade against the enemies of Sikhism. These were identified as the elderly Sikh leaders who had grown weak in the faith and, above all, the external enemy, the Government of India, which was seen in religious terms as a Hindu power inimical to Sikhism. What has been called "the logic of religious violence" took over and a religious cause legitimized violence, "for the language of warfare, of fighting and dying for a cause, is appropriate and endemic to the realm of religion."

As elsewhere, the opportunity for religiously sanctioned violence appealed strongly to young men who felt marginalized by the economic and social changes taking place in the Punjab. They became recruits for a campaign that led to the murder of many thousands of civilians and, in the attempts by the authorities to end the insurgency, the death or disappearance of thousands of militants. Human rights groups, both in India and abroad, have reported that the security forces adopted brutal methods, including torture, detention without trials, and summary killings of suspected militants and of civilians who may have helped them. However upsetting, the authorities now point to a return to elected government and normal conditions throughout the state by 1992 to justify their harsh actions during the insurgency.

While preservation of its territorial integrity from external enemies and internal insurgencies taxed the nation's energies and resources, conflicts over the creation of a sense of a national identity consensus through language and religion have also strained the unity of the nation. In regions, both language and religion have been rallying points for national unity, but in India as elsewhere in South Asia, they also have often been divisive.

The choice of Hindi, the most widely spoken of India's 12 major languages, as the national language provoked bitter debates in the Constituent Assembly and throughout the country in 1948 and 1949. But the demand in the 1950s for the creation of linguistic states posed an even greater threat to Indian unity The states, or provinces as they had been known during British rule, had been formed largely for administrative convenience or as a result of conquests at different periods, but in 1920 the Indian National Congress demanded that the country be divided into states that reflected the language and culture of the different regions.

The subject was raised again shortly after independence, but Nehru postponed action, seeing that the formation of linguistic states posed a threat to Indian unity by emphasizing regional, not national, loyalties. There were serious outbreaks of violence as powerful groups in the different regions pressed for linguistic states. In a revealing statement, Nehru said how dismayed he was as he watched what was happening in the country. The struggle that had gone on for a free and united India seemed to be endangered and he was, "face to face with the centuries old India of narrow loyalties, petty jealousies and ignorant prejudices engaged in mortal conflict and we were simply horrified to see how thin the ice upon which we were skating was."

The process of reorganization was finally resolved, with most of the country eventually divided on the basis of the dominant language group in the different regions. Those involved in the process were aware of how potentially dangerous this was to the unity of the country The States Reorganization Commission noted in its report that a unitary form of government with the divisions based on purely administrative considerations would have been the best solution, but, mindful of the violence the demand for linguistic states had created, the report concluded in laconic understatement that, "in the existing circumstances, this approach would be somewhat unrealistic."

The issue of religion is potentially more divisive than language. A carefully worded statement on the right to freedom of religion was included in the constitution of India. In 1977, a constitutional amendment interpreting the freedom of religion clause declared that India was a secular state. In the Indian constitutional usage, a secular state is defined as one that guarantees freedom of worship, treats individuals as citizens irrespective of religious affiliation, and does not support any particular religion. This insistence on India as a secular state was a recognition of the religious pluralism of Indian society, which includes 700 million Hindus, 125 million Muslims, 21 million Christians, and 18 million Sikhs.

The partition that created Pakistan on the basis of religion led in a few months to the killing of half a million people, both Hindus and Muslims, and a migration from one country to the other of perhaps 12 million people. Beyond that trauma, numerous communal riots have led to the deaths of many hundreds of people. Because of the bitter realities of violence associated with religious identity, a secular identity seemed necessary. Nonetheless, in a direct challenge to the secular state, many well-organized groups argued that secularism undermined the only true basis of Indian nationality, Hinduism. The overwhelming majority of Indians, these groups argued, identified themselves as Hindu-participants in the culture that deeply molded Indian civilization, not just in terms of religious practices, but in art, literature and styles of living.

The most vigorous exponent of this definition of Indian nationality was a powerful organization, the Rashtriya Swayamsewak Sangh, and its many related groups, most notably the Bharatiya Janata Party (BJP), which in the past 15 years has emerged as a major force in Indian electoral politics. The leaders of such groups are often referred to as "Hindu fundamentalists," suggesting a primarily religious motivation, but this term is misleading. "Hindu nationalists" is a more accurate description, for their aim is not to create a theocratic state, run by priests as spokesmen for a deity rather, it is to create a modern nation-state in which the ideology of Hindu nationalism, to which they have given the name "Hindutva," would be the guiding force for national unity.

The proponents of this nationalism identify as its enemies the religious and cultural traditions of Islam and Christianity, aided by the advocates for secularism in what they regard as the denationalized, Westernized Indian elites. This conflict over the nature of Indian nationalism was dramatized in December 1992, when a mob of militant Hindu nationalists destroyed the Babri Masjid, a mosque believed to have been built by the Mughal Emperor Babur between 1526 and 1530 on the site of the birthplace of Lord Rama, a widely venerated deity. The destruction of the mosque was seen as a dramatic assertion of the victory of the Hindu nation over the Muslims, who had once conquered India centuries earlier. In the next few days, riots broke out in a number of towns and cities, most notably in Mumbai (Bombay), where hundreds of people, mostly Muslims, were killed. India is unhappily accustomed to violence, but these events appeared to signal "a shift away from the fragile political consensus of religious neutrality, the secular state, that held together the diverse ethnic, religious, and social communities since independence, toward the new configuration of a Hindu nation."

Cultural symbols deeply rooted in the dominant cultural tradition have a powerful unifying potential, but, given the diversity of Indian society, Hindu nationalism has difficulty finding a unifying voice. Many members of the Hindu upper classes view Hindu nationalism as a deeply divisive force, while the lowest classes view it as an attempt to restore historic patterns of upper caste dominance and the Muslims see it a threat to their existence as a community. For these reasons, a careful political analyst concludes, "Unless the democratic system breaks down, or there is a major external crisis, Hindutva nationalism cannot sweep the country." While this is probably true for immediate electoral prospects, there can be little doubt that Hindu nationalism will continue to have enormous appeal, even if it does not express itself overtly in the electoral victory of a specific party.

Shortly after the secession of Bangladesh in 1971, Professor Rounaq Jahan summarized the problems of Pakistan by noting that the difficulties of nation-building were compounded by the fact that the ruling elites had to perform simultaneously the two independent, and at times contradictory, tasks of state-building and nation-building. India inherited a functioning state when it became independent, symbolized by the grandeur of New Delhi, while Pakistan had to make do with the hastily cobbled together facilities in the temporary capital of Karachi.

In terms of state-building, the first 10 years of Pakistan's existence can be characterized as an attempt to govern a country with a population of about 75 million (in 1950) divided into two areas separated by a thousand miles of Indian territory, with an unstable power structure. The structure consisted of a Constituent Assembly of 79 members as a central government, a governor-general with great executive power, elected provincial assemblies in the four provinces in West Pakistan and one in East Pakistan, a civil bureaucracy and a military establishment.

From the beginning, three issues posed a challenge to both state-building and nation-building. The first was the position of Islam as the dominant ideology of Pakistan. The second issue posing a challenge to state- and nation-building was the existence of regional differences within Pakistan. A third source of conflict was how power was to be shared within the governing structure. The irony of the nation-building process was that Pakistan, unlike India, seemed to begin with an accessible and easily comprehended unifying ideology of Pakistan as a homeland for Muslims in South Asia. This was the point Muhammad Ali Jinnah made in 1943 when consolidating his claim to be spokesman for India's Muslims.

Envisioning a Muslim homeland, he declared, "Never before in the history of the world, has a nation rallied around a common platform and a common ideal in such a short time as the Muslims have done in this vast subcontinent.... Never before has the mental outlook of a nation been unified so effectively." Why was the outcome so different from this vision, which had some basis in reality? The answer is surely that an appeal to found a nation on Islam, or indeed on any religion, in a region as complex as the Indian subcontinent would face enormous difficulties. What was wrong with Jinnah's vision was spelled out with brutal clarity by Maulana Maududi, a powerful theologian, when he reminded Jinnah that true Muslims did not believe in government by the majority, but rulership by God under the laws of Islam, not those made by a democratic majority: "In the sight of God, Muslim nationalism is just as cursed as Indian nationalism."

The failure of Islam as a political ideology to create a unified nation was shown with shattering force in the secession of East

Bengal and its emergence as the new nation of Bangladesh in 1971. Even before this, however, Islam became a source of disunity as attempts were made to spell out its place in the national life. There were a number of contentious issues that illustrated the divisiveness of Islam in South Asia. One was defining the nature of the new state. Pakistan has enacted four constitutions in 30 years, with many revisions. The first one, adopted in 1956, saw Pakistan as a modern, democratic state. Yet, it was also to be an Islamic Republic, with no laws repugnant to Islam. As one scholar has noted, ideologically Pakistan was suspended, "between the ambiguity of her founder's call for a Muslim homeland and the varying expectations of the majority of the populace for an Islamic state."

The regional conflicts that emerged after the formation of Pakistan were related to the new political arrangements, but as Stephen Rittenberg has shown in his study of the independence movement of the North-West Frontier Province, they were rooted in ethnic and tribal differences within the region itself as well as with the larger arena of the nation. The major tribal group in the province, the Pakhtuns, had ethnic loyalties and social organization that "have given provincial politics a stability which has survived the periodic upheavals in Pakistani politics since independence."

This was true in large measure of the other three divisions of West Pakistan-Sind, Baluchistan and Punjab-but stability for dominant groups within each of them meant friction with each other and with the central government. The largest of the provinces, East Pakistan, with a greater population than the rest of the provinces combined, was to become the test case for national unity, since from the beginning this region was marked from the beginning by a sense of alienation from West Pakistan. There were many complaints of unequal treatment in the allocation of government resources and of positions within the military and the civil bureaucracy, but the clearest indication of the depth of this bitterness came, as it had elsewhere in South Asia, over the issue of a national language.

East Pakistan was the most linguistically homogenous region in South Asia, with the overwhelming majority of the people speaking Bengali. But the central government decided to make Urdu, widely regarded as an "Islamic language," the national language of Pakistan. Student groups protested the imposition of Urdu and demanded that Bengali also be recognized as a national language. This student activism represented a wider unrest in society and, in 1956; Bengali was declared a national language along with Urdu.

By this time, however, more than sub-nationalism had developed: Articulate leaders were demanding social change and autonomy for East Pakistan. This first phase of Bangladeshi separatism, dependent upon free elections and political representation was halted when "the established political institutions were swept aside, and the civil-military bureaucracy, in which Bengal representation was minimal, assumed power in the country." The abrogation of civil power was the result of the third source of conflict within Pakistan, a struggle for power within its governing structure, particularly after the new constitution came into force in 1956, giving elected representatives more power. General Ayub Khan, who assumed power, justified the military takeover in 1958 on the grounds that the state was in danger of collapse, as it was torn by regional animosities, religious strife and racial differences.

In their mad rush for power, the elected politicians whom he had overthrown had shown that "the country and the people could go to the dogs as far as they were concerned." The ulema, or Muslim religious leaders, were also to blame, for instead of Islam promoting the unity of the country, their version of the faith was dividing it.

The ulema, Khan argued, were against the creation of a modern state because they feared power would pass from them to the educated classes. Khan asserted that what was needed to unify the country was a strong central government that would encourage industrialization in order to raise the standard of living of the poor give Pakistan a place in the world and end the bickering of corrupt politicians. A somewhat different, and persuasive, reading of the reasons for military rule has been given by Ayesha Jalal.

While not denying the effect of politicians on the political process, she suggests that the alliance of civil bureaucrats and the military was stretching the "ambit of central authority in order to give a long delayed impetus to their ambitious plans to industrialize and militarize Pakistan, while at the same time nurturing their own recently forged links in the international arena." Ayub was forced from office, however, partly because of the failure of his regime to meet the economic needs of the masses and partly because he was unable to maintain an alliance among the military, the bureaucrats and the industrialists whom he had encouraged.

Ayub was succeeded not by a civilian but by another military leader, General Yayha Khan, against whom East Pakistan revolted. Yayha Khan's government responded with startling brutality, killing perhaps a million civilians, but India's intervention led to the defeat of the Pakistan Army and the emergence of a new country, Bangladesh. Pakistan is not and never was, in the pejorative phrase attributed to Henry Kissinger, a "basket case," but its simultaneous search for statehood and national identity has been a daunting task.

Pakistan's military defeat in East Pakistan by India in 1971 led to the fall of Yayha Khan and the establishment of a civilian government under Zulfiqar Bhutto, who attempted to move the state away from its heavy dependence on the military. His failure was dramatized by the seizure of power by the military in 1977 under General Zia, again on the grounds that the civilian politicians did not have the ability to maintain law and order. Bhutto was arrested and executed in 1979 on a murder charge.

General Zia's regime attempted to give unity to a dispirited and divided country through a vigorous program of Islamization, combined with economic development and strict control of the press and political parties. Islamization meant an attempt to introduce traditional Islamic law and social customs, as spelled out in detail in an ordinance in June 1988, making shari a (revealed law) the supreme law of the land. This met little resistance from the masses, who followed such customs in any case, but the educated elites regarded such efforts as a futile attempt to impose standards that ran counter to the thrust of modernity. General

Zia's death in an airplane crash in 1988 led to a return to civilian government and the re-emergence of electoral politics, which resulted in the election in 1988 of Benazir Bhutto, the daughter of the executed former prime minister.

The president of Pakistan, Sardar Leghari, dismissed her from office during her second term in 1996 for misgovernence and corruption. To some observers, her subsequent electoral defeat in February 1997 seemed to replicate the fate of other civilian governments at the hands of the military, even if behind the scenes. Others, more optimistic about electoral politics, saw it as the ability of the president, in a use of constitutional powers validated by the Supreme Court, to safeguard the state.

While the danger of disunity in South Asia from religious, linguistic and ethnic differences have always been stressed in the rest of South Asia before independence, there seems to have been little perception of such danger in Sri Lanka, either by the British rulers or the leaders of political parties, until it became independent in 1948. In contrast to the fearful communal killings that marked the birth of statehood in India, Pakistan and eventually Bangladesh, the transfer of power in Sri Lanka was remarkably peaceful. The government of the first prime minister, D.S. Senanayake, concentrated on the economic development of a society characterized by high literacy, a developed political system and a social order where the division between rich and poor was not as striking as elsewhere on the subcontinent.

There were, however, very powerful forces at work within the island that combined to threaten the existence of the unitary state established in 1948. Economically, the country was faced with growing unemployment and the inability of the government to pay for the extensive social welfare programs. These problems became involved with ethnic, religious, and linguistic issues as well as struggles for power between the two families that dominated Sri Lankan politics, the Bandaranaikes and the Senanayakes.

The most explosive issue was the question of making Sinhala, the language of the ethnic majority, the Sinhalese, the national language. The appeal of Sinhala-and its potential for disunity-was increased by the fact that it was closely identified with

Buddhism, the religion of the Sinhalese majority. If this came to be the case, English would cease to play its traditional role in government, education and business. The disadvantaged group would be the Tamil-speaking minority, about 18 percent of the population, which was mainly Hindu by religion. The Tamils had originated in Tamil Nadu in south India, some having come to Sri Lanka many centuries before, while others had come in the 19th century during the period of British rule. They form the majority of the population in Jaffna, the northern district of the island.

Perhaps the clearest way to summarize the development of fierce ethnic antagonism leading to violence that threatened to overwhelm the state is through a brief chronology. In 1956, Bandaranaike's government moved to fulfill election promises to make Sinhala the only official national language and to recognize Buddhism as the national religion. This movement received militant support from the bhikkhus, the monks who had great influence in the countryside. Rioting broke out in 1958, in which hundreds of Tamils were killed.

In 1971, a serious insurrection that had no direct connection with the language issue exploded when bands of students, known as the Janatha Vimukti Peramuna (JVP), who were not supported by any major political party, began an attack on government institutions. The government had inadequate arms to fight back, but quickly received help from India, the United States and Great Britain.

The insurrection was halted only after an estimated 15,000 insurgents were killed. Although the government won, in the judgment of two scholars with exceptional access to sources in Sri Lanka, there is no mistaking the historical significance of the insurrection: "It was the harbinger of political violence on an unprecedented scale ... of which groups of Tamil activists (in the period 1975 onwards) have been the most prominent exponents." Furthermore, the JVP was not fully crushed, and in the 1980s continued to assassinate political leaders.

Groups of young Tamils, melding language grievances and claims of economic discrimination, became increasingly violent and, appealing to ethnic separatism, they demanded independence for the Jaffna region. After 13 soldiers were killed by the Tamil militants in 1983, fierce riots broke out in other areas of the island, and thousands of Tamils were killed. From this point on, the Tamil insurrection ceased to be an internal affair and became a regional one, with India as a major player. It was well known that the militants, especially the most violent group, known as the Liberation Tigers of Tamil Eelam (LTTE) were being trained and armed into a formidable guerrilla force in the Indian state of Tamil Nadu, a few miles across the Palk Strait from Jaffna, with the knowledge of the Indian government.

Out of desperation, but with considerable political courage given that there was intense anti-Indian sentiment in Sri Lanka, President J.R. Jayawardene sought an accord with India governing the deployment of Indian armed forces known as the Indian Peace Keeping Force. However, this well-armed force had little success in controlling the LTTE. In the face of strong criticism from within Sri Lanka, the Indian government withdrew the Indian Peace Keeping Force, with memories of the problems that the Soviet Union encountered in Afghanistan and the United States in Vietnam when fighting determined guerrillas. Sri Lanka's long agony continued, despite high hopes raised by peace talks in early 1995 between the LTTE leaders and the Sri Lankan government. In the summer of 1996, the LTTE, although driven out of the towns and into the jungles, killed more than 1,000 soldiers at an army base.

According to Marshall Singer, the model for the LTTE leaders is the situation in Israel: The Israelis' only hope for peace was to agree to a settlement in Gaza and on the West Bank, which they may see as "something short of a separate country," but "the Palestinians see it as an independent state." Is there any conclusion that can be drawn from 50 years-which is a long time in the life of any modern notion-of the dual quest for statehood and nationhood by the major states of South Asia, with their vast populations, material resources, and immensely rich legacy of civilization? One is, of course, that none have succumbed to the pressures of insurrections, civil wars and militant movements for secession.

This is true even of Pakistan, which lost half of its population but retained the framework of the original state. Another conclusion is one drawn by an Indian analyst, Bharat Wariavwalla. Surveying the insurrections and secessionist movements in India, he argues that they have resulted from the attempt to impose a concept of "nation" upon India's many ancient communities, leading ironically to disunity, rather than the unity that was sought. According to this view, Kashmir and Punjab are the price paid for trying to create "an imaginary nation" out of South Asia's deeply rooted multiculturalism.

One may sense the validity of this argument looking at the history of India, Pakistan and Sri Lanka, while at the same time recognizing that the loose federalism that it suggests may be unacceptable to their leaders after half a century of striving to create unitary states and to impose nationhood upon them.

RECENT TRANSITION IN GOVERNANCE

The current transition in the ideological foundation, theoretical basis, and practical orientation of governance is a worldwide phenomenon affecting almost all nations, including those in South Asia. This recent transformation-which is largely identified with neo-liberal ideology, neoclassical theory, and neo-managerial practices-has taken place with a view to reinvent, reengineer, or revitalize overall governance in different countries. In fact, the very idea of governance has recently been reconceptualized to encompass almost all domains, branches, sectors, and levels of government in favor of autonomy, participation, and transparency, and restructured to incorporate business-friendly ventures such as privatization, deregulation, and liberalization.

Apparently, this indicates a significant departure from the postwar construction of a welfare state, planned development, and an expansive public sector in developed and developing nations. As such, this basic shift in governance represents, and has been enhanced by an historical transition in the very formation of the state in line with the neo-liberal assumptions of market superiority, anti-welfares, non-intervention, and free trade and exchange.

These neo-liberal tendencies of the state can be observed in South Asian countries such as Bangladesh, India, Nepal,

Pakistan, and Sri Lanka. Under such a newly emerging neo-liberal state, the scope, objectives, structures, functions, and strategies of public governance have also undergone considerable changes guided by the businesslike neo-managerial ethos and principles resembling the so-called "new public management" in developed nations. The traces of this new public management model and its principles, concepts, and techniques, can be found in the major reform initiatives undertaken recently by governments in different parts of the world.

The globalization of such market-driven mode of governance through the advocacy, persuasion, and pressure of international forces, especially international financial agencies, has certainly affected the governance systems in South Asian countries that are heavily dependent on these agencies for external finance and technical assistance. In most developing countries, including those in South Asia, the imposition of such market-led governance has been accomplished by these agencies through the so-called structural adjustment program, which now represents one of the most primary preconditions to receive external assistance from any donor agency or country.

In this chapter, the main objective is to examine the features of this newly emerging mode of governance in the context of South Asia comprised of countries such as Bangladesh, Bhutan, India, the Maldives, Nepal, Pakistan, and Sri Lanka. Another goal is to critically evaluate various economic, political, and administrative conditions created by, or at least coincided with, the adoption of this new governance system in these countries. This analysis may help demonstrate the effectiveness of new governance in relation to such societal conditions that exist in each of these countries. However, before exploring the features and implications of current governance, the chapter briefly describes the context and genealogy of overall governance in South Asia.

South Asia is a unique region with considerable cross-national diversities, similarities, and contradictions. It is composed of countries as small as the Maldives with an area of only 298 sq. km. and a population of about 200,000, and countries as big as India with an area of 3.3 million sq. km. and a population of nearly one billion. There are also variations among countries in terms of the levels of income and living standard-the highest in Sri Lanka and the Maldives and lowest in Bhutan and Nepal. The ethnic and religious compositions also differ among these countries. For instance, in terms of dominant groups, there are Bengali Muslims and Hindus in Bangladesh; Indo-Aryan and Dravidian Hindus and Muslims in India; Punjabi and Sindhi Muslims in Pakistan; Sinhalese and Tamil Buddhists and Hindus in Sri Lanka; and Brahmin, Chetri, and Vaishya Hindus and Buddhists in Nepal.

These variations in the complex nexus of geographic and demographic size, ethnic and religious composition, economic condition, and political system in South Asia often transcend national borders, affect peoples in the neighboring countries, and lead to various forms of intraregional conflicts. Conversely, these countries have also similarities in terms of common historical roots, colonial experiences, cultural beliefs and lifestyles, cross-border ethnic and religious identities, and modes of governance.

With regard to modes of governance, despite the above contextual variations, South Asian countries have been quite similar in terms of the objectives, structures, functions, attitudes, and standards of governing bodies despite the variations in government typologies ranging from parliamentary democracy in India and Sri Lanka to monarchy in Nepal and Bhutan to occasional military rule in Bangladesh and Pakistan. These similarities in different dimensions of governance among South Asian countries can be found in the pre-colonial, colonial, postcolonial, and current periods.

During the early pre-colonial phase, a systematic structure of governance emerged in the region-evolving from of the Vedic Era (25001500 B.C.) to the Mauryan period (321-185 B.C.) with an emphasis on territorial division, law and order, revenue collection, external security, and judicial administration. Beginning from 1206 A.D., the later pre-colonial phase under Muslim rulers (particularly under emperors Shershah and Akbar) saw the emergence of a more comprehensive territorial administration and a centralized structure in the executive, judicial, and military spheres of governance.

In terms of the nature of relationship among various domains of governance, this pre-colonial tradition was characterized by the fusion of politics and administration, the absence of democratically elected governing bodies, the dominance of paternalistic state apparatus over economic production and trade and commerce, and the subordination of private capital and entrepreneurship to the state. However, a modern system of governance in South Asia evolved mainly under the British colonial rule encompassing all countries in the region except Nepal.

It was based on systematic classification, defined structure, merit-based recruitment, regular salary system, institutional training, and so on. The later stage of colonial rule witnessed more contestation and negotiation between the colonial power and the local elite for a greater national share of high-ranking positions, and for further indigenization of governing institutions and processes through legal and constitutional reforms. This discourse on sharing power in public governance-which was pursued predominantly under conceptual categories such as covenanted vs. uncovenanted public officials and provincial vs. imperial civil services-took place within the overall structure of colonial hegemony with the local elite as its subordinate constituent.

As a result, like the other colonized regions of the world, South Asia hardly transcended the colonial legacy of governance characterized by elitism, secrecy, centralization, formalism, rigidity, and social isolation. A central feature of such colonial mode of governance was the modernization of the administrative system while overlooking, and often suppressing, development in political institutions, which resulted in an overdeveloped administrative apparatus at the expense of political development in most countries of the region. In addition, since the primary mission of such colonial governance was to enhance resource extraction through state control, the avenues for promoting local private capital and indigenous entrepreneurship remained limited.

This colonial structure was reinforced further by the prevailing social structure based on the caste system that allowed minimal autonomy for and assigned a lower rank to the merchant class. Such external colonial and internal social structures represented the major obstacles to capitalist development in the region. In fact, the rigidly hierarchical colonial structure and the unchangeable caste system served complementary purposes: both the colonial administration and the high-caste elite needed each other to perpetuate their hegemonic controls over the low-caste majority, to prohibit capital accumulation based on free competition irrespective of caste identity, and to suppress the potential of any public uprising.

The postcolonial period began with the promises of rapid socioeconomic progress based on a development-oriented mode of governance, although in reality, the colonial legacy continued in South Asian administrative systems in terms of institutions, structures, norms, and attitudes. However, this developmental orientation in governance-which led to a considerable amount of academic discourse on the so-called "developmental state" and "development administration"-represented certain shift from the above colonial mode of governance.

This shift in governance became evident in its state-centered approach, expansive scope, decentralized structure, and development-oriented objectives like poverty eradication, income generation and redistribution, higher living standards, self-reliance, and nation-building. South Asian countries such as Bangladesh, India, Nepal, Pakistan, and Sri Lanka adopted this statist model of governance in favor of planned development to improve conditions in all major sectors, including agriculture, industry, commerce, education, health, and transport.

Although the later part of postcolonial period saw significant changes in the nature of regimes in South Asia-including the end of one-party dominance in India, rise and fall of one-party state (with socialist leanings) in Bangladesh, reemergence of military rule in Pakistan, weakening of monarchical power in Nepal, and increase in presidential power in Sri Lanka-there was always the priority of state-centered development agenda in these countries.

In each of these South Asian cases, the role of the private sector remained subservient to the state-led governance irrespective of such regime variations. In terms of outcomes, although the history of developmental governance is replete with negative images such as inefficiency, bureaucratism, corruption, and mismanagement, it made certain progress in providing basic services, generating employment, building infrastructure, maintaining law and order, and reducing foreign ownership and control.

The effectiveness of such governance was often challenged by the constraining contextual factors ranging from interstate hostility to natural disaster, religious conflict to excessive population growth. In most South Asian countries, however, the recent two decades have seen almost a reversal of the above historical legacy of state-led governance that dominated the pre-colonial, colonial, and postcolonial periods. This unprecedented historical shift in governance in the region reflects and resembles the current global trends of changes towards the dominance of market forces, weaker role of the state, erosion of the public sector, priority of microeconomic efficiency, and businesslike transformation of the public sector.

The move toward such a market-driven governance in South Asia was not only caused by the failure of the previous state-centered approach, it has also coincided with the market-friendly changes in international political economy, including the collapse of socialist states, delegitimation of state planning, imposition of structural adjustment program by the donor agencies, worldwide expansion of large corporations, and stronger alliance between the state and private capital.

In line with such global trends, since the mid-1980s, Bangladesh has increasingly moved away from the planned-development approach and embraced market-led reforms irrespective of differences in the past ideological inclinations of the ruling parties. Based on the prescriptions of structural adjustment, the market model of governance was endorsed by the two consecutive military regimes, and it became consolidated further under the elected civilian governments of Khaleda Zia (1991-96) and Sheikh Hasina (1996-present).

The current ruling party (Awami League) under the leadership of Sheikh Hasina has decided to continue such pro-market governance despite the party's past ideological bent toward socialism. The government has taken initiatives to divest more state enterprises, attract local and foreign private investors, and liberalize all economic ventures in favor of private entrepreneurs. Similar move toward market-led governance can be found in Bhutan where the government has encouraged participation of the private sector in various enterprises since the late 1980s.

In the case of India, the government has been quite determined to debureaucratize or "degovernmentalize" the pubic sector by reducing the government's share holdings and maximizing private ownership and control. The process of market-led governance initiated by the former Prime Minister Rajiv Gandhi in 1984, has gained momentum during subsequent governments that pursued liberalization, expanded capital markets, deregulated licensing system, reduced import restrictions, and encouraged the business sector.

A major emphasis of India's recent five year plans has been on the development of private sector, and its New Economic Policy aims to reduce the scope of public sector. In addition, in recent years, India has been aggressively pursuing policy measures to attract foreign investment in various sectors, especially through its Foreign Investment Promotion Board.

Similarly, in Nepal, since the mid-1980s, the government has undertaken various measures to transform public governance into a market friendly venture. It has moved to reduce state intervention, liberalize trade and industry, deregulate prices, relax administrative controls, divest public enterprises, and downsize the overall public sector. Such changes in governance can also be observed in Pakistan, which accepted the International Monetary Fund (IMF)-initiated structural adjustment program requiring the removal of trade barriers, reduction in restrictions on foreign investment, withdrawal of control over finance and exchange, and divestment of state enterprises.

In such a restructuring of governance, Sri Lanka has also been quite active, especially in terms of shifting the role of government from direct intervention to indirect facilitation, transferring state assets to the private sector, reducing the size of bureaucracy, minimizing import restrictions, and creating a conducive atmosphere for the private sector. The above description shows how in the current market-friendly global context, the legacy of state-centered governance has increasingly given way to market-driven governance in South Asian countries. This shift in the mode of governance implies a considerable change in the configuration of relationship between the state, capital, and society. In addition, these changes have serious socioeconomic implications for each of these countries. However, it is necessary to explicate the specific nature of current changes in governance in greater detail.

In the above section, the chapter has delineated the major contexts and origins of various modes of governance and their changes in South Asian countries. It emphasized that during the recent two decades, in the region, there has been an unprecedented transition in governance in terms of recent historical departure from the traditional interventionist state, and the endorsement of a market-friendly approach to public sector management. Like other developing regions of the world, this recent transition in governance has taken place under the externally imposed or internally endorsed structural adjustment program representing the contemporary reform agenda of international agencies.

In this section, the specific dimensions of this transition in governance are explained in terms of the following: (a) changes in government initiatives and institutions, (b) reforms in public sector structures, (c) shifts in strategic or policy priorities, (d) adjustments in task orientations, and (e) changes in performance criteria and standards.

CHANGES IN INITIATIVES AND INSTITUTIONS

In recent years, there has emerged a new genre of government initiatives and institutions in South Asian countries. In the past, these developing countries undertook varieties of development-related initiatives such as long term development plans, poverty eradication programs, rural development strategies, and affirmative action measures for low-caste citizens and women. In line with such initiatives, these countries also established certain institutions or organizations, including national planning agencies, public service commissions, local government authorities, and series of public corporations. Although many of these institutions have not disappeared, with new initiatives, their objectives and functions have changed, and certain new institutions have also emerged.

In Bangladesh, the government has endorsed the globally popular initiative known as "good governance"-especially under the auspices of the World Bank and the IMF-which recommends a smaller public sector and a stronger government-business relationship. These recommendations are repeatedly echoed in the World Bank's recent publications on Bangladesh, including Government That Works.' Reforming the Public Sector (1996. and Bangladesh: An Agenda for Action (1997.

This minimalist ethos is also visible in initiatives such as the recent Public Administration Sector Study (1993. and Public Administration Reform Commission (1997.. Among the new institutions, the major examples include the Privatization Board, Board of Investment, and the proposed Deregulation Commission and National Commission for Reforming Government. The main agenda of such institutions is to enhance the processes of privatization and private investment in Bangladesh.

In India, the government took various initiatives during the 1990s to enhance the efficiency of overall governance system: these include the appointment of an Administrative Reforms Commission by the central government, creation of Administrative Reforms Departments at the provincial level, classification of government activities into core and non-core activities with an objective to transfer the latter to private parties, and rationalization of various laws and rules.

The government has also introduced a series of new institutional measures in line with the new market-led governance. More specifically, the government has established the Disinvestment Commission and the Disinvestment Fund to accelerate the process of privatization, and the Investment and Project Monitoring Cell to provide information and guidance to private enterprises. With regard to foreign investment, there are certain relatively new institutions such as the Indian Investment Centre, the Foreign Investment Promotion Board, and the Foreign Investment Promotion Council. In addition, the government has created the Institute of Smart Governance to enhance the systems of service delivery.

Similar to India, Nepal introduced an Administrative Reform Commission in 1991, which made recommendations to downsize the civil service, streamline public sector activities, and expand the scope of the private sector. Nepal also has the Privatisation Committee and the Industrial Promotion Board to implement some of the market-led initiatives and policies.

In Pakistan and Sri Lanka, there have emerged similar institutions-including the Privatization Commission and the Board of Investment in Pakistan, and the Privatization Commission and the Public Enterprises Reform Commission in Sri Lanka-to facilitate divestment and privatization transactions. In Pakistan, moreover, the Economic Reforms Act of 1992 represented a concerted government effort to move toward pro-market governance.

The above market-driven changes in government initiatives and institutions in South Asia are quite unique not only in terms of the relative lack of similar examples in the history of governance in the region. These new initiatives and institutions are also unique in terms of the fact that although they have been introduced by, and constitute a part of, the state, they aim to diminish the scope and role of the state itself, and thus represent an anti-state position. Therefore, such changes reinforce the argument that the current reform initiatives have more to do with the influence and pressure of external forces (such as international agencies and transnational corporations) than the choices of internal power blocs (the ruling party, the military, and bureaucracy) associated with the state.

REFORMS IN SCOPE AND STRUCTURAL COMPOSITION

In South Asian countries, as in other developing countries, the structure of governance has traditionally been based on expansive size and scope of the public sector on the one hand, and the principle of close supervision over such colossal state bureaucracy to ensure accountability on the other. The post-independence period, especially between the 1950s and 1970s, saw a rapid expansion of the size and scope of public sector in terms of its command over financial and human resources and its coverage of diverse socioeconomic sectors. Although there was a growing emphasis on structural decentralization at the local level, such a colossal and all-pervasive governance system required various means of control and accountability, although these mechanisms were not always effective.

Since the mid-1980s, however, the scope and structural pattern of governance have significantly changed in South Asian countries. This is quite evident in recent government reforms to downsize the public sector, streamline public expenditure, and restructure ministries and department into autonomous agencies. In fact, initiatives were already undertaken in the 1980s by certain South Asian government to reduce or freeze public employment in South Asian countries. The World Bank reported that in the case of Bangladesh, various government departments and agencies were planned to be downsized; the redundant public sector employees were to be retrenched; and more than 7500 workers were already retrenched in state-owned textile mills.

In India, in the name of debureaucratizing, demonopolizing, and rightsizing governance, strategies have been undertaken to reduce central government employment by 30 percent over a period of 10 years. It was found as early as 1995 that some 125,000 workers were retrenched in the industrial portion of the public sector. In the case of Nepal, the government considered privatisation as a means to downsize public bureaucracy, and introduced the strategy of freezing all vacant positions in public offices.

In its 1992 report, the abovementioned Administrative Reform Commission strongly recommended downsizing the civil service and streamlining the public sector; and during 1992-94, the newly created Administrative Reform Monitoring Unit succeeded to considerably reduce the number of civil servants in Nepal. Similar scenario also exists in Sri Lanka where the government adopted the recruitment freeze and early retirement policies, and retrenched thousands of employees.

In addition to the current downsizing exercise in South Asia, the remaining part of the public sector (after retrenchment) is being transformed into businesslike agencies based on unprecedented structural autonomy in finance and personnel matters. In the case of Bangladesh, the World Bank conducted a study of public sector management in 1996, and prescribed decentralization in decision making through the creation of autonomous agencies. However, it is suggested that the sustainability, jurisdiction, and financial viability of such autonomous agencies in Bangladesh require constitutional guarantee.

In India, the Divestment Commission recommended an increased level of autonomy for state enterprises, followed by the guaranteed financial and managerial autonomy of 11 major enterprises and 97 smaller enterprises. The purpose is to enhance the operational freedom of these organizations. Nepal has also assigned autonomous status to organizations such as the Rural Energy Development Board.

Similar trend of structural autonomy can be found in certain sectors in Pakistan. For example, the Pakistan Railway has been converted into an autonomous agency and the Pakistan Telephone and Telegraph into an autonomous public company, with a view to providing an increased level of operational autonomy to these public sector organizations. Sri Lanka, on the other hand, has decided to move towards greater autonomy in personnel management by delegating the power of its national public service commission to the newly created provincial service commissions. Most South Asian countries, especially India and Pakistan with their federal structures, have decided to increase the autonomy of provincial governments in delivering services within their own jurisdictions.

SHIFTS IN THE STRATEGIC PRIORITIES

South Asian countries have been traditionally known for their post-independence strategies of nationalization, protectionism, and strict regulation of the private sector in line with national objectives such as economic self-reliance, minimal foreign ownership and control, income redistribution, higher living standard, and nation-building. But since the early 1980s, the strategic priorities have increasingly shifted towards privatization, liberalization, and deregulation with a view to expanding the market forces, accelerating economic growth, encouraging foreign investment and ownership, and taking part in global competition.

Such a strategic transition in governance is more visible in Bangladesh and India, which used to have certain socialist predispositions and believed in socioeconomic progress through planned development led by the interventionist state and its bureaucracy. The current market-led orientation represents almost a reversal of this earlier policy stance.

More specifically, the privatization strategy has been adopted by all South Asian countries in their major economic sectors. In Bangladesh, privatization has affected sectors such as textile, steel, sugar, power, natural gas, oil exploration, port, telecommunication, transport, banking, insurance, and tourism. According to some figures, by 1990, Bangladesh privatized as many as 609 industrial enterprises; and in the early 1990s, it completed administrative formalities for privatizing another 28 major enterprises. In the case of India, the government has allegedly taken a more gradual approach to privatization. During the period 1991-98, it privatized 39 enterprises out of 240, and by March 1998, the total value of privatization transaction was Rs. 112.57 billion.

However, since 1998, the rate of proceeds from disinvestment has increased. In Nepal, the privatization program expanded under the Nepali Congress Party, but slowed down under the Communist Party of Nepal that did not oppose privatization but questioned its methods. Of the total 60 state enterprises in Nepal, many have already been privatized while others are under consideration. The major sectors affected by such privatization ventures, include fertilizer, banking, salt, cement, power, textile, insurance, water, sugar, tobacco, bus, telecommunications, and airlines.

In Pakistan, the recent ruling parties have been strongly committed to the market-led policy of privatization irrespective of their previous differences in policy agenda. They consider privatization as a chosen option to enhance the country's economic progress. By 1991, privatization program was applied to 97 out of 118 state-owned industrial units in sectors such as automobiles, energy, fertilizer, cement, chemicals, food products, transport, and telecommunications.

Sri Lanka has also been active in pursuing the privatization strategy that began in the late 1970s. More than 50 state-owned companies have been sold, although the government has been more cautious to completely withdraw price controls from sectors like petroleum, railway, roads, telecommunications, airlines, and electricity. However, it sold significant portions of Gas Company in 1995, Steel Corporation in 1996, and the national airline and telecommunications in 1998 to various foreign investors. The government has also decided to raise more revenues by selling enterprises in sectors such as light manufacturing and tourism.

Another recent major strategic change in governance in South Asia has been toward the liberalization of trade and investment. In the case of Bangladesh, the government has taken initiatives to liberalize foreign investment in most sectors, allow maximum foreign ownership and repatriation of profits, reduce import duties, provide tax holidays and tax exemptions, arrange one-stop shop for investors, guarantee protection to foreign investment against nationalization, and ensure unhindered access to local banks and financial institutions. India has also moved toward similar directions in liberalization.

It has reduced trade barriers and corporate tax rates, introduced tax exemptions on export earnings, permitted foreign equity investment of up to 51 percent in major industries (100 percent in some sectors), allowed foreign companies to use their brand names, and guaranteed export firms to have duty-free imports. The Nepalese government has also adopted this liberalization option related to trade and foreign investment with a view to supplement domestic private investment and enhances technology transfer. In the case of Pakistan, the government has introduced varieties of incentives for foreign investment, including the ownership and repatriation of capital, duty and tax free imports, exemption from foreign exchange control, and full protection of foreign investment.

These incentives, however, are more attractive in Pakistan's newly created "export processing zones" where the foreign investors can enjoy complete exemptions from federal and provincial taxes, foreign exchange controls, insurance regulations, and import restrictions.

Almost similar position has been taken by the Sri Lankan government to allow total foreign ownership in most sectors, ensure maximum exemption of foreign investors from various regulations and restrictions, provide one-stop services and conducive infrastructures, and guarantee (constitutional) the safety of such investments.

ADJUSTMENTS IN TASK ORIENTATION

In most South Asian countries, the traditional task of governance was its direct production and delivery of goods and services such as health care, education, transport, agricultural inputs, industrial infrastructure, and even basic food items. The state and bureaucracy assumed primary responsibilities to meet public needs and direct future socioeconomic development. But under the emerging market-led governance in South Asia, the primary task of government has changed from being the leading agent of production, distribution, and development to an indirect facilitator of such socioeconomic activities that are increasingly assigned to the private sector.

In other words, the main task of public governance now is to assist the private sector in producing and delivering goods and services. Such a market-led reorientation in the task of governance is compatible with the abovementioned policy trends such as withdrawal of state intervention, reduction in public sector activities, and transfer of public assets to the private sector. This change in task orientation is becoming more evident in countries such as Bangladesh, India, and Pakistan.

In the case of Bangladesh, the government has increasingly assumed the task of downsizing state agencies, promoting the private sector, supporting market forces, and facilitating market-led economic growth. Various ministries in India have also undertaken measures to simplify rules and procedures in order to facilitate market-led policies like liberalisation and divestment that strengthen the role of the private sector.

The emphasis is on making governance less bureaucratic and rule-bound and more businesslike and customer-friendly. Thus, beyond transferring public enterprises to the business sector and withdrawing controls from private enterprises, the government aims to create a conducive atmosphere within which market forces can flourish. During 1994-96, India undertook a project known as "Government and Development" with an objective to educate state-level officials about the benefits of market-led policies, and encourage them to nurture an attitude of facilitating business sector activities.

For this business-friendly orientation in public governance, the Nepalese government has also set the priority at the highest policymaking level to clearly define the role of the state vis-a-vis the private sector in pursuing economic development. The agenda, of course, is to assign the leading role to the private sector, and render the task of the state to that of facilitating business enterprises. In the case of Sri Lanka, the examples of this move toward such a supportive role of the state include some recent projects- e.g., the Private Infrastructure Finance Project and the Public Enterprise Reform Technical Assistance Project-which aim to facilitate private investments in various services formerly provided by the public sector.

This change in the task of governance to serve the private sector is also evident in the increasing alliance or partnership between the public and private sectors. In recent years, the Bangladesh government has openly expressed its intention to form partnership with the private sector, especially foreign investors.

In India, the scope of public-private partnership has expanded due to the growing frequency and intensity of alliances and linkages between the government and international firms. There have also been an increasing number of policy dialogues between business executives and state officials in Uttar Pradesh, Punjab, Haryana, Rajasthan, and Himachal Pradesh-these dialogues aim to change the orientation of governance in favor of business entrepreneurs. Similar trends toward more public-private collaboration, consultation, and exchange can be found in other South Asian cases such as Nepal, Pakistan, and Sri Lanka, although it is not easy to transform the region's traditional bureaucratic attitude and culture dominated by secrecy, suspicion, and risk avoidance.

It should be mentioned, however, that the above task reorientation in governance in favor of the private sector may have negative implications in terms of conflict of interest between civil servants and business enterprises, compromise of general public interest, and marginalization of small businesses and disadvantaged groups. In the case of India, the current administration seems to have stronger alliance with foreign investors than local businesses. As Bidwai mentions, the government has spent more time and energy in courting multinational corporations than promoting local firms and small industries.

CHANGES IN PERFORMANCE CRITERIA AND STANDARDS

During the postcolonial period, as South Asian countries attempted to enhance socioeconomic progress based on planned development, the performance of government were to be assessed by the extent to which it could realize objectives such as poverty reduction, public welfare, income equality, self-reliance, and better living conditions. Although these performance criteria were hardly realized in practice, they were officially stipulated in all long-term development plans of these countries.

In addition, performance standards were also implied in the formal public service norms like accountability, representation, neutrality, equality, and justice, although these standards were often violated by public institutions. Under the newly emerging mode of governance based on businesslike objectives and market values, these earlier criteria or indicators of performance have largely been sidelined by a new set of performance standards such as growth, efficiency, competition, entrepreneurship, value-for-money, and customer orientation. In fact, the current state policies (privatization, deregulation, liberalization) in South Asia have largely been based on rationales or standards such as growth, efficiency, economy, and competition. These businesslike rationales have become common among most Asian countries pursuing such market-driven state policies.

Within South Asia, Bangladesh, India, Nepal, Pakistan, and Sri Lanka have used these standards in justifying their recent reforms in governance. For example, Bangladesh has pursued reforms in its government auditing (under the initiative known as Reforms in Government Audit) in order to enhance public sector performance in terms of economy, efficiency and effectiveness. India is putting greater emphasis on the in-service training of public employees to improve administrative efficiency and effectiveness. In Nepal, the current criteria or standards of delivering public services are speed, efficiency, and effectiveness.

In short, all these countries, under the framework often set by international agencies, have put increasing priority to these standards of efficiency, economy, and competition in public governance, although the earlier emphasis on welfare, equality, self-reliance, and representation has not been completely withdrawn. In addition to this growing significance of market-based standards, another new standard of performance is the level of satisfaction expressed by the individual "customers" of public services, which is quite different from the performance of public sector as perceived by the public or the "citizens" in general. This shift in performance standard toward the satisfaction of customers or consumers, which began in advanced industrial nations, can be observed today in most developing nations, including those in South Asia.

The term "customer" is now frequently used by the governments in Bangladesh, India, Nepal, and Pakistan while introducing new state policies, designing public sector reforms, implementing economic programs, recruiting new employees, and undertaking civil service training. In other words, one of the main indicators of public sector performance today is whether its customers are satisfied with its services. In this regard, some South Asian countries have adopted the so-called citizen's charter or client's charter resembling similar practices in developed nations.

India has decided to introduce such a charter at the federal and state levels in sectors such as railway, telecommunications, postal service, hospital, electricity, and so on. In the case of Bangladesh, there was discussion on adopting a similar charter, so that customers could express their grievances. However, the fact remains that the current concern for customers' satisfaction as an indicator of public sector performance is relevant mainly to the buyers or receivers of public sector services; it does not have much use for those who cannot afford to purchase such services.

NEW GOVERNANCE SYSTEM IN SOUTH ASIA

In the above discussion it has been explained how the overall governance has changed and a new mode of governance has emerged in South Asia in terms of its initiatives and institutions, scope and structural composition, strategic priorities, task orientation, and performance criteria and standards. At this stage, it is necessary to examine the major implications of such newly emerging market-led governance system in the region.

This section presents the scenarios of current economic, political, and administrative conditions under the new governance system in South Asian countries, in order to decipher the implications of such new governance. It is possible that these contemporary conditions in these countries may not necessarily be the direct results of the new governance system. However, the discussion will at least demonstrate whether the rationales and claims made by the advocates of this current market-led governance-such as better economic conditions, more political transparency, and higher administrative efficiency-have any validity in terms of real life societal conditions.

Although the period of new market-led governance in the 1990s saw some improvement in the rates of economic growth in South Asian countries, the fact remains that the region represents 22 percent of the world population but shares only 1.3 percent of the world income. In fact, during 1990-98, the number of people below the poverty line in the region increased from 495 million to 522 million.

In terms of specific country cases, the percentage of population below the poverty line is 42.7 percent in Bangladesh, 40.9 percent in India, 42 percent in Nepal, 34 percent in Pakistan, and 40.6 percent in Sri Lanka. In terms of Human Poverty Index (HPI) published by the UNDP, the HPI ranking for Sri Lanka is 33, Maldives 43, India 59, Bhutan 70, Pakistan 71, Bangladesh 73, and Nepal 85. These indicators of severe poverty in South Asia have often been alluded to recent market-driven reforms in the region.

In terms of living standards, South Asian countries have some of the worst records in the world. In terms of education, the overall adult literacy rate is only 26 percent in Nepal, 35 percent in Bangladesh and Pakistan, and 48 percent in India, although it is high in Sri Lanka (90 percent) and the Maldives (93 percent). In terms of other dimensions of living standards, the situation is quite critical in some of these countries.

For instance, in Bangladesh, about 66 percent of all deaths under the age of five is attributable to malnutrition and 50 percent infants are born underweight; in Pakistan, about 50 percent child deaths are caused by malnutrition; in India, nearly 226 million people have no access to safe drinking water and 640 million have no sanitation facilities; and in Nepal, more than 50 percent people have no access to potable water and 80 percent are without basic sanitation.

In South Asia as a whole, about 260 million people have no access to health care, 337 million are without safe drinking water, 830 million lack sanitation facilities, and more than 400 million are without adequate food. Thus, it is no wonder that the ranks of Human Development Index (HDI) are dismal in the region-Sri Lanka ranks 90, the Maldives 93, India 132, Pakistan 138, Nepal 144, Bhutan 145, and Bangladesh 150. These indicators do not show much improvement in living standards under the current market-led governance, which prescribes even further reductions in government spending on subsidized basic services such as health and education that are desperately needed by the majority poor in South Asia.

Such a dismal scenario of living standards may even look more critical if one takes into consideration the extreme level of economic inequality in South Asia, which has worsened during the period of promarket governance. In terms of national-level economic indicators such as external debt and balance of trade, South Asian countries have performed negatively under the new mode of governance. The condition of external debt, which was already expansive during the 1980s, worsened further in the 1990s. Between 1990 and 1997, the total external debt increased from $12.8 billion to $15.1 billion in Bangladesh, $83.7 billion to $94.4 billion in India, $1.6 billion to $2.4 billion in Nepal, $26.7 billion to $29.7 billion in Pakistan, and $5.9 billion to $7.6 billion in Sri Lanka.

Similarly, the situation of the current account balance worsened between 1980 and 1997: from -$844 million to -$902 million in Bangladesh, -$2.9 billion to -$5.8 billion in India, -$93 million to -$460 million in Nepal, and -$868 million to -$3.7 billion in Pakistan. These indicators imply the deepening external dependence of these South Asian countries. Thus, despite the current rhetoric of higher growth rates based on market-driven governance, the actual conditions of poverty, inequality, living standards, external debt, and trade balance have hardly improved in these countries.

POLITICAL CONSEQUENCES

The contemporary changes in governance based on promarket assumptions, corporate structures, and businesslike functions and orientations, have considerable implications for various political issues in South Asia. First, although the articulation of such governance has often been associated with democratization, it may have created adverse impacts on democracy itself. For example, the political institutions in South Asia have traditionally known to be weak or fragile due to excessive bureaucratic power, military intervention, and factional conflicts based on race, religion, and caste.

Under the current market-led governance, such fragile political institutions, especially the members of legislature and cabinet, have become even more vulnerable to internal and external business interests often demanding politically unpopular policies, such as divestment, retrenchment, user charge, and subsidy cut, which usually lead to job losses and declines in subsidized services. In other words, the elected political leaders may respond to the demands of narrow business interest at the expense broader public interest.

Second, the market model of governance has certain critical implications for the configuration of power structure involving the state, the market, and the public. More specifically, due to its redefinition of service recipients as customers (led by utilitarian individual desire) rather than citizens (guided by citizenship rights and collective public interest), this model of governance may lead to the individualization or fragmentation of the public, and thus, to the disempowerment of citizens in relation to the state and the market.

This is more probable today when there is a stronger partnership or alliance between the state and the private sector discussed above. It has been pointed out by Hildyard that in the case of India, the government has even taken measures to train the national police force by Western security experts to protect the property of foreign investors; and while the democratic space has expanded for the upper-class elite, it has shrunk for the lower-class majority who are also the victims of market-led governance.

In addition, the people's power based on their citizenship rights to basic services and to ethnic and gender representation is likely to be compromised due to an overemphasis of the current governance on market-based competition and efficiency and on commercialized service provisions. According to a 1999 survey, the percentage of people perceiving the legal protection of their rights by government is only 30 percent in Pakistan and Sri Lanka, 36 percent in Bangladesh, 46 percent in India, and 51 percent in Nepal.

The survey also shows that the percentage of people believing that women and minorities are well represented in governance is merely 13 percent in Nepal, 33 percent in Pakistan, 37 percent in Bangladesh, and 43 percent India and Sri Lanka. In other words, there is strong skepticism among people with regard to the protection of their rights and representation under the current governance system in South Asian countries. Third, the outward economic orientation of new governance-terms of greater openness to the world markets, emphasis on global competitiveness, and fetish for foreign investment-has made the state in South Asia less autonomous from external forces, especially international agencies and transnational corporations.

The diminishing autonomy of the state in Bangladesh, India, Nepal, Pakistan, and Sri Lanka, is quite evident in its hesitant adoption of recent market-led reforms (deregulation, liberalization, privatization, devaluation) under the influence or pressure of international financial agencies such as the World Bank, the Asian Development Bank, the IMF, and so on. Thus, although the contemporary state in South Asia appears to be relatively indifferent towards the adverse impacts of its market-led reforms on citizens' entitlements and living standards, it has become more responsive to international pressures or demands.

ADMINISTRATIVE OUTCOMES

One of the major rationales for introducing the current market model of governance in South Asia has been that it would improve administrative performance, enhance public service transparency and integrity, and strengthen public confidence in governance. However, after two decades of reforms in governance, these rationales have hardly been realized in the region. First, in terms of public sector performance, there has not been any significant improvement in most South Asian countries. According to the above mentioned 1999 survey, the percentage of people unhappy with the quality of public education (primary level) is 31 percent in India, 37 percent in Nepal, 48 percent in Pakistan, 60 percent in Sri Lanka, and 63 percent in Bangladesh.

With regard to the quality of health care, the percentage of unhappy people is 46 percent in India, 54 percent in Nepal, 64 percent in Pakistan, 67 percent in Sri Lanka, and 73 percent in Bangladesh. A similar scenario of public unhappiness exists in the case of public infrastructure. These examples imply that although the current market-led governance has been endorsed in the name of better performance, the general public may not have such a sense of improvement. In fact, the current trends of employment cut and budget cut may exacerbate financial and personnel constraints in the public sector, and thus worsen its performance in terms of quality and availability of its services.

Second, the claim of greater administrative integrity under market-driven governance is equality suspect, because the situation of bureaucratic corruption has hardly improved in South Asian countries. In fact, the major components of this new mode of governance-such as managerial freedom, financial autonomy, and public-private partnership-are likely to make corruption endemic in these countries. In the case of Bangladesh, some of the recent surveys show that the percentage of respondents perceiving various government services as highly corrupt is 97 percent for the police service, 91 percent for customs, 90 percent for income tax, 89 percent for the judiciary, and 82 percent for the secretariat.

Similar scenario of extreme negative public perception regarding administrative corruption exists in India, Pakistan, Nepal, and Sri Lanka. Even the elected political leaders are perceived to be highly corrupt by most people in these South Asian countries. In fact, a significant percentage of people think that the situation of such administrative and political corruption in these countries has worsened during the last five years.

In other words, instead of overcoming corruption, for many people, the situation has deteriorated further during this age of market-led governance. Finally, the negative perception regarding the performance and integrity of political and administrative institutions is likely to adversely affect people's trust in governance, and thus its public legitimacy. It is quite ironic that although the contemporary ruling parties in South Asia have often used the rhetoric of reducing and replacing bureaucratic power by expanding the scope of market forces, especially to strengthen their electoral support, these parties themselves now have problem of maintaining public trust in their political agenda. In Bangladesh, the government is often seen by the public as unaccountable and unresponsive.

In other South Asian cases, a considerable portion of the public-49 percent in India, 48 percent in Pakistan, and 82 percent in Sri Lanka-does not believe that political parties represent their interests. In other words, the current mode of governance (including both the administrative and political realms) may face a serious problem of legitimation due to the growing negative public perception of its performance and integrity. The cynical public attitude towards this market-led governance may exacerbate further due to worsening economic conditions and growing sense of powerlessness among the poor constituting the majority in South Asian countries.

The colonial and postcolonial formations of governance in South Asian countries have been imitative of foreign models rather than indigenous contexts. In this regard, the current market-led mode of governance is not an exception, its associated principles, objectives, functions, structures, and norms originated mostly in advanced capitalist nations. The adoption of such a market model of governance in South Asia involved both the external pressure (coercion) of various agencies and the internal choice (consent) made by governments, not to mention the fact that such coercion and consent themselves became reinforced and legitimized by the globalized market ideology during the past two decades.

One main justification of following such a market-led model is the failure of the earlier state-centered governance discredited by the international advocates of market ideology. There is no doubt that the state-centered approach in South Asia-although it made some contribution to overall socioeconomic progress-had serious limitations in terms of excessive intervention, unmanageability, inefficiency, aloofness, unaccountability, and cronyism. However, the current alternative model has its own set of problems discussed above.

The market model of governance has the potential to reduce bureaucratic power, enhance administrative efficiency, and reinforce responsiveness, but it has been relatively ineffective to improve the situation in South Asia. In fact, the period of current governance has coincided with the abovementioned recent trends of economic, political, and administrative disorders in the region. A relevant question then is with regard to the actual reasons behind embracing such a market model despite its minimal effectiveness and negative consequences. In this regard, a major dimension of analyzing reforms in governance-which is often overlooked by conservative intellectuals-is the vested interests of various local and international powers behind the official rhetoric of such reforms packaged in positive words and jargons.

In South Asian countries, beyond the external pressure and influence discussed earlier, the current public sector reforms and policies were considerably motivated by tangible benefits reaped by certain internal power blocs. For instance, in the case of Bangladesh, the investors in recently privatized industries made windfall profits by selling the industrial sites and buildings, and about 80 percent of the recent government loans to the private sector have been by influenced by the elected political leaders.

In India, some of the sound and highly profitable public enterprises were heavily under priced and sold at one-third to one-seventh of their market values, and many of these enterprises were subsequently bought by the affluent business elite close to the government. It has been pointed out by Ghosh that the structural adjustment program adopted by the market-led governance in India, has benefited the affluent 10-15 percent of the population while marginalizing the rural poor.

In the case of Pakistan, some of the major beneficiaries of market-driven policies are business firms, top bureaucrats, and influential political leaders and their relatives involved in buying and selling the undervalued, privatized assets and shares. A similar scenario can be observed in Sri Lanka where a significant percentage (ranging from 10 to 50 percent) of privatized state-enterprise shares has been offered to employees free of charge, and many high-ranking public officials have made fortunes by buying privatized assets at extremely low prices.

These are just few examples of how certain vested interests, especially the political, administrative, and business elites, have gained from policies and reforms adopted under the current market-led governance in South Asian countries. Thus, beyond the official rhetoric and advocacy, there are private interests of various groups that might explain one of the most critical reasons for endorsing this governance.

Such internal interests have been quite powerful and active in perpetuating a positive image of the market model of governance. The external factors-including the loan conditionalities attached to structural adjustment program imposed by donor agencies, the collapse of socialist states and discredit of state-centered models, and the worldwide expansion of private capital and triumph of neo-liberal ideology-also played critical roles in instituting and reinforcing such market-led governance in South Asia, In this regard, a series of critical studies may be needed to examine further the actual causes and consequences of this new mode of governance in the region.

9

Human Rights Drama Featuring Burma

The World Trade Organization ("WTO"), an organization described as "arguably the most boring international group in the world," recently held a ministerial conference that drew a huge group of demonstrators, showing the growing resentment that large numbers of people feel toward the WTO. The establishment of the WTO in 1994 and its corollary system of dispute resolution in 1994 provided a strengthened means of resolving trade disputes, in comparison to the earlier General Agreement on Trade and Tariffs ("GATT"). The only way that a panel report containing recommended remedial provisions can not be adopted is for a Member country to appeal the report, the parties to agree to non-adoption, or for a consensus of the Dispute Settlement Body ("DSB") to agree upon non-adoption.

In addition, the Dispute Settlement Understanding contains heightened enforcement provisions that establish a procedure for the DSB to monitor compliance with the report and approve sanctions by the complaining country if non-compliance is found. While the DSB has succeeded in strengthening enforcement of GATT and its related agreements, it may also be seen as a major source of the growing resentment of many people toward the WTO.

By authorizing a non-judicial body the ability to resolve questions of violations of an international agreement, and by agreeing to be governed by resultant sanctions, the WTO Members have sacrificed a major aspect of their sovereignty.

Certain issues, even ones justifiably removed from the sphere of "free-trade," are now, according to the WTO and the DSB, beyond national legislation. Therefore, in many circles, the WTO is seen not only as the embodiment of capitalist corporate ideals, but also as a supranational enforcer able to impose those ideals on unwilling nations.

With nations ceding the power to legislate in certain areas and subjecting themselves to an international enforcement mechanism, questions naturally arise. Does the agreement relate rationally to the areas in which it is empowered to act? Does the international organization charged with this power, and the agreement under which it operates, take into sufficient consideration the ancillary goals and ideals of the member nations of the agreement?

If not, do other methods of achieving these ancillary goals exist in the international arena?

This chapter, by analyzing the dispute that has arisen out of the Massachusetts-Burma selective purchasing law, posits that in the recent fervor to attain the goal of free trade, the idea that "trade serves at best as an instrument for achieving goals societies seek" has been lost. As a consequence, the ability of nations to legislate in certain areas-those either marginally related to the concept of free trade or vital enough to warrant exceptions to the strict application of free trade agreements-has been severely compromised.

Unfortunately, this may hamper the ability of sovereigns to deal with the issue of human rights in countries that are seen as consistently violating the most basic rights of its citizens.

Applying the GPA in this manner may further alienate the WTO and the notion of free trade generally, in the minds of a public already dissatisfied with WTO policies and procedures. As a result, this type of application of the GPA may be detrimental to the cause of other free trade agreements in the future. In making these arguments, this Chapter argues that international trade agreements should recognize that "trade is a means to an end, not an end in itself."

THE CURRENT BURMESE REGIME'S VIOLATIONS OF HUMAN RIGHTS

The least contentious issue in the entire dispute about the Massachusetts Burma Law is the existence of gross violations of human rights in the present Burmese regime. The Court of Appeals for the First Circuit expressed this notion succinctly with the following statement: "There is one matter on which the parties are agreed: human rights conditions in Burma are deplorable." Consequently, the court did not inquire further into the matter. While perhaps not completely germane to the legal controversy put before the District Court of Massachusetts and the Court of Appeals, the issue of the existence and the extent of human rights violations in Burma should have been given more than cursory attention in the subsequent legal dispute. Therefore, in an effort to provide a more complete picture of the situation than has generally been exposed by legal proceedings and constitutional analysis, a short history of the current Burmese regime and its treatment of its citizens is necessary.

Burma, officially named the Union of Myanmar, lies in Southeast Asia, bordered by Bangladesh, China, India, Laos, Thailand, the Andaman Sea, and the Bay of Bengal. Slightly smaller in size than Texas, Burma is plentiful in natural resources but has remained in poverty for much of the time since its independence from the United Kingdom in 1948. From 1886 until its independence, Burma was treated as part of British India, and one writer has commented that the legacy of colonial rule greatly influenced the isolationism that remained the trademark of the nation until the late 1980s.

This isolationism found its greatest expression in the rule of General U Ne Win, who became dictator after a 1962 military coup ended fourteen years of fledgling democracy. Aided by tumultuous internal strife among the many ethnic minorities in Burma; national fears of incursion by neighboring countries; a single party political structure; complete power over the national press; and strict controls on ingress of foreign journalists and egress of Burmese citizens, the General propelled his country along the "Burmese way to socialism."

This ultra-nationalist policy based upon communist principles sequestered Burma from both the Communist Bloc and the Western community. Under General U Ne Win's control, the country virtually shut itself off from the rest of the world, enforcing a "non-aligned policy" that, until only recently, prohibited the nation from forging any strong strategic or economic alliances and kept public attention from focusing on Burma.

Due to continual clashes between ethnic minorities; the harsh political and social controls over the populous; the lack of attention paid to the regime by the world community; a culture of accepting adversity as an element of strong Buddhist beliefs; and a Burmese trait of selfless respect for authority, General U Ne Win faced little opposition from his countrymen until March 1988, when student protests began in earnest.

THE DECLINE IN THE BURMESE ECONOMY

In the fall of 1987, the Burmese government withdrew a large amount of currency from circulation in Burma. The move was possibly aimed at stifling the drug trafficking industry, which appeared to be run largely by ethnic rebel armies. The effect, however, was to significantly deplete the savings of many ordinary Burmese people. Students protested this decision, but the protests remained small. Apparently, the students were unable to garner any great support for their protests, possibly due to the deference to authority mentioned above; the long history of living under authoritarian rule; and an economy that may have been healthier than most observers could see from the official statistics.

The withdrawal of currency, though, occurred at a time when the Burmese economy was weakening even further. Public sentiment in the fall of 1987 was not strong enough to propel a backlash against the government, but after a few months of living under harsher economic conditions, things began to change. Western influences possibly added to the growing rancor. Reports in early 1988 suggested that, despite extreme isolationism, the government reluctantly tolerated Western tourist excursions.

Tourists brought in U.S. dollars, which became a staple of the Burmese economy, fostering a black market that paid approximately seven times the government exchange rate. Also, western movies, music, and television shows entered Burmese culture, adding a breath of diversity long denied by the xenophobic military regime. Following a sharp decline in the official economy, firsthand experience with the power of a strong currency, and imported visions of Western freedom, the Burmese people replaced their docility with public protest.

Early in 1988, the death of a student provided the impetus for the people of Burma to express their long-restrained dissatisfaction with the government. In March, an argument between students and villagers in a Rangoon tea shop led to the death of one student, apparently due to police action. Students, angered by the death, began a series of protests that lasted approximately one week.

Many believe that the student protests arose out of the earlier fall protests, which had stagnated due to lack of support. Although largely unreported in the Western press, protests continued in the following months as support increased. In July, the protesters achieved one of their goals; twenty-six years after seizing control of Burma, General U Ne Win officially resigned as head of the government, citing the pro-democracy student protests, which ended in the deaths of numerous citizens. Although officially out of office, many believed that U Ne Win remained in control of the country throughout the several subsequent changes of official leadership of Burma; even today, he likely continues his influence.

General Sein Lwin, appointed by the government, took control from General U Ne Win on July 26, 1988. The General had been in charge of the riot police that attempted to contain the earlier protests. Due to this notoriety and the belief that the resignation of General U Ne Win was merely a ruse, the protests ending the twenty-six year reign of the dictator continued in Rangoon. Across the country, minor disputes between ethnic minorities continued to erupt into full scale anti-government protests, and the military and riot police continued to brutally suppress the rioters.

It was reported that the military, at times, fired into groups of unarmed women and monks. A letter endorsed by 170 lawyers of the Rangoon Bar Council, a Burmese governmental organization, asserted that during the rioting, "the army shot and killed nurses on duty, people in their homes or coffee shops, and pedestrians in the streets." After holding power for just seventeen days, and under extreme pressure from fierce rioting, General Sein Lwin resigned the presidency of Burma.

In the final five days leading up to his resignation, the government acknowledged that ninety-five people died in the violence, but other reports listed at least 3000 deaths in Rangoon alone. One week after the resignation of General Sein Lwin, the first civilian leader of Burma in twenty-six years entered office. Attorney General Maung Maung, one of only two civilian members of the presidential cabinet, was selected the next president of Burma by the ruling government.

Many in Burma believed that he had been chosen to appease the people, and to give the impression that military rule was at an end, while control remained with the military establishment. However, even if Mr. Maung Maung was able to wield power him and not merely as a puppet of General U Ne Win, he still would have been a very objectionable leader in the eyes of the Burmese people. Mr. Maung Maung had close political and ideological ties to U Ne Win and had personally inscribed the principles of the "Burmese Way to Socialism" into the Burmese constitution of 1974.

The Burmese people believed that, even if Maung Maung could exert independent control, the principles and ideologies that resulted in the economic devastation and the disregard for basic human rights in Burma would still be enforced. The protests for democracy against the government continued, drawing millions into the streets. Outraged at the brutality of the suppression of protests in Burma and convinced that the unrest and danger would not be quelled by the most recent change in government, the U.S. Senate and the House of Representatives each penned resolutions condemning the violence in Burma, and the U.S. Department of State prepared for the evacuation of U.S. citizens from Burma.

In another attempt to appease pro-democracy activists who protested in the streets to express displeasure with the recent change in government, Maung Maung promised democratic elections later in the year. The promise did not change the attitude of the Burmese people and did little to quiet the public protests, because many believed that General U Ne Win continued to hold power. After twenty-six years of dictatorial control, few believed that U Ne Win would acquiesce to a call for real democratic reform.

For approximately one month, the protests against the rule of Maung Maung continued, during which time various groups contemplated the idea of forming an interim government. The former Prime Minister of Burma, U Nu, who had lost his position in the coup of 1962, actually formed an interim government but did not receive support from the public or other opposition parties. The most prominent opposition leaders concluded that the current regime would have to resign before an interim government could be formed.

Any interim government would be doomed to failure without the support of the military because of the military's vital role in Burmese society and politics. Unless the current government resigned, the formation of an interim government would force the military-historically very loyal to U Ne Win and the ruling establishment-to decide whom to support. The opposition forces were not willing to wager that the military would disavow historic allegiances in favor of a newly formed, idealistic government. Therefore, the opposition parties waited, hoping that Maung Maung would commit to democratic reform.

In September, Maung Maung ordered the resignation of all military personnel and civil servants from the Burma Socialist Program Party ("BSPP"), the ruling political party. On September 18, perhaps in response to the forced resignation of the military from the BSPP, another change of government occurred in Burma. The Defense Minister, General Saw Maung, appointed by former ruler Sein Lwin over the summer, initiated a military coup to take complete control of the Burmese government and set up the "Organization for Building Law and Order in the State." This military council enumerated its position when it stated: "in order to halt the deteriorating conditions on all sides all over the country, and for the sake of the interests of the people, the defense forces have assumed all power in the state."

Once again, the Burmese people believed that the change in the government was not an actual shift in power. One reporter described the apparent military takeover as a "false coup" designed to maintain the power of the BSPP-still be headed by U Ne Win-with a weak puppet as the officially recognized head of the government. This interpretation comports with the analysis that the forced resignation of the military from the BSPP-intended to signify to the Burmese people that the upcoming elections would be truly free and not influenced by the military-was a political tactic rather than an accommodation of future democratic elections.

By effectively abolishing the BSPP, the government wanted to be perceived as acceding to the public's desire to end the one party system of rule in Burma. However, combined with the military coup that followed shortly thereafter, almost certainly led by U Ne Win, the only effect was to rename the persons in control of the government. From the speculation that the coup was a reaction by the military to its forced resignation from the BSPP, one may draw the conclusion that the forced resignation was designed to anger the members of the military.

Military anger with the BSPP would shift its loyalty from the official party to the leaders of the ensuing coup. Therefore, in the eyes of the public, the official government would change hands, and the military would change allegiances, but no real change of power would occur. Whether the change in government was in name only or was a real shift in power, the effects remained the same. Shortly after the coup, the military dispersed demonstrators in Rangoon, and the council, headed by General Saw Maung, ordered a curfew and banned groups of more than five people.

Less than a month after the takeover, the new government killed 1000 civilians and fired thousands of government workers. One reporter claims that videotapes of the violence after the coup show soldiers killing wounded students after the demonstrators were dispersed. Rangoon was described as being under "virtual military occupation," and thousands of students were reported to be fleeing to areas controlled by ethnic rebels in hopes of obtaining military training and arms.

Also, although Saw Maung again promised free elections, the elections originally scheduled for late in the year were rescheduled to "sometime in 1989," or only after "three conditions were met: peace would have to prevail; the battered rail and road network would have to be made secure; the basic food and shelter situation would have to be improved." With the effects of twenty-six years of social, political, and economic stagnation to frustrate the achievement of these criteria, the military government showed that it planned to retain its hold on Burma for the indefinite future, with elections coming only when the government so desired.

In an apparent attempt to temper the repression and to bolster the promise of free elections, the Saw Maung regime permitted political parties to form. 233 parties formed by April 1989, including the National League for Democracy ("NLD"). Named as General Secretary of the NLD was Daw Aung San Suu Kyi, the daughter of General Aung San, who had been the major force in the independence movement in Burma in the 1940s, but who was assassinated shortly before Burma gained its independence from Britain in 1948.

Over the next few months, Suu Kyi gradually assumed the role of popular leader of the NLD and spokesperson for the democracy movement in Burma. In early 1989, the military government of General Saw Maung, which came to be known as the State Law and Order Restoration Council ("SLORC"), set a general time frame for the democratic elections but continued its attempts to repress dissent. In March, after protest rallies, the SLORC renewed arrests of dissenters, hauling in approximately 1000 people, including 300 members of the NLD.

In July, the SLORC put Aung San Suu Kyi and another leader of the NLD under house arrest, not allowing them contact with other NLD members or leaders. Reports indicated that the government continued to arrest anyone that advocated human rights or democracy, attempting to eradicate dissent in Burma. According to a senior Western diplomat, "The government seems to be clearing the field of anyone in opposition. People who were active last year continue to be picked up."

Due to the continued detention of large numbers of political dissenters, the government removed regular criminals from many of the jails to make room for political prisoners. The main jail in Rangoon reportedly released 17,000 criminals to free space for opponents of the government. Reports also claimed that the government often detained individuals with no political ties or involvement for up to five days in harsh conditions and released them with an admonition not to become involved in politics. In the weeks leading up to the one-year anniversary of the massive protests in which thousands of people had been killed, the military detained at least 1,000 members of the NLD to stifle any commemoration of the previous year's events.

REGIME REFUSES TO ACCEPT RESULTS OF DEMOCRATIC VOTE

Despite the efforts of the government to stifle public dissent and detain political protesters, elections set for May of 1990 occurred on schedule and appeared uninfluenced by corruption, though they could hardly be called fair. The ban on gatherings of more than four people continued to be enforced, squelching public debate, and each party running for election was allowed only one campaign address, which was censored.

In spite of daunting challenges it faced: election restrictions; the detention of thousands of its members; and the continued house arrest of its two main leaders, the NLD captured more than eighty percent of the parliamentary seats for which it was vying. Not surprisingly, the ruling military regime, embodied by the National Unity Party, the successor to the BSPP, won only 10 seats out of 485.

Despite the landslide victory of the NLD, the prospects for a change in the actual government of Burma were dim. Prior to the election, the ruling regime stated that before any exchange of power would occur, a new constitution would have to be drafted by the new parliament. After the election, the military stalled attempts by the NLD to take power. Although the NLD appeared ready to submit a constitution based on the democratic constitution of 1947, under which Burma had been governed until 1962, the military refused to meet with the NLD and refused to call a national assembly to begin work on the new constitution.

Throughout the following years, the military regime continued its repression of the members of the NLD and to stall the process of writing a new constitution. Aung San Suu Kyi was kept under house arrest until July 1995, when the military felt that the democracy movement had lost enough momentum so as to threaten no longer the military regime. At various times, the military proposed measures to begin forming a constitution, but these efforts often included the requirement that the military be given a large role in any future government.

Needless to say, these measures were seen as unacceptable to the proponents of true democratic reform. Aung San Suu Kyi, after her release from house arrest, began to work on the drafting of a new constitution with the NLD, but the military government indicated that such a document would not be accepted. By enacting a law that made the writing of a rival constitution a crime, the military clearly expressed its intent to maintain a firm holds on any constitutional process in Burma.

This intent has not dwindled in the ensuing years. In 1999, nine years after the democratic elections, a Burmese governmental official stated: "You can't cry over spilled milk now. And if you're going to stick to demanding that the government should hand over power, I don't think that is very realistic."

HUMAN RIGHTS ABUSES OF THE REGIME

The 1988 protests and the ensuing actions of the Burmese government provide a chilling account of the reprehensible abuses that the Burmese regime imposed upon its people to retain and strengthen control of the country. The killing of thousands of protesters; the arrest, detention, and torture of many thousands of other protesters; the detention of hundreds of members of opposition political parties, including the leaders of the main opposition unit; the severe restriction of social freedoms; and the extreme repression of virtually all democratic ideals serve to introduce the human rights abuses present in Burma today.

The list of other abuses of which the Burmese regime is accused includes: extrajudicial killing; torture; forced labor; forced child labor; forced relocation of entire villages; rape committed by military personnel; invasion of personal privacy; confiscation of personal property; restrictions on access to information; repression of religious activities; and discrimination against ethnic minorities. Since journalists have been either banned completely or severely restricted in the areas that they could visit alone, and since no foreign or national human rights organization has been allowed to operate in Burma, the scope of human rights abuses in Burma has been severely underreported.

The primary source of information has been refugees who have escaped to bordering countries, such as Thailand. From these reports, which detail scores of brutal acts, one indication of human rights abuses of the Burmese military has been the apparent ease and nonchalance with which it has indiscriminately killed fellow citizens. The program of extrajudicial killings in Burma was extensively detailed in a report issued by Amnesty International.

Although issued in 1988, reliable sources indicate that the program of extrajudicial killings, especially of ethnic minorities, continues presently. In its efforts to control the ethnic rebellions that have plagued the country since its independence in 1948, the military regime of Burma has subjected the inhabitants of various ethnic regions to extreme abuse and death in a number of ways.

Reports indicate that to ensure that militant rebel factions receive as little support as possible, the government has often placed entire villages under strict control: 1. restraining free movement; 2. relocating villagers; 3. allocating the amount of food or money that the villagers may possess; and 4. maintaining strict curfews. Persons that are caught in violation of these controls are sometimes killed on sight. Amnesty International stated in its report: "Porters and guides caught trying to escape are often killed, as are villagers who run away when they hear the army is coming." Although the SLORC has often denied these abuses and cited its attempts to "make peace," evidence shows: the military has continued in the 1990s to kill villagers for having real or alleged sympathies for anti-government forces.

In addition to killing villagers and those allegedly supporting local insurgents, the military common tortures its detainees. One rice farmer interviewed by Amnesty International described a frequent torture method used against villagers: shin rolling.

"[The interrogator] tried to force information out of me by rolling a large bamboo pole over my shins, up and down, increasing the pressure until the skin began to strip off... After a few minutes of this treatment, the skin came off, but the guy kept rolling the bamboo over the exposed bone, causing terrible pain."

Other favorite methods of torture include: 1. detention in underground pits; 2. wrapping victims' heads in plastic sheets until the victim nearly suffocates; 3. near-drowning; and 4. near-strangulation. Many Burmese people are also killed when the military forces villagers to work as porters. These porters are most often used in the areas of Burma in which the government is fighting ethnic insurgencies. The military, often facing mountainous terrain with no roads and having no mechanized transport, uses human labor to carry food, ammunition, and other supplies, and uses locals familiar with the geography of the region as guides for their military expeditions.

Not only are the villagers forced to labor for the military; they are rarely, if ever, paid for their work, and they are also maltreated and forced to engage in dangerous activities for the benefit of the military. Reports suggest that porters are frequently mistreated for not carrying a large enough load or for not walking quickly enough. Porters are also frequently worked to death or killed for not working hard enough. In addition to using conscripted porters to perform grueling manual labor, the military also forced them to act as human danger detectors its forces. Reports show that porters are frequently forced to walk ahead of the military through areas that are suspected of being mined.

As human mine sweepers, these civilians-pulled from their homes or from the streets of their villages-are forced to risk their lives. Also, accounts relate that porters have been forced to dress in the uniforms of the army to patrol insurgent areas unarmed. In these patrols, the civilian porters serve as defenseless decoys for the army, drawing the fire of rebels and alerting the military to their location.

Until the late 1980s, the porters were mainly used to support military operations in ethnically controlled insurgent areas, but with the gradual opening of the Burmese economy after 1988, the government began using forced labor for infrastructure projects as well. These projects included the building of railroads, an airport, roads, and an oil pipeline.

During the period 1992-97, Human Rights Watch/Asia estimated that approximately two million Burmese people were used for forced labor to make the Burmese infrastructure more attractive for foreign investment and tourists. Current reports indicate that the institution of porterage is still widely used in Burma. "The forced use of citizens as porters by the army-with attendant mistreatment, illness, and sometimes deaths-remained a common practice" in 1998, according to the United States Department of State. The State Department report of human rights conditions in Burma in 1999 stated:

The Government did not honor its repeated pledge to prevent its officials from using their authority under the country's Towns Act and Villages Act to mobilize forced labor. In June the Government responded to sanctions that the International Labor Organization (ILO) imposed on it for its use of forced labor by unilaterally withdrawing from the convention on forced labor administered by the ILO.

Along with the indiscriminate killing of citizens and the imposition of forced labor upon civilians, the military government also commonly practices forced relocation of citizens. As part of the "four cuts" strategy to disable ethnic rebels-cutting off food, funds, information, and recruits to the insurgents-entire villages are often relocated away from areas of rebel activity.

The new locations often lack even the most basic features of adequate living areas, such as sanitation facilities, access to water, electricity, and health care facilities. From 1988 to 1990, the government relocated an estimated 500,000 people from their homes. Further, as Burma attempts to attract foreign investment, the government began to relocate citizens not only to counter ethnic conflicts, but also to hide "shanty towns" from the view of investors, and to renovate possible tourist areas.

In addition to various forms of military brutality, Burma also engages in overt ethnic and religious discrimination. Burma recognizes three different levels of citizenship, each with different levels of rights: full citizenship, associate citizenship, and naturalized citizenship, each with different levels of rights. A full citizen must prove Burmese ancestry back to pre-1823 British occupation.

An associate citizen is one who had one or more ancestors who were citizens of another country. Finally, a naturalized citizen is the offspring of a full citizen and an associate citizen. The discriminatory efforts focus on associate citizens, who are not allowed to own land, hold elected office, or become doctors or engineers. Associate citizens are also severely restricted in their movements within the country. Indirect discrimination also occurs, in that many ethnic minorities who could prove the requisite ancestry back to pre-colonial times are effectively barred from obtaining their citizenship documents. The government has often failed to register these people by making the registration process unavailable in local areas, and associate citizens are frequently not allowed or unable to travel to central locations to register.

Religious intolerance hostility toward non-Buddhist religions occurs frequently in Burma. The military regime has long enforced a policy of promoting Buddhism as the "true" religion of the Burmese people, attempting to instill in the populous the belief that to be a "true Burmese," one must follow Buddhism. The government has forced the conversions of children to Buddhism, destroyed Christian churches, and conscripted Christians and Muslims to build Buddhist religious facilities. In order to maintain a dictatorial hold on Burmese society, the military has repressed freedom of expression for the past thirty-eight years.

Foreign sources of information were largely unavailable for much of this period, with access to foreign newspapers and magazines subject to government censorship. Domestic media services are controlled completely by the state. Domestically produced books, magazines, and films are scrutinized by a "Press Scrutiny Board." Since most materials are submitted to the board only after substantial expense has been incurred by the publisher, publishers use self-censorship to ensure that their investment will not be wasted by subsequent government revisions. In addition, censorship violations potentially result in seven years in prison for publishers, providing a healthy incentive to stay on the censor's good side.

The effects of censorship and the lack of access to foreign printed material cannot generally be circumvented by electronic means. Realizing that electronic communication could deal a damaging blow to the repression of speech and the isolationism favored by the ruling elite, Burma enacted laws requiring a license for any facsimile machine or computer modem. In addition, for most of the 1990s, the government closed the universities to prevent further student protests.

THE BURMESE LEGAL SYSTEM

The Burmese legal system provides few rights to prisoners and detainees. Many prisoners are detained for up to three years without a trial, and trials do not provide prisoners with most basic judicial norms. Defendants are often denied access to counsel before and during trial. When defendants are allowed counsel, the attorney often simply bargains with the judge for the least harsh sentence for his client. Members of the NLD are usually denied counsel, and when counsel is available for political prisoners, one report suggests that the counsel's role is mainly to serve as mere moral support for the defendant.

Even if counsel played a normal role in court proceedings, the judiciary in Burma is subjected to influences that make it unlikely to act independently in its decisions. First, the judiciary is tied to the military rulers of Burma. The SPDC appoints the members of the Supreme Court of Burma. With the approval of the SPDC, the justices select the lower court judges.

This naturally presents conflicts, most notably in trials of political prisoners, where it is believed that the government exerts its influence to determine the outcome of the trial in advance of any proceeding. Also, bribery appears rampant in the judiciary. The judges typically earn an equivalent of $300 per year, providing ample incentive for parties to attempt to buy their way to a favorable decision. By many accounts, the people of Burma have become increasingly dejected by the continuing history of brutal repression in their homeland.

Few would argue that the present situation in Burma is not a saddening example of a people being subjugated to the whims of a powerful military elite. What does provoke heated arguments, though, is the method by which to express the world's desire for the situation in Burma to improve, the manner in which influence should be used to encourage or compel Burma's regime to respect the most basic human rights of its citizens, and the tools to be used to promote peaceful transition from repressive regime to just governance.

INTERNATIONAL SANCTIONS ON BURMA

Beginning in 1988, in response to the brutal repression of the student protests in Burma, the international community enacted measures intended to ease the tensions in Burma and compel the military regime to appreciate and respect human rights. Due to the internal political, economic, and social situation in Burma, however, these measures have largely failed to effect any substantial change in the Burmese regime. Because of the "Burmese Way to Socialism" instilled by General U Ne Win, Burma remained economically isolated from the rest of the world for twenty-six years.

Although the country possessed vast reserves of natural resources such as oil, natural gas, timber, and precious gems, a failure to economically exploit these resources caused Burma to fall from a "rich" country to one of the poorest countries in the world, garnering a vast amount foreign aid. Knowing that a large part of Burma's capital flows came in the form of aid, the first response by countries wishing to influence Burma was to cut off this aid. Believing that without the foreign aid, the Burmese regime would be more willing to change, the major suppliers of aid to Burma cut off most non-humanitarian aid in late 1988.

In October 1988, three large aid donors, the United States, West Germany, and Japan, halted aid to Burma. The combined yearly aid to Burma of these three countries equaled approximately $152 million, and Burma also lost an additional $200 million in Japanese loans. Burma's foreign reserves dwindled, and the country was described as "virtually bankrupt." These decisions to halt aid showed the contempt the world community felt for the brutality of the military regime during the summer of 1988, and were designed to influence the government to change its tactics.

Rather than weakening authoritarian control of the country in order to regain foreign aid, the government-for the first time in approximately twenty-six years-opened its borders to foreign investment. Not surprisingly, many investors initially remained wary of entry into such a volatile market, but a few, mainly in Thailand, were tempted by the abundant natural resources Burma had to offer and immediately capitalized on the new market. Through a gradual increase in the amount of foreign investment, Burma was able to compensate at least partially for the loss of direct aid formerly supplied by foreign governments.

According to data reporting the levels of Foreign Direct Investment (FDI) in Burma, $56 million of FDI was attained in 1989-90, with the United States and the Netherlands representing the largest contributors. By 1990-91, the level of investment had increased to $225.1 million, with the United States and the Republic of Korea being the largest investors. The cutoff of aid from Western countries was also ameliorated by increased Chinese interest in Burma. After the 1988 student protests, the military became increasingly aware that future social disturbances posed a great threat.

The military was also concerned about the likelihood that past and future political uprisings would provide an impetus for the many ethnic insurgent factions to increase rebellious activities to take advantage of the disarray caused by the massive protests. In light of these realizations, the military leaders of Burma began purchasing large amounts of arms from China in 1989.

With a more intimate relationship between China and Burma forming due to the arms sales, China saw an opportunity to increase its influence on Burma. From this strengthened relationship, Burma received greatly increased trade ties with China and opportunities for Chinese development loans. Desiring to wield as much political influence in the region as possible, China established a relationship with Burma that it strove to maintain.

Even though Burma may have wished to retain a more independent relationship with China, it now had a "Big Brother," with all the added implications, to provide needed economic and military support. Increased trade with China reduced the coercive effect of the cutoff in foreign aid. Therefore, one traditional method of influencing rogue states proved completely ineffective in Burma.

Diplomatic and humanitarian attempts to deal with the oppression of the Burmese people have proven to be equally ineffective. In addition to ending aid to Burma, the United States imposed an arms embargo, which was easily circumvented through Burma's relationship with China. A 1995 visit to Burma by Madeline Albright, then-U.S. Permanent Representative to the United Nations, engendered excuses and justifications by the Burmese government for its past actions, rather than a dialogue geared toward the resolution of the tensions between Burma and the rest of the world.

As the Association of South-East Asian Nations (ASEAN) prepared to accept Burma into the economic group, the United States and the European Union retracted their opposition to the joinder of Burma to the group, calling for ASEAN to take the lead in encouraging talks between the opposition and the military government. The UN has repeatedly issued resolutions condemning Burma for its abuses and calling for an end to the violation of human rights in the country, but to no avail.

The UN High Commission on Human Rights established the position of a Special Rapporteur ("Rapporteur") for Burma in 1990 to make trips to Burma and report on human rights situations. For a few years, the Burmese regime allowed the Rapporteur entry to Burma; then, in 1996, the government denied the Rapporteur access and has since not allowed the UN official into the country.

The International Society of the Red Cross negotiated with the SLORC to gain access to political prisoners. Finally, in 1995, the Red Cross, completely discouraged by the military regime's failure to grant access to the prisons, withdrew from the country. Subsequently, the Red Cross has been able to return to Burma and obtain limited access to prisoners, although it has claimed that many political prisoners were removed from a prison in Rangoon so that the Red Cross would be unable to see or speak with them.

In addition, the Burmese government has continually rebuffed the efforts of the International Labor Organization ("ILO") to secure Burmese adherence to its international obligations. In retaliation, the ILO effectively ejected Burma from the organization and will not allow re-admittance until Burma stops using forced labor.

WEAKNESSES OF CONSTRUCTIVE ENGAGEMENT

While it is obvious that various diplomatic measures and the withholding of aid have failed to promote respect for human rights in Burma, the next step remains unclear. Some groups argue that sanctions should be continued against Burma and should be tightened, while others tout "constructive engagement" as the proper tool for promoting human rights and democracy. Proponents of constructive engagement argue that, all too often, sanctions fail to have a substantial effect on the practices of that country.

In addition, it is argued that economic sanctions have negative repercussions that inure to the innocent citizens of a rogue state, outweighing any benefit from the sanctions. Therefore, instead of relying on an ineffective tool that harms the people it intends to help, proponents of sanctions insist that economic incentives and the benefits from profitable economic activity will more effectively promote the same aims as sanctions. In sum, proponents assert that capitalism will triumph.

The principle behind constructive engagement is that with free trade, instead of sanctions, rogue states are allowed and encouraged to enter into economic transactions with whomever they please. These economic transactions will cause capital flows into the country, very often in the form of foreign direct investment. Proponents of constructive engagement argue that these increased capital flows and the resulting increased wealth for citizens in the country, from either new jobs created by foreign investors or increased demand for existent production capacity, will gradually lead to political and social changes.

It is often claimed that in developing countries with poor wages and poor labor conditions, the introduction of foreign-owned businesses will heighten labor standards and the level of pay. Proponents argue that the higher labor standards to which foreign businesses have become accustomed outside of the target country will eventually affect the target country's labor system, almost as if by social osmosis. It appears that adherents to the policy of constructive engagement believe that, by entering foreign markets, businesses, rather than maintaining the status quo of the host country and taking advantage of the opportunity for cheap labor and the ability to circumvent costly standards of treatment, will infuse the labor climate of the target country with greater pay and worker protection in the long run.

Proponents argue that the increased economic and social wealth for the citizens of the target country and its increased presence in the world community, will generally lead to faster improvement in the political and social situation than with sanctions.

This improvement appears to be possible in two general ways. First, the country and its political and social climate, through the influence of wealth, security and foreign values, may "evolve" from a restrictive or oppressive state into a more open, protective state cognizant of, and responsive to, its citizens' appeals for change. This evolution would be aided by private and public appeals to the government for change.

Governments supportive of economic ties with the target country could use the increased interactions between the two governments to state privately their concerns and desires for reform and could offer future incentives (the classic carrot and stick situation). The same appeals could be made publicly, and foreign governments could threaten to sever economic ties, appealing to the economic self-interest of the country and its people. The second possibility is that the increased wealth, security, and power of the citizenry will manifest itself in increased political dissent.

As the fruits of engagement are distributed throughout the economy, a "middle class"-motivated by the taste of what economic and social freedoms have to offer-will develop with the intense desire to change the government and the increased power to do so. The theory suggests that change would occur through rebellion against the country's current government. What the proponents of constructive engagement for Burma fail to realize, though, is that the conditions necessary for the policy to be effective are not present in Burma. As Madeline Albright noted after her trip to Burma in 1995, "`Constructive engagement' must be, in fact, `constructive.'"

To be constructive, the policy must be able to work its influence upon either or both of two factors. First, if a base level of respect for the rights of the citizenry exists, increased economic and social integration with the rest of the world may subtly influence the target country and its leaders to gradually allow change in the country. Eventually, the theory says, greater involvement with more refined and respectful nations will cause the target country to evolve into a country more conscious of the need for, and more willing to allow, greater protection and freedom for the people.

The influence for change would come about not only from an internal evolution of respect for the populace, but also from external pressures. To maintain the increased involvement with the rest of the world, the target country would seek to create an air of respectability in itself. The views of foreign nations would gain in stature as the target country attempts to promote itself as a country worthy of continued and expanded economic engagement. Secondly, increased economic activity with the outside world could work its influence upon the people at large, rather than the government.

As the theory goes, increased demand for the nation's labor force and the creation of new jobs that accompanies the influx of foreign investment will cause an increase in the wealth and stability of the people. Buoyed by small tastes of what economic and social freedom could entail and strengthened physically and morally by newfound wealth, the people will have greater incentive and capability to throw off the control of their intolerant regime. Upon further analysis, it seems that the policies, politics, and economic realities present in Burma are not conducive to the goals of constructive engagement.

For the past thirty-eight years, the military regimes of Burma have shown a willingness to murder, torture, enslave, repress, and discriminate against the citizens of the country. In the twelve years since the technical ouster of General U Ne Win, Burma has resisted change, even in the face of political and economic pressure from much of the world community. Even after the large increase in the levels of foreign direct investment in Burma since 1988, no real strides in the realm of respect for human rights have occurred.

The combination of many factors largely unique to Burma may account for the failure of economic cooperation with the outside world to have positive effects. The first, and perhaps most subtle factor to be considered, is the social and political climate that has been predominate in Burmese recent history.

Long before the present regime instituted its own social and political repression, British colonialism repressed and abused the Burmese people, creating an air of distrust of foreigners to form in the Burmese consciousness. After British colonial rule ended, Burma was allowed little time for this distrust of foreigners to wane before General U Ne Win instituted his "Burmese Way to Socialism," officially instituting fear and distrust of anyone or anything non-Burmese.

For twenty-four years, Burma was effectively cut off from the rest of the world, not only economically, but also socially and politically. Simply put, Burma has not had the necessary time to evolve from a nation fearful of the influences of foreigners to a nation that can be subtly and positively influenced by mere economic cooperation with the rest of the world. For such intangible and indirect changes to occur in the national mindset or the social and cultural norms and morays of the Burmese people, there must be a conduit through which capitalism can succeed. Unfortunately, for Burma, such a conduit remains largely lacking.

One way in which involvement may positively affect the general social and political climate in a target country is through the increased flow of information. With greater access to a wider variety of sources of news and opposing viewpoints, the populace may begin to think more for it, may begin to question the status quo, and may feel more confident in its own expression of dissent. Also, the people may learn that they are not as alone as they once thought.

Not only may they feel themselves to be an increasingly greater part of the world community, sharing in the events of the day and the ensuing discussion and dialogue, but they may also see that the world actually cares about their domestic situation. Sympathizers never before known of may be revealed, providing moral support and feeding the people's hope and determination to be free. In Burma, however, the flow of information is anything but free. Despite increased engagement with the outside world, censorship still rules the day.

Foreign newspapers, magazines, films, television, books, and videotapes all face distribution restrictions. Those media sources legally allowed into Burma or produced domestically face heavy state censorship, which that eliminates any material likely to damage the image of the present regime. Technological innovations may also prove incapable of increasing, to any large degree, the flow of information to Burma. Fax machines, computer modems, and other devices that would enable the free, or at least less restricted, influx of information and that would allow the outside world to have a degree of unrepressed contact with the Burmese people continue to be strictly controlled by the military regime.

Although in some areas the enforcement of these strict controls has been lax, the laws requiring licenses for these devices remain in force, awaiting enforcement when the junta deems it necessary. Direct contact with foreigners interested in seeing positive change in Burma could also prove to be a conduit of information, but this would not occur today in Burma. Foreign journalists continue to be severely restricted in their ability to even enter Burma and once there, in the ability to have contact with the opposition.

Humanitarian non-governmental organizations ("NGOs") are permitted only a very small presence in Burma, and human rights

NGOs face an outright ban on operations, thereby limiting the contact between aid workers and the Burmese population. The government usually grants tourists limited duration visas to certain restricted areas, thereby limiting the contact they may have with the people. In any event, the Burmese people may remain wary of having meaningful contact with foreigners, even if and when the opportunities may present themselves. The threat of harassment and possible detention remains over the heads of citizens that discuss anything other than mundane matters with foreigners.

Another factor needed for "constructive engagement" to attain its goals is the ability of foreign investment or other increases in economic activity to economically and socially benefit the people of the target country. In theory, a stimulated economy will produce not only financial benefits for those employed directly as a result of new or increased foreign investment, but will also stimulate the economy of the country in general by widely dispersing the increased wealth and attendant benefits.

In this model, workers employed by or, as a result of, increased foreign investment will receive better pay and treatment than those in the typical domestic employment will. The increased wealth will be spread to the community at large, promoting general economic growth. Employees receiving better labor standards will become accustomed to the more humane treatment and will be more likely to demand similar treatment in the future.

The stimulated economic growth will lead to improvements in infrastructure, allowing the growth to be sustained and heightened. The government, through increased inflows of cash, will be able to provide improved social services for its citizens, leading to a happier, healthier, and better educated populace that will be increasingly desirable to foreign employers, providing ever increasing opportunities for sustained economic growth. Eventually, economic growth will lead to the formation of a middle class with a heretofore unknown power of political persuasion, better able and more willing to express its views to the government and more likely to have its views listened to by those in political power.

Economic integration will tend to provide a gradual shift in the political and social climate in the host country. Through capitalism, respect for and protection of the population and its basic human rights will either evolve naturally in those in political power, or will be superimposed upon the rulers of the country through the will of a populace with increased political and economic power and the influence of foreign industry and governments. The target country will likely be quite intent on maintaining economic ties with these foreign players and will therefore be more susceptible to political and moral persuasion by those whom the target country wishes to keep happy.

As logical and reasonable as the model of constructive engagement may seem, it is difficult to believe that economic activity, without more, may lead to a positive shift in the political and social climate of Burma. Unfortunately for the people of Burma, the social and political situation in the country and the increased economic interaction outside Burma tend to lessen or even negate the potential benefits from "constructive engagement." First of all, Burmese citizens may actually receive an extremely small amount of the financial rewards of economic engagement with foreign firms and investors. Approximately one-third of the foreign investment in Burma flows to the oil and natural gas industry, which remains under state control.

Rather than private businesses or individuals capitalizing on the profits and opportunities from one of Burma's greatest assets, the state receives nearly all of the benefits: offering itself as the sole joint venture partner for foreign firms in this field. Furthermore, approximately one-third of all investment in Burma is accounted for by the tourism and hotel industry, in which the military regime also plays a large role. The government also maintains a monopoly in the export of rice, the prime agricultural product of Burma, and in teak wood, pearls, jade, other gems, metals, and minerals. The Burmese government also controls the fisheries, communications, public utilities, defense, and banking and finance industries.

A 1995 International Monetary Fund report stated that government-run monopolies controlled fifty percent of all Burmese exports and controlled forty percent of all imports. The government's explicit monopolistic control of vast areas of the economy serves only as an introduction to the role of the state in the Burmese economy. In addition to maintaining economic control by holding monopolistic power over certain industries and resources, the Burmese government also wholly owns a huge number of operations in all areas of the Burmese economy.

Despite recent efforts to privatize a small percentage of these holdings, in early 1999, the government still owned 1,609 enterprises in Burma. These holdings are largely in the form of State Economic Enterprises ("SEEs") operated by diversified governmental ministries. However, a number of enterprises are also owned and operated directly by the military, providing foreign currency for the maintenance of economic stability and military political control.

The government, rather than the population as a whole, receives the greatest amount of direct benefits-profits and cash flows-from increased economic ties with the outside world. In theory, this would not absolutely prevent Burmese society from receiving the benefits of economic integration, assuming the government engaged in some beneficial redistribution of the new wealth. However, this does not appear to be the case in Burma. The expenditures of the government have historically been to support the military. Speculation on the percentage of the government's budget spent on the military ranges from approximately thirty-three percent to sixty percent.

From 1988 to 1999, the Burmese military expanded from a force of approximately 180,000 troops to at least 350,000. Given that during this time Burma was not involved in any aggressive or defensive military actions with other countries; had no real outside enemies against which to defend; and junta entered into cease-fire agreements with a large number of ethnic rebel factions, this military buildup was less of a protectionist security measure, and more of an attempt to perpetuate the power and control of the ruling military government.

Some foreign corporations recognized the failure of "constructive engagement" to positively affect the Burmese government. Levi Strauss pulled out of the country in 1992, stating that "Under present conditions, it is not possible to do business in Myanmar without directly supporting the military government and its pervasive violations of human rights."

As public sentiment against the military regime in Burma grew stronger over the following two years, Liz Claiborne also decided to cease its Burmese operations, articulating the following reasoning for its withdrawal: "Though the facilities with which we work have complied with our strict human rights standards, we cannot support the activities of this country's current government." The most telling example of how economic engagement may support or promote continued violations of human rights in Burma may be the Yadana natural gas pipeline, a project that has brought the subject of human rights violations in Burma into the U.S. legal system.

In this novel litigation, the plaintiffs are attempting to hold Unocal, a California oil company, responsible for acts of "forced relocation, forced labor, torture, violence against women, arbitrary arrest and detention, cruel, inhuman or degrading treatment, crimes against humanity, the death of family members, battery, false imprisonment, [and] assault," allegedly committed by the Burmese military in furtherance of the pipeline project.

The theory of the case is that the actions of the Burmese military in relocating villagers; forcing villagers to work on infrastructure projects related to the pipeline; forcing villagers to work on the pipeline itself; and committing various other human rights violations may be attributable to Unocal. This is because the SLORC, the alleged cause of these abuses, acted as an agent for the Myanmar Oil and Gas Enterprise, Unocal's partner in the Yadana joint venture.

Unocal denies that any human rights violations have occurred because of the pipeline project and those actions by the military government are completely separate from Unocal's role in the joint venture. Two documents obtained by human rights groups, however, suggest that Unocal implicitly and explicitly knew of, and may have been complicit in, human rights violations related to the Yadana pipeline project. Whether or not Unocal is deemed legally responsible for these alleged acts, the reports support the contention that serious human rights violations have occurred in Burma because of the pipeline project. This negates, at least in the short term, much of the argument that economic engagement with Burma will promote the social and economic welfare of its citizenry.

One possible benefit of constructive engagement is the distribution of economic benefits from foreign investment throughout society. One method to attain this goal is to use a socialist approach, in which the government reaps the greatest benefit and redistributes it through social welfare programs. In part due to the tremendous assets expended on the military, the government has failed to provide increased social services to the Burmese people. The Burmese education system has been devastated by the disinvestment in social and human re sources.

Formerly a leader in Southeast Asia in terms of education, Burma has slipped greatly in the last few years. In the mid 1980s, the country boasted an official literacy rate of 78.6%. It appears that Burma has not been able to maintain this figure in the 1990s, with only twenty-five percent of the children that enroll in school completing the mandated five-year educational program and thirty-nine percent of school-age children not attending school at all, largely because of the cost.

Theoretically, primary education in Burma is free, but parents are required to pay the costs of textbooks and various supplies and also to make contributions for school improvements; as a result, many families in Burma are unable to utilize the educational system. Those parents that are able to afford these costs often face additional costs. As the salaries of teachers remain quite low, they sometimes extort additional payments from parents to supplement their income, and, at times, parents must pool together their money to pay the teachers' salaries.

Although the status of health care in Burma has improved in the last few years, much more emphasis needs to be placed on health and medical services in the country. The government has been slow to provide increased services. In 1998, only sixty percent of the Burmese population had any access to primary public health services, the second lowest figure in the region. In remote regions, this figure may be much lower. In addition, doctors are paid meager salaries in Burma, necessitating supplements to their incomes. To achieve this, doctors often engage in private practices apart from their government positions.

This not only makes access to health care more expensive, but also tends to alleviate health and medical statistics in Burma, since only figures gathered by health care workers in their official capacity are tallied for official statistics. Therefore, the true incidence rate of such diseases as AIDS, malaria, and tuberculosis may not be known, causing the health situation in Burma to look more favorable than the real situation.

Despite a doubling in 1997 of the budget for health services, supplies of equipment, drugs, and other medical supplies, the number of treatment facilities, and the amount of money for health care worker salaries remain inadequate to provide sufficient services to the people of Burma. Malnourishment remains a prevalent problem in Burma (approximately forty-three percent of children under five-year old are mildly or moderately malnourished, and approximately sixteen percent are severely malnourished). Access to sanitary drinking water also remains a large problem (approximately sixty percent of the population has access to safe and convenient water sources).

Through the aid of various NGOs, opportunities for Burma to deal effectively with these problems exist. Despite the increased wealth provided to Burma by economic engagement, the government has failed to utilize this wealth and opportunity. The lack of attention focused on the improvement of educational and health services for the people of Burma not only shows a disregard for the welfare of the population, but also provides indications that development and economic integration with the outside world may not prove to be sustainable in the country.

The nature of economic ties with Burma supports an argument of constructive engagement in general, or as applied to certain countries with special circumstances. As noted earlier, constructive engagement must actually be constructive to have a positive effect. Many believe, however, that engagement with Burma actually serves a detrimental purpose in that economic ties with the country-both directly and indirectly support-the military regime.

After a visit to Burma in 1995, Madeline Albright noted the direct and indirect support that economic ties with the country engender for the military government. She commented on the how hard relief organizations in Burma have to work to ensure that relief actually went to the citizens in need, rather than to the government itself. She added: "Democracies should be ashamed to encourage their businesspeople to be `first in Burma' for this would provide the SLORC with the booty it needs to resist mounting pressure for a political opening." This "booty" consists of not only physical assets, but also the possibility that economic assistance and integration show implicit international acceptance of the military regime's practices and policies.

With the military regime's virtually omnipresent presence in the Burmese economy, particularly with regard to foreign investment and trade, economic engagement-touted by many as the vehicle of choice for engendering political and social change in Burma-may not prove "constructive." Rather than providing direct monetary benefits to private citizens, engagement with Burma tends to direct foreign capital and profits to the government, enriching the ruling junta and providing it with the assets necessary to continue the repression of the Burmese people that has become typical over the last thirty-eight years.

APPLICATION OF THE MASSACHUSETTS BURMA LAW

In 1996, Massachusetts became the first state in the nation to take its own stand against the government of Burma. Buoyed by the previous success of anti-apartheid divestiture laws, and the increased public attention focused on the repressive regime of Burma, Massachusetts passed "An Act Regulating State Contracts with Companies Doing Business with or in Burma (Myanmar)."

Commonly referred to as the "Burma Law," the Act aimed to severely restrict the commercial ties between Massachusetts's state agencies and any entities economically tied to Burma. To achieve its aims, the statute prohibits any state agency, state authority, or either house of the Massachusetts legislature from procuring goods or services from entities listed on a "restricted purchase list." The restricted purchase list, established by the secretary of administration and finance, includes all the entities that are deemed to be "doing business with Burma (Myanmar)" and is directed to be updated at least once every three months.

Certain exceptions to the prohibition are contained in the Burma Law, such as an exemption for the situation in which procurement is essential and the only offer or bid for the procurement contract comes from an entity on the restricted purchase list. In addition, a general exemption applies to entities operating in Burma for news-reporting purposes or for purposes of providing goods or services for international telecommunications, and an exemption allows the requisition of certain medical supplies from an entity on the restricted purchase list.

The last exception, covering procurement contracts for which bids from both listed and non-listed entities have been received, allows a covered state entity to purchase from an entity on the restricted purchase list only if "there is no comparable low bid or offer by a person who is not on the restricted purchase list." A "comparable low bid or offer" is defined as a bid or offer that is within ten percent of the lowest received bid or offer.

In effect, a ten percent surcharge is added to each bid or offer received from a listed entity, and the procuring agency or authority is then allowed to take the lowest bid or offer. In sum, these exceptions, although well enumerated, seem rather sparse in practice.

In the two years in which it has been in force, the Burma Law proved to be effective in causing a few companies to pull out of Burma and has, arguably, had much greater indirect effects by focusing public attention on Burma and its repressive regime. Just seven months after enactment of the law, four large companies: Apple Computer, Eastman Kodak, Philips Electronics, and Hewlett-Packard ended their ties with Burma to avoid the Burma Law..

Although perhaps not directly attributable to the Burma Law, J. Crew, Levi-Strauss, Motorola, and Walt Disney also pulled out of Burma in 1996, apparently in response to the growing boycott against companies involved with Burma. In January 1997, PepsiCo, Inc., which had been a major target of a consumer boycott, because of its business in Burma, completely ended its relationship with the country, citing "our assessment of the spirit of current US government foreign policy."

Implicit in Pepsi's statement was a concern about impending U.S. sanctions against Burma. However, because there was debate in Congress as to the appropriate level of sanctions, from limited restrictions on certain business activities (which would have allowed Pepsi to retain its then present involvement in Burma) to complete disengagement, a "wait and see" policy could have been followed by Pepsi. By taking action before federal sanctions passed, it is logical to assume that Pepsi was concerned not only with federal sanctions, but also with the possibility of stricter state and local sanctions influenced by the Burma Law, as well as with the pressure of growing consumer discontent.

William Weld, the Governor of Massachusetts at the time of the passing of the Burma Law, expressed a corollary purpose of the law: "it is my hope that other states and the Congress will follow our example and make a stand for the cause of freedom and democracy around the world." [sic] This goal was satisfied to a certain degree. Since the enactment of the Burma Law in Massachusetts, fifteen cities, including Los Angeles, which passed its selective purchasing law after the Massachusetts law was held unconstitutional, and two countries have passed legislation relating to Burma.

Perhaps most importantly for business interests, the Massachusetts law and its consequent constitutional challenge has aided supporters of boycotts against companies doing business in Burma. Massachusetts state representative, Byron Rushing, the drafter of the Burma Law predicted that if states and localities are unable to use selective purchasing laws: "What you'll see is a lot more individual boycotts of companies." Speaking of such consumer boycotts aimed at members of the National Foreign Trade Council ("NFTC"), the lobbying group suing to invalidate the Burma Law, commented: "Potentially, it could be a very serious problem for some companies."

The enactment of the Burma Law in 1996 received attention in a group of law review articles both attacking and defending the Act's constitutionality. The arguments against constitutional validity focused mainly on Massachusetts's invasion of the exclusive realm of foreign relations power of the federal government. The Supreme Court, in two cases in 1937 and 1942, described the foreign affairs power of the federal government as "Complete power over international affairs is in the national government and is not and cannot be subject to any curtailment or interference on the part of the several states. In respect of all international negotiations and compacts and in respect of our foreign relations generally, state lines disappear."

It later stated that "[I]n our dealings with the outside world the United States speaks with one voice and acts as one, unembarrassed by the complications as to domestic issues which are inherent in the distribution of political power between the national government and the individual states." A review of these cases indicates that they dealt with the Roosevelt-Litvinoff Agreement between the United States and the Soviet Union, and thus can be largely distinguished from the Massachusetts case. The Litvinoff Agreement cases concerned the applicability of New York law in relation to application of the Agreement. New York argued that application of the Agreement, which would have entailed implicit validation of the Soviet nationalization of Russian businesses, violated New York public policy.

One may therefore argue that the opinion of the Court stands for the proposition that state law may not contravene federal laws or agreements already in place, rather than the proposition that States may never engage in activity that relates to foreign countries.

Possibly the only Supreme Court case that has dealt explicitly with state infringement on the foreign affairs power of the U.S. Government is Zschernig v. Miller. In Zschernig, the Court set a general guideline for the determination of whether a state statute impermissibly interferes with the foreign affairs power of the federal government.

The court concluded that the statute under scrutiny "has a direct impact upon foreign relations and may well adversely affect the power of the central government" and "seems to make unavoidable judicial criticism of nations established on a more authoritarian basis than our own."

The Court contrasted this determination with Clark v. Allen, which held that a similar California statute was constitutionally valid. In that case, the Court concluded that the California statute would have only "some incidental or indirect effect in foreign countries" and that "the case seemed to involve no more than a routine reading of foreign laws." Therefore, the general test flowing from Zschernig involves a determination of the degree to which a state action affects foreign countries, and of the degree of scrutiny to which the action subjects foreign countries.

A state law implicating the foreign affairs power of the federal government, and not contradicting existing federal legislation or executive action, may be constitutional if it does not too greatly affect foreign countries or unduly inquire into the actions of foreign governments. Consistent application and explication of this general test-determining what is "too far"-has eluded courts dealing with the foreign affairs power. The Supreme Court has not yet explained the practical application of the Zschernig test, so one may still argue that the Burma Law does not meet the test.

In addition to the argument that the Burma Law does not facially violate the principles enunciated in Zschernig, proponents of the Act offer another theory. They argue that the considerations of the "market participant exception" that are commonly applied to the dormant Commerce Clause should also apply to the Foreign Commerce Clause and the foreign affairs power.

Under this theory, considerations such as (1. whether a state acts as a market regulator or purchaser/ seller; (2. whether the state action is discriminatory in character; (3. whether a legitimate state interest exists; and (4. the degree to which a state action actually affects commerce potentially remove the negative presumption against the validity of state action in the realm of foreign affairs. In making this argument, Massachusetts argued that if it acts as a market participant, the statute is not discriminatory in nature; the statute has only indirect effects; and a "legitimate local purpose" exists to support the Act.

Furthermore, opponents of the Burma Law have argued that it is unconstitutional under the dormant Commerce and Foreign

Commerce Clauses. Like the dormant Commerce Clause, the dormant Foreign Commerce Clause vests ultimate authority over foreign commerce with the federal government, notwithstanding a lack of affirmative action by the federal government.

In addition, commentators have argued that the Court applies stricter standards to Foreign Commerce Clause issues than to traditional interstate commerce issues. The distinction rests on the premise that foreign commerce deserves heightened standards of analysis due to the interest of the federal government in maintaining a unified policy and approach to foreign commercial relations. Thus, any state action that attempts to regulate foreign commerce, absent a proper exception or congressional endorsement of that action, would seem to face an almost insurmountable challenge to its validity.

Given the real and potential problems that legislation such as the Massachusetts act posed for a number of American economic interests, the NFTC, on behalf of its members on the Massachusetts restricted purchase list, brought an action against the Burma Law asserting that

[T]he Burma Law is invalid because it 1. Intrudes on the federal government's exclusive power to regulate foreign affairs; 2. discriminates against and burdens international trade in violation of the Foreign Commerce Clause; and 3. is preempted by a federal statute and an executive order imposing sanctions on Myanmar.

1. The District Court-A Violation of Foreign Affairs Power

The district court briefly discussed the Foreign Commerce Clause and preemption arguments, but did not base the decision on either of these, instead focusing on the alleged violation of the foreign affairs power of the United States federal government. The district court broke its constitutionality analysis into two parts: whether the Constitution grants exclusive foreign affairs power to the federal government, and whether the Massachusetts Burma Law impermissibly burdens U.S.-foreign relations. In determining that foreign affairs are an exclusive federal power, the court quoted the Supreme Court's warning in Pink: "power over external affairs is not shared by the States; it is vested in the national government exclusively." The district court also used Zschernig as further support for federal exclusivity over foreign affairs, asserting that the net result of Zschernig is that states and localities must defer to the federal government if their actions will affect foreign affairs. The district court also used Zschernig to determine that the Burma Law is burdensome on U.S. foreign relations, pointing to amicus briefs from both the EU and Japan as evidence that the Burma Law violates Zschernig in that it is a non-federal law affecting foreign policy. Specifically quoting the Zschernig test, the district court stated that the Burma Law is unconstitutional because it has more than an "indirect or incidental effect in foreign countries," and a "great potential for disruption or embarrassment."

2. The Court of Appeals-Impinging on Foreign Powers of the United States

In contrast to the relatively sparse district court opinion, the Court of Appeals for the First Circuit touched on nearly all of the major arguments in its de novo review of the lower court opinion. The court of appeals first determined that while the federal government has dominion over foreign affairs, state activities in this arena are not completely excluded. Quoting the Restatement (Third) of Foreign Relations Law of the United States, the court of appeals noted that states may have a role in foreign affairs, so long as their actions do not "impinge upon the authority or the foreign relations of the United States." Thus, the central question is whether the Burma Law impedes the foreign relations of the United States. The court of appeals responded that it did, citing the district court's focus on the disruption the law has caused within the EU and ASEAN, among others.

Massachusetts argued that Zschernig stood for the proposition that a state may lawfully intrude on the federal government's foreign power dominion if the interest is sufficiently strong. However, the court of appeals struck down that argument by stating that Zschernig does not require a balancing test of state and federal interests, but rather that Zschernig essentially creates a foreign powers bar over which the states cannot venture. Massachusetts again tried to evade Zschernig by using Barclays Bank PLC v. Franchise Tax Board as support to limit Zschernig's scope, asserting that Barclays allows only Congress to determine if a state is violating a federal foreign affairs policy. The court struck down this interpretation of Barclays, which, if accepted, would have essentially overruled Zschernig. The 1st Circuit thus upheld Zschernig as good law.

The court of appeals continued to discuss, and subsequently dismiss, further Massachusetts's arguments for the constitutionality of the law, including the market-participation exception. The market-participation exception, which was omitted from discussion by the district court, was briefly analyzed in the decision of the court. The exception, which has been applied only in situations dealing with the dormant domestic Commerce Clause, was succinctly disposed of by the court of appeals, which determined that it explicitly had been limited to specific dormant domestic Commerce Clause instances and should not be extended. The court of appeals also determined that the law violated the Foreign Commerce Clause, mainly through facial discrimination; hindrance of the federal government's ability to speak with one voice; regulation of conduct beyond its borders; and lack of local justification for the law.

Massachusetts's final argument dealt with implicit approval, arguing that because Congress knew of the Burma Law before it passed the federal act and did not condemn the Act, Congress implicitly approved it. The state cited Barclays, in which the Court found that Congress had implicitly permitted the use of the reporting method at issue because it had studied the method and surrounding issue and considered but did not pass legislation that would have overruled the method.

However, the court of appeals dismissed comparisons to Barclays. First, Barclays concerned the Commerce Clause, not the Supremacy Clause. Second, Barclays involved taxation, traditionally a state activity, rather than foreign affairs, traditionally a federal activity. Third, Congress frequently discussed the taxation issue in Barclays, thereby making a determination of implied consent much easier than in this case, in which Massachusetts argued that virtual silence should equal implied consent. Fourth, in Barclays, Congress ultimately was silent when it came to the specific tax issue, whereas in this case

Congress passed legislation specifically relating to Burma. The last conclusion leads into the preemption argument, which although it is a small part of the appellate court opinion, this is the main-essentially sole-focus of the Supreme Court.

3. The Supreme Court-Preemption

Congressional preemption can come in two forms: express preemption, where Congress specifically states its intent to overrule existing law with a federal action, and implied preemption, which is more difficult to discern. The Supreme Court has established that implied congressional intent to preempt exists where 1. A federal statute is so pervasive that it completely occupies the area of law; 2. the federal and state law cross so often that it essentially would be impossible to follow both; or 3. to enforce the state law "stands as an obstacle to the accomplishment and execution of the full purposes and objectives of Congress." In addition to one of the three requirements above, if the statute regulates an area traditionally occupied by state law, the congressional intent must be "clear and manifest."

However, as the court of appeals points out, usually a case for preemption is the reverse situation: a state is interfering in the federal sphere rather than the federal government interfering in the arena of the states. Thus, after determining that Congress implied preemption, it is necessary to examine the state regulation to determine whether it was preempted by federal law. In Hines v. Davidowitz and its progeny, the Supreme Court established that a state law will be preempted in at least two instances.

One, when Congress, through either express or implied intent, indicates that federal law shall "occupy the field," and two, when the state law interferes with a federal law, regardless of whether Congress has occupied the field. In the latter instance, evidence of state interference includes situations in which it is virtually impossible for a party to comply with both the state and federal laws, and where "under the circumstances of [a] particular case, [the challenged state law] stands as an obstacle to the accomplishment and execution of the full purposes and objectives of Congress."

The Supreme Court found that the federal act preempted the Burma Law. The Court's reasoning was tri-fold. First, it found that Congress's intent was to authorize the President to have complete as well as flexible control over sanctions against Burma. The federal act gives the President much power and discretion in determining appropriate interactions with Burma; therefore, the Court stated that "it is just this plenitude of Executive authority that we think controls the issue of preemption."

Second, the Court determined that Congress specifically intended that economic pressure against Burma be limited, and that the Massachusetts statute, by penalizing all companies engaged in business activities in Burma, went beyond the intended congressional mandate. Thus, if Congress exempted a certain business from its actions in Burma, the Burma Law could still penalize the business, a situation the Court found to be unacceptable. Third, the Court found the state law directly conflicted with the President's authority under the federal act. Through an analysis of the Congressional Record, the Court determined that Congress intended for the President to be able to control U.S. sanctions against Burma without state or local interference.

The Supreme Court's decision is quite anti-climatic. With all of the protests and controversy surrounding this issue, the Court had an opportunity to take a definitive stand on the manner in which this country deals with human rights violators. In reality, however, the effect of the Supreme Court decision is not what is enunciated, but what is omitted. The Court, in focusing only on preemption, permits two different conclusions. The decision might stand for the proposition that the Court is completely eliminating the issue.

The Court's decision might mean that state action against foreign human rights violators is so beyond the scope of state action that it does not warrant further discussion. On the other hand, the Court might have opened the door to state and local foreign affairs actions when the federal government has not yet spoken. Thus, while the Court has answered the question specifically raised by the Burma Law, it has arguably not affected future state and local legislation. This actually could be quite meaningful. Given the relative ease of passing state and local legislation versus federal legislation, state and local laws could affect foreign governments for some time before a federal law preempts them.

This possibility leads back to issues regarding the WTO. In order for the WTO to effectively impact human rights violators, it must have the complete support of its Members. The Supreme Court decision implies that states and localities can erode the ability of the United States to "speak with one voice." This could lead to dissension in the WTO, as well as massive world pressure on the United States to close the loophole.

If the purpose of state and local legislation is to eliminate human rights violations in countries such as Burma, then closing the loophole is not the answer. As seen by the effects of the Burma Law, sub-national entities have the ability to effect change in foreign economies, which can lead to a change in human rights policies. While the WTO is supposed to be engaging in "constructive engagement," it does not seem to be working. Thus, if sub-national entities are not permitted to participate, one could argue that the top priority of the United States and the WTO is not to eliminate human rights violations through free trade but, as the Seattle protesters illustrated, to make money.

On the other hand, perhaps procurement agreements-whether local, state or federal-are not the solution to end human rights violations, especially in Burma. Burma, in its more than thirty-eight years of isolationism, is no stranger to a lack of outside investment. With the exception of the approximately twelve years that the country opened its doors, Burma has existed on its own. However, giving the country a taste of democracy through outside investment, and then withdrawing that investment after only eight years, just places Burma back on the same, albeit harmful, "Burmese way to socialism."

How can the wrongs of Burma be rectified? Perhaps free trade, without restrictions and guidelines as envisioned by constructive engagement, is the answer, despite the shortcomings of using economic incentives to improve human rights. Free trade-in its purest form-may in time give the country the taste of capitalism that it needs to break free from its oppressive regime. While the federal government and Massachusetts had human rights reform in mind when they passed procurement laws, by essentially forcing industry to retreat from Burma, they may have unwittingly reversed any potential positive steps. In fact, they may have sent Burma back into the depths of isolationism, because "Trade is a means to an end, not an end in itself."

While recent events seem to indicate that constructive engagement might not work in Burma, it is also clear that sanctions have failed as well. However, this should not end attempts to reduce the number of human rights violations in Burma. Perhaps the answer is to insure that the international community clearly communicates its condemnation of the Burmese regime through the process of constructive engagement. By using trade not purely as an economic tool as the WTO favors, but as a means to achieve freer societies, we could satisfy multiple obligations: 1. making money through the uninhibited passage of goods across borders; 2. allowing citizens to freely participate in this exchange; and 3. aiding economic development.

Although judicially settled (for the time being), the issue at hand rings loud and clear in this country and abroad. Needless to say, the protests will continue; the matter will brew; and voices will be raised in the future. Perhaps this is not a matter for the courts, or for any one country, but rather a global issue, begging for a multilateral approach and a well-devised system of sanctions. To leave the problem as it is now invites danger and disregards the slow but constant movement towards giving human rights a greater voice.